For Rowan and Duncan

ALLWORTH PRESS
NEW YORK

08 07 06 05 04 03 5 4 3 2 1

Published by Allworth Press
An imprint of Allworth Communications
10 East 23rd Street, New York, NY 10010

Cover design by Mary Belibasakis
Cover illustration by Bill Wray
Page composition/typography by Susan Ramundo

Library of Congress Cataloging-in-Publication Data
Neuwirth, Allan.
Makin' toons : inside the most popular animated TV shows and movies / by Allan Neuwirth.
p. cm.
Includes bibliographical references and index.
ISBN 1-58115-269-8 (pbk.)
1. Animated television programs–United States. 2. Animators–United States–Interviews. 3. Motion picture producers and directors–United States–Interviews. I. Title.
PN1992.8.A59 N48 2003
791.45'3–dc21
2003000759

Printed in Canada

TABLE OF CONTENTS

Acknowledgments

To all of my talented colleagues who contributed to *Makin' Toons:* Thank you. Without your help, there's no way I could have realized this project. In particular, my editors, Liz Van Hoose, Jessica Rozler, and Nicole Potter, and publisher Tad Crawford, for your guidance; my good friends and frequent collaborators Gary Cooper and Glen Hanson, for your insights; Susan and Eric Goldberg, who unlocked many doors (and shared so much of the animation trivia stored in the Cartoon Coloured vault also known as Eric's brain); Linda Simensky, who threw the portals wide open at Cartoon Network; and my sister Risa Neuwirth, animator Raul Garcia, writer/cartoonist Angelo DeCesare, and production manager Masako Kanayama, for your feedback and assistance. An extra special thank-you goes out to Bill Wray, for that fabulous and witty cover painting.

There are so many who made my research and/or image-gathering phase much easier–including the ever-amazing Howard Green and Susan Butterworth at Walt Disney Feature Animation; Margaret Adamic at Walt Disney Publishing Worldwide; Courtenay Purcell, Megan Trikilis, Joe Swaney, Diana Ritchey, and John Cawley at Cartoon Network; Kyle Feeley and Lorri Bond at Warner Bros. TV Animation; Nathan Johnson, Nicole Mazer, Richard Betz, and Tashna Newman at Nickelodeon; Jeffrey Katzenberg and Terry Press at DreamWorks; Steven Argula at Pixar; Kevin Kolde at Spumco; Tiffany Ward and Trish Lamkin at Jay Ward Productions; Linda Zazza at Blue Sky; Rick Kunis at Alan Menken's studio; Jessica Jarrett at *King of the Hill*; photographer Greg Preston; Pam Martin at Cel-ebration Gallery; and *TheDigitalBits.com*'s Greg Suarez; and *Collecting-Simpsons.com*'s Bill LaRue, for sharing their *Simpsons* interview material.

Humble thanks also go to the late Nina Bamberger, whom I dearly miss, as well as Andrew Adamson, Roger Allers, Billy Aronson, Ken Bruce, Pat Carroll, Jean Chalopin, Brenda Chapman, Ron Clements, Vanessa Coffey, Gabor Csupo, Andreas Deja, John R. Dilworth, Paul Dini, Pete Docter, Ben Edlund, June Foray, Paul Germain, Michael Giaimo, Eric Goldberg, Susan Goldberg, Marty Grabstein, Don Hahn, Mary Harrington, Stephen Hillenburg, Scott Johnston, Mike Judge, Helen Kalafatic,

John Kricfalusi, Bill Lauch, John Leguizamo, Richard Liebmann-Smith, Craig McCracken, Shaun McLaughlin, Kent Melton, Alan Menken, Candy Monteiro, Glen Murakami, John Musker, Sue Nichols, Steven Orich, Gyorgyi Kovacs Peluce, Margot Pipkin, Don Poynter, Eric Radomski, Dave Reynolds, Fredda Rose, Will Ryan, Chris Savino, Thomas Schumacher, Linda Simensky, Tom Sito, Arnold Stang, Andrew Stanton, Genndy Tartakovsky, Terry Thoren, James Tucker, Alan Wagner, Teale Wang, Aron Warner, Chris Wedge, Billy West, Scott Wills, Gary K. Wolf, and Bill Wray, who all generously agreed to share their experiences with me.

INTRODUCTION

Hi. My name is Allan. Like many of you out there, I'm a *toon-a-holic.*

My addiction began at the tender age of four, when my parents gave me my first TV set, an old black-and-white Zenith. No sooner had they placed it at the foot of my bed that I began what was to become my early morning ritual: open my eyes, scamper across the covers to flip the set on, then sit there mesmerized by the cartoon images flickering before me.

Dogs chasing cats . . . cats chasing mice . . . mice tricking cats . . . cats tricking dogs. A hapless coyote hurtling off a cliff. Bears stealing picnic baskets. A blustering southern rooster and a pugnacious chicken hawk. A cowboy horse and his Mexican burro sidekick. A prehistoric construction worker powering the family car with his bare feet. A cheerful mouse and his inquisitive pet dog. A wascally wabbit outwitting a host of verbally challenged, dim-witted adversaries. A plucky flying squirrel and a moose of dubious intellect.

And so many catchphrases, all permanently etched into my brain: "Eh, what's up, Doc?" "Exit, stage left!" "You're . . . dethpicable!" "Watch me pull a rabbit outta my hat!" "Yabba dabba do!" "Vhat is plan, darlink?" "Smarter than the average bear!" "Jane, stop this crazy thing!" "I tawt I taw a puddy tat!" "Aaaaaalvin!!!"

The toons were chaotic, wildly funny, and often sly and subversive. They fueled my imagination and helped form my comic sensibilities.

A year or two later, my mother began taking me to the movies with her, to see all the great animated features. *Lady and the Tramp* was the first, followed soon after by *One Hundred and One Dalmatians*, *Gay Purr-ee*, *The Jungle Book*, *Pinocchio*, and on and on. Suddenly, I wasn't just laughing at wild antics anymore–even though I was a young kid, I found myself absorbed by the narratives and pacing of the longer form. Oh, I still laughed, but now I was also thrilled, frightened, and sometimes moved to tears.

As I got a bit older, I realized I could actually *draw* these characters and put them through adventures of my own devising–which I proceeded to do, night and day–an experience that's shared, not surprisingly, by so many others whom you'll read about in this book. To the complete and utter mortification of my parents, I drew 'em on everything: my clothes, their clothes, painted walls, wallpapered walls, napkins, fine tablecloths, my dad's handkerchiefs, the margins of books, the soles of my own feet and even, occasionally, on paper. Wherever there was a clean surface, it was soon covered with images resembling Bullwinkle, Yogi Bear, Crusader Rabbit, or Mickey Mouse. My manic obsession with toons had taken root.

But by far the greatest discovery of all was that amazing little device called the *flipbook*. I learned that if I stapled a small stack of paper together at the bottom, drew slightly progressive poses in sequence, and then riffled through the pages, my drawings could actually move–just like the ones on TV. So *that's* how they did it–or, at least, I thought it was that simple.

Years later, of course, I learned what an involved and rich process the act of creating animation actually is–all about the writing and designing and directing and producing, and storyboards, layouts, timing, voice recording, music, sound effects, mixing, and editing that go into making a cartoon series or film. Once I was gainfully employed in the animation field, my parents would remind me of how I'd declared my intentions at the age of seven to make cartoons. I have no reason to doubt it.

My friends and I–and certainly most of you, if you're reading these words–grew up addicted to animation, consumed by our passion for it. Clearly, we weren't alone. Aside from the odd curmudgeon or two out there, *everyone* adores cartoons. Most often, they're our first introduction to humor and satire and music . . . an inescapable part of modern pop culture that crosses boundaries of language, class, and generation. More than ever before, animation is appreciated by adults as well as kids. And yet, with millions of fans happily sharing this obsession with the medium, so many people still have no idea what really goes on behind the scenes. Or what an intense labor of love it is for everyone involved.

Which brings us ever so neatly to the beginning of this book.

It's my hope that you'll find some answers in these pages that chronicle the creation of many of the most popular animated TV series and feature films from the last few decades–a period now being hailed as animation's modern renaissance. A *toon boom*, if you will.

In *Makin' Toons*, you'll hear some of the greatest practitioners of the craft, in their own words, discussing how our favorite cartoons sprang to life. Naturally, I couldn't cover every show and movie–there just isn't enough room in one book–so I tried to pick a representative cross sampling of the very best. You'll also find that most of the focus here is on projects created in the United States. The fact is, there's been such a worldwide animation explosion in recent years, if I'd tried to include the international scene, it would've required a volume three times the size of this one.

As I began my research, I was reminded of how quickly technology is advancing in the animation world. Just as in seemingly every other aspect of modern life, the computer has become more and more a part of our daily process. Some skeptics have even sounded the death knell of classic hand-drawn animation, predicting that computer-generated fare will soon replace it altogether. I believe there's room for both. Cave wall paintings aside, modes of artistic expression never get antiquated. The digital world is a considerable force to be reckoned with, for sure, but nothing to fear–if anything, it helps us to unleash our imaginations and create in ways that were heretofore impossible. We all crave a good story, and usually don't care how it's told . . . as long as it's told well.

In mapping out the structure of this book, I debated whether or not to separate the discussions of television and films. For a long time, the two were distinctly different groups. Those who worked on animated feature films didn't work on cartoon TV shows, and vice versa. In recent years, however, the line has blurred considerably. Many now move freely from one medium to another, and then back again. Hit TV series spawn popular theatrical features (like *South Park*, *Rugrats*, *Scooby-Doo*, and *Batman*) and successful animated features spawn hit TV series (like *The Adventures of Jimmy Neutron: Boy Genius*), made-for-video sequels, and Broadway musicals. So, thanks to today's cross-pollination of talent, and in the interest of keeping things lively, you'll find all the ingredients mixed together in the same stew.

You'll also notice a lot of the same names popping up from time to time in various capacities on different projects. Nothing exemplifies the nature of the animation business better–someone can work as a story artist or director on one job, then do animation or layouts on another, then write a script, then go back to storyboarding, and so on. Typically, people in this industry are extremely versatile.

Finally, they say that everyone on this earth has at least one book in them. Well, here's my first–all about something I've loved watching and working on my whole life: cartoons.

—ALLAN NEUWIRTH

CHAPTER 1
WHAT A GREAT IDEA!
How Some Tip-Top Toons Were Born

"Where do you get your ideas? Is there a rack, a file someplace where iced or quick-frozen ideas are stored, only waiting to be thawed? I am grateful to be able to answer the question sincerely and honestly: I don't know where ideas come from."

—Chuck Jones, legendary cartoon director (1989)

It's hard to pinpoint where that initial spark–the germ of a new idea–originates. An inspiration can hit you when you're standing in the supermarket, reaching for a can of baked beans. It can suddenly occur to you in the shower, or just after you've stretched out on your bed at night and turned off the light, or while you're romping with your schnauzer in the park. Without warning, your eyes can glaze over in the middle of a conversation as a thought suddenly pops into your head–a thought completely unrelated to what you were talking about.

Some of the most brilliant cartoon projects sprang to life as a fleeting notion, whereas others were hatched through a combination of concentration, hard work, and not a small amount of luck.

In our opening chapter, let's take some fleeting glances at how a few of the most popular animated films and TV shows of the past several decades got their start–and at the remarkably diverse group of people who created them. Later on, you'll read in more detail how some of these (and other) ideas were developed, designed, nurtured, and produced. Several of them were trendsetters–projects so different they created a sensation, blazing a trail for much of what followed.

To begin with, there was one motion picture that's largely responsible for jump-starting the animation boom of the last few decades. It actually began back in the mid-1970s, and it all leapt out of one man's fertile imagination . . .

THE BUNNY DID IT, AFTER ALL

Roger Rabbit Ignites the Toon Boom

Gary K. Wolf had written three well-received books for Doubleday when they agreed to purchase a fourth novel from him, sight unseen. Basically free to write about whatever tickled his fancy, he began thinking about a story–and doing research on three things that had fascinated him since he was a kid: "Comic books . . . cartoons . . . and hard-boiled private eye novels. My favorites were superhero books. *Blackhawk, Superman, Batman, Wonder Woman* . . . but I was also big on Donald Duck and Uncle Scrooge." He even belonged to a Scrooge McDuck fan club. "A penny saved is a penny earned," laughs Wolf, reciting the zillionaire skinflint's maxim. "Comic books were always big for me."

As the author struggled to somehow combine his three interests, he studied the Saturday morning cartoons. "Yeah, it's research; I'm not doing it because I like it," he told his dubious wife–yet when the "research" paid off, it wasn't the shows themselves that gave Wolf his bolt of inspiration. "All of a sudden, I realized . . . that there was something, not about the cartoons, but about the *commercials*. Y'know, I was seeing Cap'n Crunch, Snap, Crackle and Pop, Tony the Tiger, and the Trix Rabbit . . . These were cartoon characters, and they were messing around with real kids, and nobody seemed to think it was odd! That was a real eye-opener for me. I said, "'What would a world be like if the cartoon characters were *real*–if this thing that I'm seeing on cereal commercials really existed?'"

Wolf realized that he'd just had an epiphany. "It was a mind-blowing idea," he says. "I got that idea in 1975. But at that point–you know how writers are–I got really paranoid. I'm not a fast writer. I mean, it takes me a long time to write things. And I thought, 'This idea is so obvious that somebody else is gonna do it first.' But nobody did!"

So he stepped up his research, honing in on some very specific details. "I realized that if I was going to do this book the way I wanted–and have people believe it–that everything in it had to be consistent. In other words, cartoon characters in the book had to do things that cartoon characters do . . . and, if possible, the whole story had to revolve around the fact that these were cartoon characters in a real world, so that if you took the cartoon characters *out*, the story wouldn't work."

That's the part that took time. Wolf needed to consider what toon characters could do that real people could not, apart from being squashed and stretched. Once he was ready, he began banging out a murder mystery novel quite unlike any other. And he called it, *Who Censored Roger Rabbit?*

Roger Rabbit, Jessica Rabbit, and Baby Herman were the first three characters he came up with. "My hero was kind of a Disney character . . . I realized that Disney really didn't have a prominent rabbit, so I thought a Disney-esque rabbit would be good," he relates. "I wanted people to read this thing, and go, 'Oh yeah, I remember that character.' The one that was most successful was Baby Herman. My own agent came to me and said, 'You know, you're going to have trouble with this Baby Herman, because that's somebody else's character.' It worked because everybody remembers human babies from the thirties and forties cartoons and comic books. But these were all mine."

When he finally finished over two years later, he felt it was the best thing he'd ever written. So it was a real kicker when Doubleday declined to publish it. "They rejected it! First reject I'd ever had," says Wolf, who admits he was flabbergasted. The reason? The marketing department didn't know how to sell it. "It doesn't fit any genre," he was told. "There's no category for this." *One hundred and ten* rejections later, a publisher–St. Martin's Press–finally said yes.

Wolf meets Rabbit in person at Walt Disney World Resort in 1991. Disney character © Disney Enterprises, Inc. & Amblin Entertainment, Inc.

Before the book even came out, Gary Wolf's agent showed the galleys to people in L.A., who shopped it to Disney, who liked it so much they optioned it in 1980. Later on, to the author's delight, producer (and avowed toon lover) Steven Spielberg entered the picture, and the rest is history.

In 1988, *Who Framed Roger Rabbit*, a jaw-droppingly seamless blend of animation and live action, was unleashed on audiences. To the sheer delirium of cartoon fanatics around the world, for the very first time ever, Mickey Mouse, Bugs Bunny, Donald Duck, Daffy Duck, Betty Boop, and so many other Disney, Warner Bros., and Fleischer characters coexisted side by side by side in the same on-screen universe, courtesy of Spielberg's Amblin Entertainment and the Walt Disney Studios. It was a smartly written motion picture, beautifully animated and staged, with live action directed by Robert Zemeckis and animation supervised by Richard Williams. The story may have changed somewhat from the original novel, but the characters, the undertones about racial harmonies and inequities–"Toons are not better or worse than people," says Wolf. "They're just people," and most of what made *Who Censored Roger Rabbit?* unique were left perfectly intact.

Who Framed Roger Rabbit scored in a big way with audiences. And suddenly, after a long dry spell, people of all ages were interested in animation again.

A Little Mermaid Is Spawned in Burbank

The next toon was another trendsetter, redefining our perception of what an animated musical could be. It was 1985, and Michael Eisner had assumed leadership of The Walt Disney Company just one year earlier–a company that was floundering at the time. Animated musical films, once Disney's bread and butter, were by then considered relics of the past. Eisner had already hired Jeffrey Katzenberg to come in and supervise movie production at the studio, and the two immediately began to turn things around.

One notion Eisner brought with him from Paramount, a studio he and boss Barry Diller had built into Hollywood's powerhouse of the late 1970s and early 1980s, was a sort of brainstorming/pitch session they dubbed *The Gong Show* (after producer/host Chuck Barris' loony TV talent showcase). Ron Clements, already working at Disney for several years as a story artist and a writer/director, elaborates: "In January, Michael and Jeffrey gathered together a bunch of creative people–story people, directors, some animators–and everybody was to go out and find five new ideas for animated features. We'd come back in two weeks, and then we would pitch those ideas. They called it *The Gong Show* because we'd get an immediate reaction: If they liked it, we'd hear 'yes.' But if they didn't, then it got gonged."

Soon to score a modest breakthrough with John Musker on *The Great Mouse Detective* (which was nearing completion and due to be released the next year), Clements began actively searching for ideas to develop and pitch. One day, while poking around a bookstore, he spied a copy of Hans Christian Andersen's fairy tales. Plucking it off the shelf, he riffled through its pages until he reached "The Little Mermaid." A lightbulb popped on over his head: The story would make a perfect animated feature.

"I thought, this has a lot of really great elements in it! I don't know why it hadn't been done," Clements says today. In fact, Walt Disney had notions about animating "The Little Mermaid" as far back as the late 1930s. Kay Nielsen, a Danish artist on staff at the time, created some beautiful character and story sketches. Nothing much had come of it, however, and the project was shelved.

Clements sat down and wrote up a two-page treatment based on the original tale, but with a few significant changes. He turned the sea witch character into more of a prominent villain so that it would be a classic good versus evil story, and he added a happy ending wherein the heroine married the Prince.

"That was very different from the Andersen story," he notes, "where she dies at the end."

Oh, and he named the mermaid "Ariel." In other words, the basis for what was to develop into one of Disney's best animated musical films, not to mention single-handedly revive the genre, was all there in his two typed pages right from the beginning. He pitched it verbally to Disney execs at the very first *Gong Show*–and it got gonged. Apparently, the execs felt it was too similar to *Splash*, the Tom Hanks mermaid comedy that Disney had recently released. They said they'd take a look at Clements' treatment, anyway, and happily, to their credit, Katzenberg and Eisner changed their minds after reading the pages. They went ahead and put the picture into development–as yet unaware that they were setting the stage for the dawn of a new era.

THE ANIMATED SITCOM IS REBORN

Meet *The Simpsons*

In 1986, while production on *The Little Mermaid* was swimming along, another trendsetting toon was being spawned not too many miles away.

Producer/director James L. Brooks and his crew at Gracie Films were hatching a new TV series called *The Tracey Ullman Show* for the Fox network's very first season. Brooks wanted to create a different sort of comedy program–a show comprised of sketches, only longer and more elaborate than usual, performed by a troupe led by the versatile Ullman. The skits would form mini-stories, sort of a hybrid between a sketch show and a sitcom. In between the live action, he decided, he wanted to run short interstitial animated cartoons.

Makin' Toons

One of Gracie's production assistants at the time, Paul Germain, remembers sitting in Brooks' office as the producer tried to decide what the animated bits might be. As it happened, a friend, [designer/producer] Polly Platt, had given Brooks the original artwork from a Matt Groening newspaper cartoon–a framed "Life in Hell" strip, which he'd hung on his office wall. "And so he looks around the office," Germain relates, "and he says, 'Why don't we get *that* guy?' I said, 'Oh, Jim, I love his stuff–that's such a brilliant idea!' And he looked at me and he said, 'Okay, you do it. You go out and put it together.' I said, 'Whaddaya mean, *I* do it? I don't know anything about animation.' He said, 'Well, you better learn!'"

When Gracie Films contacted Matt Groening and proposed the idea, the artist was interested. Suddenly, Paul Germain was thrust into the position of putting together the cartoons for the new show. After culling through some fifty videocassettes–containing animation that ranged from okay to hideously awful–he and associate producer Jeffrey Townsend landed on a then-tiny commercial production house named Klasky Csupo.

Hungarian-born animator Gabor Csupo recalls Germain and crew thinking it would be cheaper to animate Groening's line drawings in black and white. "We said that for a comic strip, that's cool–but for a moving weekly show I think that the audience would like to see some color," says Csupo. "So we kind of convinced them, and the only reason we won is because we said we were gonna do it for the same price! They said, 'Oh, okay, well, in that case, it's in color!'"

The team initially set out to produce a cartoon version of "Life in Hell," starring a one-eared rabbit named Binky, and hired a color designer named Gyorgyi Kovacs Peluce to develop the animated look of the oddball shorts. Peluce prepared full color presentation boards to show the network, but then the deal ran into a snag. "Basically, they couldn't reach an agreement about using 'Life in Hell,' because Fox wanted to own certain kinds of rights that Matt Groening was unwilling to give them," as Germain remembers it. "He had been drawing the cartoon strip for ten years, and he didn't figure that it was anybody's but his. He wasn't gonna *give* it to Fox just because they were going to animate one minute spots–I think he was being very savvy."

Finally, Fox said to forget "Life in Hell," and asked if Gracie and Groening could think up a new, original idea. We know what the cartoonist came up with next. "He went away," says Germain. "He had two weeks to do this–and I think he did it the night before. What he did was, he drew this family. The original drawings look very different from the drawings now. They're crudely, fundamentally similar, but they're not the same."

Three artists–David Silverman, Wes Archer, and Bill Kopp–were assigned by Klasky Csupo to refine and animate the characters, and *The Simpsons* were born. In 1987, they began appearing on *The Tracey Ullman Show*, along with another quirky series of short toons that has been all but forgotten today: underground cartoonist M. K. Brown's *Dr. N!Godatu* (with characters also voiced by *Simpsons* regulars Dan Castellaneta and Nancy Cartwright). From '87 to '89, there were forty-eight *Simpsons* shorts in all before they graduated to their own half-hour prime-time series. Fox Broadcasting's gamble paid off in a big way.

An Angry Chihuahua and a Retarded Cat

Ren & Stimpy Get Their Start in the Biz

By any account, *The Simpsons* was a groundbreaking animated TV series–but it wasn't the only one of its time. Yes, my roguish readers, *there is another*. It invaded not the prime-time viewing hours, but those of the daylight–previously the domain of sugarcoated guano like *Smurfs* and *The Care Bears*–and it helped change the nature of so-called children's cartoons for years to come.

Back then, the airwaves were cluttered with bland, cheaply animated kiddie fare. It wasn't just numbing kids' brains and disheartening their parents; it was downright depressing as hell for anyone working in the animation world. Many of the most talented artists and writers were forced to toil on this stuff if they wished to earn a living at their chosen profession. Some survived it by taking a philosophical approach. "I called my first house *Casa de He-Man*," laughs director and animator Tom Sito, who worked on *He-Man and the Masters of the Universe* at the Filmation studio. "I was makin' a mint. I mean, we knew it was junk while we were working on it. But hey, sometimes they want sausage, and sometimes they want pâté."

Mostly, artists were just grinding out the sausage. But many of them yearned to be making their own cartoons–cartoons they actually cared about.

One man, John Kricfalusi, was hell-bent on reviving the kind of gut-bustingly funny, shoot-milk-out-your-nose animated shorts that his hero Bob Clampett used to create at Warner Bros. in the good old days. He eventually got his chance when a young network called Nickelodeon bought a show from him named *Ren & Stimpy*.

It really began a few years earlier, when Kricfalusi was working for a small animation studio in Los Angeles called Calico Creations. Constantly

Stimpy making sure his pal Ren is happy in "Stimpy's Invention."

scribbling his "phone doodles," the artist found himself drawing the same character, "this retarded-looking cat," over and over again. "He looked *way* more retarded than Stimpy ended up on the show," he asserts. The brainstorm for Ren came more suddenly, based on a postcard of a sweater-clad Chihuahua standing beside a woman's legs. "I thought it was hilarious," Kricfalusi remarks. "So I drew a caricature, only really, *really* perverted-looking, of this psychotic Chihuahua. And there was a guy there named Joel Fajnor who thought it was funny. He and I used to do Peter Lorre impressions, and we would just make up a million jokes. I think *he* suggested that I put that character together with Stimpy, the cat that I was drawing. It wasn't like I sat down and said 'Well, gee, I've gotta create a team of characters.' That's usually not as good as things that just happen by accident, or inspiration."

Nothing much came of the retarded cat and psychotic Chihuahua for a few months. They didn't even have names. Then, one day, Fajnor came to pick up his friend at his apartment. Kricfalusi saw him standing near the mailboxes, laughing his head off, and asked what was so funny. In the best juvenile tradition, Fajnor was cracking up at the name of the apartment manager, Ren Hoek.

"It *was* a funny name," Kricfalusi says, "so I just used it. Originally, I called him 'Ren Hoek Toad Tot.' I don't know what the hell a Toad Tot was; it just sounded weird. And I used to call a college roommate of mine 'Stimpy'–his name was Harold Duckett; he's an animator, too–but for some reason, he just looked like a Stimpy to me. And when I used to draw that cat, the name seemed to fit. So all this stuff just sort of randomly came together."

Eventually, someone–probably Fajnor again–encouraged Kricfalusi to pitch it as a series idea, so he did. With the help of then-girlfriend Lynne Naylor and pals Jim Gomez and Francis Forte, he kicked around ideas before assembling a presentation. The characters of Ren and Stimpy were nailed down early, as Kricfalusi tells it: "Ren is an absolutely psychotic lunatic, but he's completely helpless because he's so small. If he could, he'd kill you in a second; he would just tear your skin off. But he needs Stimpy–he needs someone who's got a little more girth to him, and strength to protect him, and who'll put up with his rages."

John K. pitched *Ren & Stimpy*, along with a few other animated series ideas, to anyone who'd listen. Mostly, the suits at the networks didn't know what to make of this hyper lunatic who sweated buckets as he jumped about, acting out all his nutty ideas and characters. "They were just nervously looking around," he says, "thinking, 'How can we get a security guard in here?' Whenever I pitched anywhere, it was always [whispering,] '*Call the police!*'"

But they all said no to *Ren & Stimpy*–everyone, that is, except the fledgling network Nickelodeon. And a new cartoon trend was born.

Tim Burton Shares His *Nightmare* with the World

In the early 1980s, Disney had an imaginative young animation artist/director in its employ that it didn't quite know what to do with. His drawings were too unique, too dark and different from the studio's house style. Still, he turned out a pair of distinctive animated shorts that they funded and encouraged him to create, *Vincent* and *Frankenweenie*, and a forty-five-minute, live-action retelling of *Hansel and Gretel* for the Disney Channel, all in 1982.

Around the same time, he began developing characters and designs based on a three-page poem that he'd written, inspired by the holiday TV specials he'd adored as a child–including Dr. Seuss' *How the Grinch Stole Christmas* (directed by Chuck Jones) and *Rudolph the Red-Nosed Reindeer* (filmed in stop-motion "Animagic" by Rankin/Bass). The poem began:

It was late one fall in Halloweenland,
and the air had quite a chill.
Against the moon a skeleton sat,
alone upon a hill.
He was tall and thin, with a bat bow tie;
Jack Skellington was his name.
He was tired and bored in Halloweenland.
Everything was always the same.[1]

Tim Burton attempted to get his idea produced as an animated short, a television special, anything he could. He imagined it narrated by his idol, Vincent Price, whom he'd already worked with on *Vincent*, but no one would do anything with *The Nightmare Before Christmas* until years later, after Burton had succeeded wildly as a live-action film director.

In 1990, he approached Disney–who actually owned the designs, sketches, and story outline that he'd created while working there–and a deal was struck to turn his holiday parable into a big-screen stop-motion animated feature. Burton began developing the project in a decidedly non-traditional way, telling the story to composer and frequent collaborator Danny Elfman–who would then go off on his own and write songs. So before anything was ever scripted, *The Nightmare Before Christmas* began to take shape more as an operetta. Elfman himself ended up performing the singing voice of Jack Skellington, the fearsome Pumpkin King of Halloweentown who dons a white beard and red coat in a misguided attempt to replace Santa Claus and preside over Christmas.

The finished film, produced by Burton and directed by talented stop-motion animator Henry Selick, finally opened in 1993. Although it was criticized by some as too frightening for kids, most critics raved about the movie–"Through Burton's eyes, these dark dreamscapes aren't bad places at all. In fact, they're quite wonderful," the *Washington Post* declared. In fact, the film and its songs hold up remarkably well to repeated viewings–and its popularity has only increased over the years as it slowly achieved cult status.

Giving His Creation Life . . . Down in *Dexter's Laboratory*

By the late eighties and early nineties, the cable TV networks were growing bigger and more influential. Cartoon Network had started out by programming mostly older toons, drawn largely from the Hanna-Barbera library. The big plan was always to eventually develop their own original

[1]From Tim Burton's The Nightmare Before Christmas *by Tim Burton (New York: Hyperion Press, 1993).*

series, so in the summer of 1994, the network put out the word, inviting new artists to submit their toon proposals. Those selected would be given the opportunity to create a seven-minute short that would introduce their characters. The goal from the start was to fund and create forty-eight cartoons in all–which would appear on a new series called *World Premiere Toons*. (When the network began airing the films, they re-dubbed the show *What A Cartoon!*)

With the stage set for some fresh new talents to get their big chance, into the picture walked an unassuming young Russian émigré named Genndy Tartakovsky, who says he didn't start to draw, or even know what a comic book was, until he was about seven years old and his family moved to Chicago.

"When we came here, I saw comic books all over the place," he recalls. "If you go into a 7-Eleven, they've got a rack–I think that's where I actually saw my first one–and I just fell in love instantly." But, surely, as a child in Moscow, he was influenced by all the cartoons he'd watched on TV, right? Surprisingly, no. Soviet Russia offered only one cartoon show that Tartakovsky can remember, called *Nu, Pogodi!* "The best translation is, 'Wait Till I Get You Now,' and it was a *Tom and Jerry* type of thing about this wolf chasing a rabbit," Tartakovsky recalls. "It was a very popular show. But I wasn't drawing in Russia. I started drawing *after* I discovered comic books. Then I discovered cartoons, and started watching those religiously."

Yet, as he grew older, animation didn't seem like a career option to him. He figured he would go into advertising design and do storyboards, but when he got to Columbia College in Chicago, all the classes he wanted to take were closed. "They had alphabetical registration," Tartakovsky adds dryly.

"So I was taking English and stuff, and then I realized there was an animation class, and I could fill in an elective credit." From the moment he stepped into that classroom, he suddenly realized that animation was his true calling. After two years of creating some wildly experimental short films, Genndy decided he needed more of a challenge, so he moved to Los Angeles and transferred to California Institute of the Arts (CalArts), where he met Rob Renzetti, Randy Myers, Paul Rudish, Craig McCracken, and a host of others who'd all end up working together one day.

It was during his second year at Columbia College that Tartakovsky made a two-and-a-half-minute toon called *Changes*, which just happened to feature two future (and as yet unnamed) cartoon stars. "I drew this girl, and I really liked her–I wanted to animate a girl dancing, and I decided to make my student film around her. And I thought, she's tall and skinny, what do I need for her to interact with?. . . . I'll make a little *boy,* and he can be more square and he can be a little scientist, and then he can have a lab in his bedroom. And then things started to click."

The pint-sized genius after an experiment goes awry in Dexter's Lab.

Tartakovsky pitched his idea to Cartoon Network, and in February of 1995, they aired their very first short: *Dexter's Laboratory*, which proved so successful that just a year later the network introduced it as a series.

WHOOPING SOME CARTOON ASS, POWERPUFF STYLE

Much of *Dexter*'s distinctive look came from the show's art director, Craig McCracken, another up-and-coming cartoonist discovered by Cartoon Network. McCracken, a relentless drawer and doodler from the moment he could pick up a crayon, had visions of immortality dancing in his head from an early age, when he first set out specifically to create something that would end up as his legacy.

By the age of twelve, McCracken recalls, he had begun trying to create "that one character that would be my definitive character." Of course, his young hands and mind were bound to frustrate him, and he reluctantly ended up taking his parents' advice: "Just go to art school, and just *wait*."

It was at CalArts, at age twenty, that he finally honed in on his characters. "I was already in school, so I was making films," McCracken recalls. "And I knew for my second-year student film I wanted to do a superhero type short . . . At the time, I was working on a Mexican wrestler character to be my hero. I wasn't totally sure of it yet–and I just happened to draw these three little girls, and I went, 'Wait a minute. *They're* super-

Bubbles, Blossom, Buttercup, and Professor Utonium exude love in this publicity image from The Powerpuff Girls.

heroes; it's much cooler!' It was more of a contrast, and they seemed tougher because they're so cute."

So McCracken made an animated short called *The Whoopass Girls*, designed in a sharp-angled minimalist style not unlike UPA Studio's 1950s cartoons. The short went over pretty well in school. It went over just as well when he pitched it to Cartoon Network for *World Premiere Toons*, and they ended up commissioning two animated shorts from McCracken, which both aired in 1994–but not before a name change, to *The Powerpuff Girls*.

Although it took a long time, the girls finally made it to the screen as stars of their own series. Once the fourth season of *Dexter's Lab* wrapped, McCracken got crackin' with his original creation. With pal Genndy Tartakovsky along to help produce and co-direct, the new series was put into production and began to run in 1998.

CONGRATULATIONS, MRS. LION! IT'S A BOY

The Birth of *The Lion King*

At about the same time that *Dexter's Lab* was premiering on TV, Walt Disney Pictures had been basking for a year in the glow of their biggest box office smash and one of the most beloved animated films of all time, *The Lion King* (1994). The origins of the picture have been shrouded in mystery for years–even many of the film's key creative personnel can't seem to agree on how it began. In fact, *The Lion King* was born several times–first springing to life in a casual conversation between Peter Schneider, then head of feature animation at the studio, and Jeffrey Katzenberg. During the press tour for *Oliver & Company*, the two execs were sharing a flight and loosely talking about potential films when the idea of a movie featuring lions came up. Why lions?

"Because lions are cool," says Thomas Schumacher, who was *The Lion King*'s producer from the very start and guided the project through its development. "They started talking about making a movie that had lions in it, an animal movie. There was no story, no concept, it wasn't conceived as a musical, there was nothing. Just lions." In 1989, Charlie Fink–who'd been hired by Schneider to start an animation development department at Disney–put the vague idea into the works. Several different stories were devised by various authors, and a lot of drawings were done–of lions. What emerged from all this was a story outline for a film called *King of the Beasts*, about a war between lions and baboons.

Schumacher, who had just produced *The Rescuers Down Under* (released in 1990), was asked to take *King of the Beasts* under his wing and shepherd it forward. By then, the studio had another little project well on its way into production–something called *Beauty and the Beast*–so the lion film was renamed *King of the Jungle*. This apparently didn't sit well, either.

"Roy [Disney] said, 'You can't call it *King of the Jungle*. Lions don't live in the jungle!' So it became this ongoing thing that lions don't live in the jungle," Schumacher recalls with amusement. "In fact, the king of the jungle isn't really a lion, anyway, since lions live in a *savannah*, not a jungle. This was something that eluded a number of people, I think."

The idea quickly became a problem child.

Since there was no existing story structure to fall back on, what followed were years of false starts, development that veered off in many different directions but never felt right, storylines that went unresolved, and characters–like Bhati, the young fox, and Mheetu, another lion cub–that were written in and then cut. Screenwriter Linda Woolverton (*Beauty and the Beast*) worked for about a year on various early drafts of the story. "But it was difficult to figure out what the film was actually *about*," says Schumacher, "and who was who. During this period of time, Rafiki went from being a cheetah to being a baboon . . . the whole idea of the war with the baboons had ended . . . and now it was going to be about responsibility, and about raising a cub who wants to be king–but how was that going to happen?"

Then came the conversion of the movie into a musical–which practically everyone resisted–and an inspirational trip to Africa for creative personnel, which provided many ideas that would eventually find their way onto the screen. Though the story kept evolving, moving closer to the one we know today, there still were major problems. By the time the film's first director, George Scribner, was traumatically let go, there was so much turmoil that "no one wanted to work on this project," according to director Roger Allers, who had climbed aboard in 1991, thanks to some serious coaxing by Jeffrey Katzenberg.

When Rob Minkoff was assigned to join Allers as co-director, they wisely decided to lock themselves away in a room with producer Don Hahn and a few story artists and writers for two weeks of intense brainstorming. The team took the story apart, analyzed it–especially the troubled second and third acts–figured out who the characters were, and put it back together again.

"*Then* the thing raced into production, and it was a wrestling match for the next three years," says Schumacher. Despite all its early problems, "the alchemy of this movie–which still confuses me–works," he observes. "And the very things people didn't like about it are the things that drive it." *The Lion King* went on to become a hugely successful phenomenon, spawning sequels, merchandise, a television series, and a smash-hit, award-winning Broadway musical with productions running all around the world.

Pretty as a Pixel

Toy Story Becomes the First CGI Toon Feature

Another animation milestone was set one year later, with the release of the very first movie ever to be created entirely on computers. *Toy Story* (1995) rewrote the rules about what a feature-length toon could look like and how it could be produced. It was a huge technological leap.

Hard to believe now, but when the Pixar creative team begin planning out the film in 1991, they faced a question similar to the one encountered by both Disney and Fleischer almost sixty years earlier: Would audiences who were accustomed to short-form computer-generated cartoons sit still for one that ran the length of a feature?

The landmark movie actually began as an idea for a holiday TV special. Pete Docter, *Toy Story*'s supervising animator and one of its three original creators–along with John Lasseter and Andrew Stanton–reveals the company's early strategy: "Ed Catmull–who's the president of Pixar–had long had dreams of doing a feature film using computers. He had this plan loosely in place that we would start by doing shorts, then we would do commercials ('cause shorts don't actually make any money) . . . and then we were gonna do television of some sort, working our way up to features."

In late 1990, they began developing an idea that director Lasseter and story artist Joe Ranft had hatched: Using some of the characters they'd developed already for the shorts, such as Tinny from their Academy Award-winning *Tin Toy* (1988), they'd create a TV special. Their idea turned into something they called *Tin Toy Christmas*, which they pursued until the group encountered a small problem. "The bare bones bottom budget that we could make this for was still, like, eighteen times more than what any network was gonna give us," recalls Docter. They realized they'd have to rethink their plan.

Tinny from Pixar's acclaimed short, Tin Toy.

The folks at Disney, meanwhile, had been after former employee John Lasseter to return to the fold. But instead of going back to work there again, he cannily managed to convince them to hire the whole Pixar Studio–to produce a feature film. Eisner and Katzenberg told Lasseter to come back to them when he had some ideas.

"We sat around, and we thought and we thought," says Docter. "I remember John finally saying, 'What if we took this *Tin Toy Christmas* idea and extrapolate it out into a feature?' Well, we didn't know what we were doing, so we just said 'Sure!'" he laughs. "And that was the beginning of *Toy Story*."

The original story bore little resemblance to the one we know today. Buzz Lightyear started out as *Tin Toy*'s Tinny, explains Docter. He was to be the main character–a toy that in the 1940s doesn't sell and so is put away in storage. "And it's sort of like Rip Van Winkle: When he wakes up, it's now the bustling nineties, and he's in this huge megastore like a Toys 'R' Us, where he's eventually bought by this girl."

Docter speculates that it took a year of figuring out the story and characters before they were able to lock in the basic structure. At one point, for instance, they had Tinny encounter a ventriloquist dummy. But the test of that one didn't go so well. "It was really creepy. I think a lot of people had ventriloquist dummies that attacked them as kids or something," Docter muses. Eventually, the dummy became a pull-string doll–"based largely on a *Casper the Friendly Ghost* pull-string doll that John had loved when he was really little." That doll finally evolved into a cowboy named Woody, whose personality was not unlike Andrew Stanton's. "He has this way of saying these really rude, obnoxious things," grins Docter, "but they make you laugh, so he gets away with it. And that's the way we were playing Woody."

When they finally pitched their big idea to Jeffrey Katzenberg, Thomas Schumacher, and the rest of the Disney honchos, the reaction wasn't what they'd expected. The execs felt that the story seemed too juvenile. "A lot of the elements were there, but everybody was very happy and fun and nice to each other," Docter observes. "I'd say it was charming and innocent. But the words Jeffrey used were, 'It's juvenile.' He pushed us to make it much more edgy, make the characters acerbic and angry. So then we came back, and by now we had storyboards. We showed a reel where Woody was a complete asshole. And *nobody* liked him–but it was edgy! It was really finding the balance, then, of those two things."

"From the very beginning there was a ton of back and forth on the story," Schumacher confirms. "At one point most of the crew got laid off while it went back into development–but John Lasseter always had a vision for how the characters would behave."

Toy Story ended up a solidly crafted tale, and it proved that if the storytelling is strong, the characters are memorable, and the movie's entertaining–three qualities that Pixar's first feature had working in abundance–audiences will take that leap of faith and embrace something different and new.

Mr. Hankey Goes to Hollywood

How *South Park* Got Started

Sometimes, it's all about the timing, as with one wildly popular toon that could never have seen the light of the small screen just a few years earlier.

Trey Parker and Matt Stone's *South Park* (1997) started out as a small, obscure, cheaply produced cartoon utilizing cutout paper animation. Today, it's a very big, *famous*, cheaply produced cartoon utilizing cutout paper animation–or at least the look of cutout paper, as it's now being created digitally.

Parker and Stone, who both actually grew up in South Park, Colorado (purportedly a real-life hot spot for UFO sightings and alien abductions), met and became friends at the University of Colorado. It was there that they decided to collaborate on some projects together, including a few cartoons and a low-budget independent feature called *Cannibal: The Musical*. One of the toons, whose look was inspired by Terry Gilliam's cutout animation on *Monty Python's Flying Circus*, had a simple yet touching premise: Beloved childhood character Frosty the Snowman comes to life and threatens to slaughter everyone until he's stopped by Baby Jesus and four potty-mouthed little kids–all early incarnations of the *South Park* gang. The Cartman character's name is "Kenny" in this short, now known as "The Frosty Episode," and, just as his namesake would do in countless later stories, Kenny dies.

Now that the world is familiar with Parker and Stone's sensibilities, it comes as no surprise that there was enough blasphemy and bad taste in the short to offend just about everyone. Also, no surprise that this thoroughly delighted many of the folks who managed to view it. In 1995, one such person–Brian Gradon, then a TV exec at Fox–offered the guys $2,000 to create a short video in the same style, so he could use it as a novel Christmas card to send all his friends that year.

They jumped at the offer and quickly produced "The Spirit of Christmas," in which Santa Claus battles a now grown-up Jesus at a local shopping mall. Adequate.com's *South Park* Web site quotes one of the creators talking about the cartoon:

"I did the animation using construction paper cutouts," Trey Parker says, "and we both improvised the dialogue, screaming obscenities at each other in my basement while my mom was baking fudge upstairs. It cost $750 and we pocketed the rest." That Christmas, Graden sent the video out to eighty people, who promptly copied it and made it their card, as well. And so on and so on. "By February, we were hearing about it from every state; friends of friends in New York were telling us, 'Metallica saw your video and they loved it.'"

As the story goes, actor George Clooney also went crazy for the short, making another 150 dubs to send out to all *his* friends. The momentum kept building to a fever pitch, finally prompting Parker and Stone to head to Hollywood together and try to sell their idea as a series. The pair found themselves sleeping on people's floors at night and making the rounds during the days. Most networks were too apprehensive to put a show about foul-mouthed kids on the air every week–but not Comedy Central.

"When I saw 'The Spirit of Christmas,' I thought it was the funniest thing I've ever seen," network CEO Doug Herzog told *Animation Magazine*'s Sarah Baisley in 1997. "My first instinct was, if we can find a way to make it airworthy, we need to do this and be in business with these guys."

It premiered that summer with its first episode, "Cartman Gets an Anal Probe," with the kids still voiced by the show's creators. Sure, the stream of four-letter words spouting out of Cartman, Stan, Kyle, and Kenny's mouths are bleeped or muffled, but we know what they're saying. *South Park* the series has been consistently–and lovingly–crudely animated. It's also totally irreverent and wickedly funny. Another holiday-themed show, "Mr. Hankey, The Christmas Poo" (in which a sweet, singing, dancing brown turd teaches the town the true meaning of Christmas), may have plumbed new depths in tastelessness, but no one could deny it was flat-out hilarious.

The TV show spawned a successful theatrical animated musical film, *South Park: Bigger, Longer, and Uncut* (2000), which proved even raunchier than the series. Suddenly, the constraints of television didn't apply, and the kids could curse and swear–in both dialogue and song–openly. The film was slapped with an "R" rating by the Motion Picture Association of America, but that didn't stop millions of kids and adults from flocking to see their favorite show blown up onto the silver screen. One of the film's songs, "Blame Canada," was even nominated for an Academy Award! Although it didn't win, many felt that the satiric *South Park: Bigger, Longer and Uncut* musical number was robbed, in, uh, large part, due to the movie's cheerful vulgarity.

In 2002, Parker and Stone decided to kill Kenny off for good. Hard to say if he'll stay dead, though, considering the kid's track record at resurrection. Regardless, the TV series will be around for a long, long time.

Middle-Aged White Guys Make It to *King of the Hill*

South Park wasn't the only enduring prime-time animated comedy show to hit the air in '97. Flush from the success of his unexpected (and long-running) hit on MTV, *Beavis and Butt-Head* creator Mike Judge was encouraged to create something for the Fox network to run following *The Simpsons* on Sunday nights. "I had met with all the studios, and I think they said, 'Oh, okay, so he's not a scary guy with swastika tattoos or anything,'" the affable Judge muses in his Texas studio.

Fox offered Judge a deal, and he set about trying to think of an idea for a show. What came to mind pretty quickly were four neighbors he remembered from Dallas: "We had bought a house up there and it was kinda like, they were always out in the back, drinking beer in the alley, y'know?" This recollection, combined with his penchant for doodling middle-aged white guys in his sketchbooks, led straight to the creation of the characters Bill and Dale. Judge's work had begun.

Mike Judge's original drawing that inspired Fox's hit prime-time series, King of the Hill.

"I had a different Hank originally," he explains. "I kinda mellowed him out a little bit, and just kinda made up Boomhauer. . . . I'd done it like a panel cartoon of four guys with beers. Originally, I was gonna do an animated short of basically those four guys standing around looking down at an engine, arguing about what's wrong with it–which is just something I saw growing up all the time, on my paper route. . . . There's, y'know, guys standing out there with their beers going, 'Uh . . . it's the carburetor.' I just started from there."

Somewhere along the way, Judge decided to write a pilot script and do some more drawings based on the blue-collar guys. His managers saw the idea as a potential new TV series, and brought in then co-executive producer of *The Simpsons,* Greg Daniels. "That was around the time the *Beavis and Butt-Head* movie was starting to go," recalls Judge. "I'd already written a pilot and done the drawings . . . so he came in and did a rewrite."

Daniels refined Mike Judge's basic premise without losing its flavor, making changes both subtle and broad in the pilot script. Perhaps most significantly, he added the character of Hank Hill's nubile eighteen-year-old niece, Luanne, to the household. "And then, he kinda got the show up and running while I was doing the *Beavis and Butt-Head* movie. He did all the work of finding the writers," says Judge. "He was really the show runner. He had added some good stuff to the pilot, so I thought it would be good to put his name on there, make it his reputation, too, not just mine. At that point, I was like, 'I'll share the success if I can share the blame,'" he adds wryly.

They called their new series *King of the Hill* and centered it around proudly Texan, hardworking blue-collar everyman Hank Hill (voiced by Judge), his wife Peggy (Kathy Najimy), their son Bobby, niece Luanne, and neighborhood buddies Dale, Bill, and gibberish-spouting Boomhauer. It struck a chord with viewers from the very start, and became one of Fox's most popular shows.

NOW THAT'S AN UGLY BABY

Shrek Happens

As you can see, every couple of years or so the entertainment biz experiences a film or TV series that can only be described as a phenomenon. The eighties and nineties offered several, and the new millennium ushered in its very first with a hideous green ogre and his pals who belched, farted, and wisecracked their way to stardom on the big screen.

When Pacific Data Images/DreamWorks' feature *Shrek* opened in 2001, no one knew for sure how audiences would embrace the film. The young studio had already had a few smash hits, but all in the live-action arena. None of their ambitious animated projects–*Antz* (1998), *The Prince of Egypt* (1998), or *The Road to El Dorado* (2000)–had taken off quite the same way, and with partner Jeffrey Katzenberg overseeing things, the comparisons between DreamWorks and Disney were unavoidable. Could Katzenberg replicate the kind of success he'd achieved at Disney, where he had presided over *The Little Mermaid, Beauty and the Beast, Aladdin,* and *The Lion King,* several of the biggest hits in the history of animated cinema?

Shrek sprang from the mind of noted author-illustrator William Steig, who in 1990 created a simple thirty-two-page picture book entitled, appropriately enough, "Shrek!" It told a tale about a nasty green ogre who's perfectly pleased with his repulsive appearance, and goes off "slogging along the road, giving off his awful fumes" after his parents have "hissed things over" and "kicked him good-bye." Along the way he encounters a witch, a dragon, a donkey, a knight in armor, and, finally, a hideous princess who's even uglier than he is. As foretold by the tale's witch, Shrek and the princess marry, with the bride clutching a cactus instead of the usual bouquet of flowers.

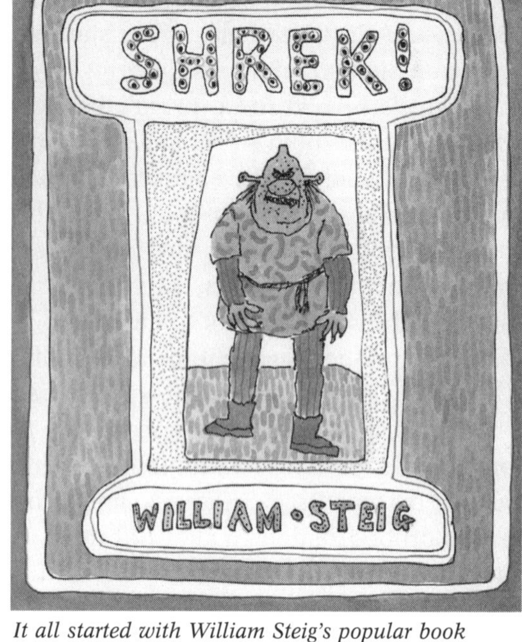

It all started with William Steig's popular book about the green ogre.

The story was a favorite of kids and adults everywhere, including the young son of producer John H. Williams. It was Williams who brought the book to the studio and said, "Hey, I think this would be a good movie." He was right. "He liked to say that he had the story pitched to him by his kindergarten child," laughs Andrew Adamson, one of *Shrek*'s two co-directors.

A large measure of the film's success can be attributed to its irreverent tone, essentially deconstructing the genre by telling a modern fairy-tale within a parody of classic fairy-tales. From the start, there's no mistaking where the movie is headed: The very first piece of business in *Shrek* is literally Shrek doing his business–in an outhouse. And there's plenty more off-color humor laced throughout the rest of the film. Because *Shrek* lampooned so many traditional characters and stories ("Pinocchio," "Snow White and the Seven Dwarfs," "The Three Little Pigs," and so on), it was assumed far and wide that Disney was its intended target. Toss in the Jeffrey Katzenberg connection, and could there be any doubt?

The filmmakers claim that all they were trying to do was tell a funny story that had heart, yet at the same time poke fun at the genre's tried and true conventions. But Katzenberg and his crew knew what people would think once the picture opened. They were so keenly aware of this that they took the unusual step of defusing any potential controversy–by inviting about twenty Disney execs to screen the film before it opened to the general public. The execs loved it.

The following year, *Shrek* nabbed one tribute after another, winning the very first Academy Award for "Best Animated Feature" (an Oscar category that artists in the industry had been fighting for forever, and which finally became a reality in 2002), along with similar honors from the National Board of Review, the Annie Awards, Los Angeles Film Critics, and many others.

Dawn of a New Ice Age

The award-winning DreamWorks film turned out to be just the first salvo in a volley of well-received digitally animated features that opened in rapid succession. Pixar's excellent *Monsters, Inc.* (2001), Nickelodeon's kid-friendly *Jimmy Neutron: Boy Genius* (2001), which became a wildly popular TV series a year later, and Twentieth Century Fox's breakout theatrical hit *Ice Age* (2002) were all released within months of each other to eager audiences.

The idea for *Ice Age* had been kicking around at Fox for at least a year before director Chris Wedge and his crew at Blue Sky Studios got involved. "Producer Lori Forte came up with the original concept," Wedge explains, "and the simple storyline was developed inside the Fox animation division."

The project had been earmarked for director Don Bluth, but that was before the studio closed down his animation facility in Arizona. Since Fox already owned Blue Sky–they had purchased the New York–based CGI animation company back in '97–it made perfect sense to turn to them. As Wedge elaborates, "We were developing a project with Fox at that point, which they decided *not* to make–it was a William Joyce book–and so, basically, we were just looking for something to do. They said, 'Well, take a look at this.' So I read *Ice Age*, and it was the best one-and-a-half acts of a script that I had read in a long time. It cranked it up, but then it had problems, that first draft did."

The original script was written by Michael G. Wilson, "who gets credit for the story, and deservedly," Wedge states. "But the tone of it was significantly different–it was more of an action-adventure thing with a lot of cataclysmic fighting, and it wasn't a comedy at all. Fox said, 'We'd like to make this a comedy. You think you can do that?' And that's what we signed up for." The producers brought in another screenwriter, Michael Berg.

"Michael came on board about the same time I did, around the beginning of 1999, in the early spring," says Wedge. "We just started jamming on the story together."

Ice Age tells of an unlikely team of prehistoric animals: Manny, a large, hairy, antisocial woolly mammoth (voiced by comedian Ray Romano); Sid, an irreverent, lovable little sloth (John Leguizamo); and Diego, a scheming saber-toothed tiger (Denis Leary). While the three journey together to bring a human infant back to its family, the tiger is secretly leading them into an ambush–where his pack awaits, hungry for revenge against

Scrat–a breakout star–makes a break for his life in Blue Sky/Twentieth Century Fox's surprising hit, Ice Age.

the child's tribe of hunters. Along the way, an unexpected bond develops among the trio, giving Diego pause on whether or not to continue with his sinister plan. Throughout the film, we periodically see a madcap, recurring character that all but steals the show: Scrat, a tiny, hapless, saber-toothed squirrel who's desperately trying to bury an acorn in the snow and ice.

"It's a very simple story, almost formulaic," Wedge admits. "But because the characters are so well-chiseled, it gave us a lot of opportunity to just have fun with the animation. I never liked the 'Three Prehistoric Mammals and a Baby' idea, because that really wasn't what it was for me. In fact, I did everything I could to *play down* the core idea that they have to get this baby back to its family. We just wanted to make it more about these three characters, and less about their predicament."

Ice Age went on to become a mammoth hit worldwide, putting both Blue Sky Studios and Twentieth Century Fox solidly on the map in the animation feature market.

CHAPTER 2
PUTTING IT TOGETHER
How Four Humongous Cartoon Hits Were Developed

"You've never heard of The Gladstones? The Gladstones couldn't be cleared for use. The rights [for the name] were held by somebody else, so that's why it had to be *The Flintstones*."

—Ed Benedict, designer and developer of Hanna-Barbera's classic series

Obviously, great ideas are not enough. Millions of wonderful ideas are out there even now, floating undeveloped on clouds in Idea Heaven . . . or rotting in Development Hell, that popular hot spot where ideas go to languish and roast for all eternity. Every animated series or feature has to go through the process of figuring out what it is, how it'll work best, who the main characters are, what they look like, what comprises their world, and so on. So many choices to be made . . .

And it can take time. Developing a toon project requires a lot of patience.

With a live-action film, development usually centers on the script. Nothing can proceed until it's locked in, having gone through as many rewrites and drafts as the producers deem necessary. With an animated feature, the writing of the script and the visual development go hand in hand, all happening at once. "In animation, you have to make the film before you make the film," points out *Shrek* producer Aron Warner, whose background was largely in live-action production until he joined DreamWorks. "You have to storyboard the entire film, edit it, put the voices to it, and look at it over and over and over again until it's right. In live action, you don't have those opportunities. You go out and shoot, and if you're lucky you can go back and do reshoots of a scene or two . . . but usually, you aren't that lucky."

Developing a cartoon TV series requires just as much fortitude. When a network gives the producers a green light, everything kicks in at once: working out the character designs, the environments, the props, the animation style. Finding the right voices. Creating the stories and scripts and storyboards. Recording the actors and adding sound effects and music. Editing it all together and delivering six or thirteen or twenty-six shows by a certain date, so the network can schedule it, promote it, and get it on the air.

While all shows and films have a certain development process in common, the way they go about it is often very different. In our second chapter, let's take a closer look at how four projects in particular were put together–two smash hit TV shows, and two incredibly popular films–starting with an ogre who took home the first ever Academy Award for Best Animated Feature.

He's Mean and He's Green

Bringing *Shrek* to the Screen

When the crew at DreamWorks began developing *Shrek*, one of the first things they did was find a voice for the title character: Chris Farley, the large, hyper comedian who'd gained fame on TV's *Saturday Night Live*. Farley was hired and brought into the recording studio to begin laying down lines from the script, still very much in progress at that point. By all accounts, he was marvelous as the ogre. The board artists and writers began sketching and planning out the film, with Chris' characterization as the centerpiece of the story.

Early on, the producers considered a technique known as *motion capture* to animate *Shrek*'s characters. A sizable crew was hired to run a test, wherein sensors were placed on an actor's arms, knees, shoulders, and so on, and a computer would capture those points as the actor performed . . . comprising data then utilized to build a CGI model based on his movements. According to those who saw it at the time, the motion capture test was just *ugly*. One staffer likened its appearance to that of "a guy dressed in full body character costume who walks through a theme park, shaking hands with little kids."[1]

In May of 1997, Jeffrey Katzenberg, underwhelmed with the results of the test, decided to cut the film's crew down substantially. Those who continued to work on *Shrek*, now just a handful, were moved to a smaller facility to concentrate on the story. Development of the production continued, going through its fair share of early turbulence–directors came and went, some of them burning out while others hopped aboard.

[1]*The technique, following further development, was used to brilliant effect on the character, Gollum, in* Lord of the Rings: The Two Towers *(New Line Cinema, 2002).*

Andrew Adamson joined the team that year and hit the ground running, partnering with Kelly Asbury to co-direct. As he quickly got himself up to speed, Adamson notes, "We were gaining a sense of what we wanted the film to look like. We were actually doing a lot of the design in miniature. In fact, we played for a while with the idea of using computer-generated characters over miniature backgrounds . . . and that was really what helped us find the look of the picture, even though we ended up doing it entirely computer-generated."

Some of the most important sets–such as Shrek's home–were crafted as miniature models, meticulously sculpted and painted. The artists sought to create a stark contrast between Shrek's very swampy, organic environment and the tyrannical Lord Farquaad's pristine kingdom. They studied the appearance of Hearst Castle, several popular ultra-sanitized theme parks, even the work of Nazi architect Albert Speer, mixing it all together to create Dulac, Farquaad's vision of heaven on Earth.

And through it all, the story kept changing and changing.

"We started pretty much in the tone that *Shrek* is now. Y'know, light, fractured fairy-tale, balls-to-the-wind craziness. Probably too crazy," story artist Ken Bruce reveals. "Jeffrey pushed for more focus on relationships, and on feeling, emotion, and empathy . . . and a lot of the wacky stuff went out the door. We went *so* far into a serious *Shrek* that pretty soon our boards were looking like 'Shrek's List'–so dead serious, and so emotionally overwrought, that we had a completely different film. It turned into a sort of humorless quest."

The struggle to figure it all out would sometimes get stuck on a single story point, such as the part where evil Lord Farquaad dispatches Shrek to fetch Princess Fiona from a castle tower where a fire-breathing dragon is guarding her. "We wanted to know *why* Fiona was up in a tower," Bruce recalls. "And Jeffrey kept saying that it doesn't matter, she's just up there, we won't address it. He was absolutely right. But we were creating incredible, convoluted back stories to explain what the hell she was doing up there! And, in fact, the answer to that question was in the mirror sequence. We're in a fairy-tale world, and the Magic Mirror tells us that there are three maidens and one of them just happens to be up in a tower. And you never question it. But *we* sure did."

Then, in the middle of everything, something terrible happened: Shrek died.

Chris Farley had already recorded over a third of his dialogue when he was found dead of a drug overdose at the age of thirty-three. This was nothing short of disastrous, on many levels. The world lost a talented and funny man, but Chris Farley wasn't merely the voice of Shrek–he *was* Shrek. Much of what the filmmakers had been developing was based on Farley, in subtleties, in mannerisms, and in the acting. "Chris had that emotional weight," notes Bruce. "Chris could make you cry."

On at least five increasingly frustrating occasions, the crew gathered to screen the filmed storyboards as *Shrek* plodded on. Each one was markedly different, but still, the right direction seemed to be eluding everybody. Morale began to flag more than once as they all struggled to find their way.

"You always go through that at some point on a film," producer Aron Warner points out, "but it was a particularly low group 'cause we didn't know where the movie was going, and we didn't have a lead actor." What they did have were endless brainstorming sessions to try and figure it all out. Plus, they had Steven Spielberg advising them along the way, and Katzenberg squarely in their camp, always nudging them forward, never letting them give up hope.

In 1998, co-director Kelly Asbury left the struggling film to helm another animated feature at the studio, *Spirit: Stallion of the Cimarron* (2002). Vicky Jenson, who'd been a story artist on *Shrek* for a few months at that point, came on as Andrew Adamson's new and final co-director. Rather than divide up their responsibilities as some other co-directors have done in the past (as in, "you take art direction, I'll take story"), the two decided to divide the movie itself in half, so that, although they would both spend time on each other's scenes, at least the crew would know who to go to with specific detail questions about those sequences. "We both ended up doing a lot of everything," Adamson says. "We're both kinda control freaks, and we both wanted to do everything."

Shortly after the final directorial change, the story crew experienced a revelation. "For some reason, we went and dug out the very *first* screening," Ken Bruce says. "You have to imagine, we had completely forgotten what we had boarded. . . . We put the tape in, and it was like it had fallen from the heavens! It was like God had dropped the tape and said, 'Here's the film you should work on.' It had its problems, but we all looked at it and thought, 'What's wrong with this?! Why can't we just do *this* film? This has got it all there–y'know, when there's a problem we can solve it–but it's lean, it's mean, it's clean, it communicates. It's *Shrek*!'"

The movie that ended up on the big screen is considerably different, of course, but that was the turning point for the filmmakers. As Bruce puts it, "We spent two years going in the wrong direction only to find out that what we had started with was pretty darn good. But that's the process. Sometimes you need to do it all *wrong* to find out what's all *right*."

Things began coming together even more so once they found their new Shrek–in the person of Chris Farley's former *Saturday Night Live* cast mate, Mike Myers. Myers had already moved on to even greater fame and success with *Wayne's World*, his *Austin Powers* movies, and other projects–and the filmmakers were thrilled to get him. He quickly began recording Shrek's lines, and everyone was newly energized. Ideas were flooding in from all sides now–story points became clearer, people came up with fresher gags and comedy bits–and the momentum of the whole project took a forward motion and never let up from that point on.

Along the way, however, they encountered yet another curious bump in the road. Myers' voice for Shrek was sort of a bland North American/Canadian accent, and not terribly distinctive.

"We sat down and watched the film," Warner says, "with Mike and Steven Spielberg and Jeffrey, in a very rough form, with probably about half

Author/illustrator William Steig's original conceptions of Shrek and that "jabbering jackass," Donkey.

of [Myers' performance] having been recorded, and a few sequences having been animated. Mike went away to think . . . and came back and said, 'You know, I can do better.' And we all said 'okay, let's try it.'"

Myers felt Shrek should have a Scottish accent, so he and the filmmakers worked out a whole new back-story for his character. "We didn't want to go too broadly Scottish, because we wanted to make sure that American audiences would understand it. Sometimes, I see Scottish films here [in the United States], with *subtitles*," chuckles Andrew Adamson, who hails from New Zealand. "And I look around and go, 'Come on, what's wrong with you people?!' But the whole idea was that Shrek was second-generation, and his parents were Scottish ogres who'd moved to Dulac. So we wanted to do a slightly lighter accent, and make it sound kind of like he'd grown up with Scottish parents and lived in this environment. There were times where we'd say, 'You didn't sound Scottish enough there,' or, 'You sound *too* Scottish there,' and he would work with us on that."

Bit by bit, the film began to come together.

The irreverent tone they'd played with earlier was blended with some of the heart and empathy that Katzenberg had been striving for. The idea to lampoon all the fairy-tale characters, which hadn't been part of the story at all before, entered the picture and picked up steam with gag idea after gag idea. Contemporary pop culture references and satiric jabs at other films, like *The Matrix* and *Crouching Tiger, Hidden Dragon,* began working their way into *Shrek*. The directors and producers, many of them from live-action backgrounds, introduced another element to give *Shrek* a unique feel: using familiar pop tunes and golden oldies to move its story forward. New covers of songs like "On The Road Again" and "Try a Little Tenderness" were strategically integrated into the film's score.

The story that finally emerged in *Shrek* was a simple one, which allowed the writers to weave many verbal jokes and sight gags into the fabric of the film:

Shrek, a surly loner, suddenly finds his swamp overrun with famous fairy-tale characters who've been banished from the realm by the short, anal retentive despot, Lord Farquaad, who's looking to clean up his pristine fiefdom. Befriended by a motormouthed donkey, the ogre appeals to Farquaad to undo the damage he's wrought–and the tyrant agrees, but on one condition: that Shrek journey to a far-off castle where beautiful Princess Fiona is imprisoned, defeat the dragon that protects her, and bring the lovely girl back to be Farquaad's bride. So donkey and ogre set off on their quest–with many twists and turns along the way.

As they were nearing completion of the project, Katzenberg prodded the filmmakers to revise *Shrek*'s ending in order to "go out with a big laugh," something they'd initially resisted. Instead of wrapping up the tale with a storybook closing over Shrek and Fiona as they rode off into the sunset, they finally decided to add a musical number which brought all the fairy-tale characters back onto the screen, in a rousing, comedic cover of "I'm a Believer" recorded by Smash Mouth and Eddie Murphy.

Shrek's development had been a long and rocky road, but what emerged was a true crowd-pleaser that sent audiences filing out of the theater with grins plastered to their faces. The vast majority of critics were enchanted, as well–despite the grumblings of a few, like the *Chicago Tribune*, who felt that *Shrek* "isn't nearly as visually pleasing as the Pixar/Disney collaborations," and one or two others who carped about the film's lowbrow humor. The movie was nevertheless an unqualified box office smash and the recipient of numerous awards, including that first Oscar for Best Animated Film. *Shrek* was hailed by some wags as "a celebration of the right to be cranky" . . . something DreamWorks was anything but.

JUST YOUR TYPICAL YELLOW CARTOON FAMILY

Turning *The Simpsons* Shorts into the Most Popular Animated Series in TV History

Most babies are born privately, and allowed to grow up and mature away from the public's prying eyes. Not so with *The Simpsons*, which was literally birthed on air, and had to grow up in front of millions of TV viewers every week on *The Tracey Ullman Show*. That it survived, much less evolved into what is inarguably the finest prime-time animated series ever made, is a modern miracle. When it began as a series of short interstitial cartoons sandwiched between the longer form sketches on Ullman's comedy series, the design and animation were crude, but startlingly different from any animation we'd ever seen on the tube.

No one involved with the show will tell you it was easy. *The Simpsons* took a fair amount of time to find its voice–literally. If you listen to Dan Castellaneta as Homer in the forty-eight shorts or in Season One, you'll hear a rather sharp-tongued and punitive parent, who gradually evolves into the lovable buffoon we all know today. "I think he was doing sort of a variation on Walter Matthau, initially," says Paul Germain, who, as associate producer, directed all the voice recordings for the short cartoons. In fact, the entire series went through a similar evolution–growing slicker, more sophisticated in both style and technique–as it found itself.

Makin' Toons

When Gracie Films first began to produce the short *Simpsons* cartoons, Matt Groening's original layouts were in black and white, just like his comic strips. It was color designer Gyorgyi Peluce who took the drawings of the oddball family and colored their skin yellow. Why yellow?

"Because it reads very well," she states. "I wanted the facial characteristics, the facial information when a character moves or talks, to always read well wherever they go." She perceived Groening's uniquely crude *Simpsons* designs as "a breakaway from all the concepts that we had ever learned about animation. Definitely as far away from Disney as it could possibly be." To her, they were a kind of folk art, which called for primary colors. And she had another, much simpler motive: "I wanted to make them look good!"

Peluce also gave the backgrounds their distinctive bright and colorful pastel hue, so that the characters and their world would be unified.

Klasky Csupo producer and co-owner Gabor Csupo with Gyorgyi Peluce, the color stylist who gave The Simpsons *their distinctive yellow skin.*

In 1987, Klasky Csupo, a small studio that had been producing commercials, titles, music videos, and trailers, began their most ambitious project to date: producing *The Simpsons* shorts. "It was so much fun," recalls Gabor Csupo. "But it was a lot of pressure, too, because I only had two or three animators, and we had to do basically a minute, a minute-and-a-half every week. You know, crank it out. And Gyorgyi was not only designing the colors–she was painting [cels and backgrounds]. We had a little mini-factory going."

Matt Groening would script the cartoons and draw out the sequences. "They were more like a comic strip guy's version of storyboards," says Germain. "Then, we would record the voices and cut it together like a radio play." Artists David Silverman, Wes Archer, and Bill Kopp would then refine the boards, time out the sequences, and do the layout drawings and animation. By the time it was shot and developed, sound effects were added, and the track was mixed, overall turnaround time worked out to about a month per segment. It was a hectic pace–and the budget was ridiculously low–but they were all happy to be working on something that felt so original and new.

The Simpsons' first animation producer, Margot Pipkin, remembers the all-for-one and one-for-all spirit that prevailed in those early days. "Matt Groening was working out of his garage in Venice [California] at the time," she recounts fondly. "We all went over there . . . he had a party in this tiny little house, and we all crammed into his garage where he did the work–it was so *underground comics*, those shorts."

The classically dysfunctional toon family was voiced by two supporting players from Ullman's show–Dan Castellaneta and Julie Kavner–plus two other talented actors, Nancy Cartwright and Yeardley Smith, hired specifically to voice Bart and Lisa. Interestingly, Tracey Ullman never performed a voice for the cartoon series that ran on her own program. "She didn't want to do a voice; she was too busy . . . so she let other people in the cast do voices," Pipkin says. Ullman took a very active hand in the creation of her show, which was chiefly composed of live-action comedy sketches–sharply performed and written.

Gabor Csupo describes the network's low expectations in the beginning: "They were just little short cartoons; they didn't really care too much. They said, 'Oh, okay, no one's gonna watch these, these are just bridges anyway between the brilliant Tracey Ullman sketches.' And then it turned out to be the other way around–everyone was watching *The Tracey Ullman Show* for the *Simpsons* cartoons!"

In 1989, James L. Brooks pushed Fox to turn *The Simpsons* into a series of its own. "It became clear that people were enjoying these little one-minute cartoons every bit as much as the show–maybe more," Paul Germain notes. "The executives at Fox, like every other executive in town, were saying no adult will ever watch animation. Well, we had about an hour of these short cartoons, and we would show them instead of having a warm-up comic, before the live filming of *The Tracey Ullman Show*. We would run these for the audience, and they were cracking up. I would sit there with the Fox executives and point and say, 'Do you see how they're laughing? Don't tell me adults aren't gonna watch this. They will!'" Executive producer Brooks refused to give up, and was finally able to convince the network.

Paul Germain helped guide The Simpsons *onto the air as a series, and later went on to co-create* Rugrats *and* Recess.

Everything changed when *The Simpsons* got picked up by Fox as a weekly half hour. "We'd never produced a series before," Csupo says today. "But they saw how hard we worked on the little cartoons, and they trusted us. And I hired producers who worked in the industry, who'd produced weekly shows before. And so, I think, from fifteen or sixteen people, from one week to another, we had to hire, like, another fifty people."

Right away, production time lengthened considerably. It now took at least two months to write and edit each script, followed by six to seven more months of storyboarding, drawing layouts and key poses, working out the timing, recording the voice tracks, and so forth. Animation production now had to be farmed out to overseas studios, where large crews could turn out the amount of footage required for a weekly series. It also meant that several different units had to be working on various episodes simultaneously.

Ken Bruce was one of the layout artists and animators on *The Simpsons'* first full season. "The genius really came from the writing. We all knew we were animating a brilliant radio play, with characters that were certainly difficult to draw–they're deceivingly difficult to draw, and animate, and turn. Now, it's all solved, but back then, we were solving that on a day-to-day basis. For a while there, we were making it all up as we went along. David Silverman and Wes Archer, mostly, were really instrumental in creating that big *black book* [the show's visual bible]. But we were all creating it in production. We were *discovering*–that first season, we were discovering what was working, and what wasn't."

The artists discovered that they had to change the feel of the show considerably. The underground quality of the shorter *Simpsons* cartoons, in a longer format, just seemed off model–the characters' appearance wasn't consistent from shot to shot, or scene to scene. So the crew had to deal with that problem early on. As producer Pipkin puts it: "Omigod, it was awful! We had to suddenly do an about-face, get really clean models, send them overseas, forget the underground look."

Although Groening and Brooks entrusted Pipkin and her crew with the daily nuts-and-bolts assembly of the physical production, she feels that both men remained as close to hands-on as they could be. "Brooks would look at everything," she raves. "And we met with Matt Groening several times a week, to show him boards, to show him designs . . . he was *very* involved. And he was very clear about what he wanted from the series. It was cutting-edge humor, but when it started getting too mean, he would pull it back. He knew where to push it to, and where to bring it back. Working with Matt was a pleasure."

Simpsons executive producer Brooks already had a formidable track record in TV and motion pictures: Emmy-winning writer and producer of *The Mary Tyler Moore Show*, *Taxi*, and *The Tracey Ullman Show*, and multiple award-winning director and writer of the films *Terms of Endearment* and *Broadcast News*. But he hadn't yet mastered a working knowledge of animation production. There was a considerable learning curve involved, as Pipkin remembers from a meeting they had when the very first color print came back and Brooks studied it with her: "Jim Brooks asked, 'Well, where's my coverage?' And I kinda looked at him blankly: 'Coverage?' And then it dawned on me–he wanted a three-camera show. He had no idea that he was only gonna get back one shot . . . he wanted to see another angle."

Was he embarrassed that he hadn't known that? Pipkin laughs. "Oh, no. When they're at that level, they don't get embarrassed. They just yell at you: '*Why didn't you give me coverage??!*'" She explained that in animation, there's no such thing. Since every image has to be drawn, animated, and painted, having to produce extra shots of the same scene would be like shooting three shows. "But, I mean, of course he picked it up immediately . . . he's a very, very smart man."

One thing the producers knew *very* well was writing. And they knew what they wanted: an animated series with the feel of a live situation comedy. "They wanted a different kind of humor–different from what we were used to in cartoons. And that was the hardest thing to bridge," Pipkin notes. "They wanted a far more sitcom kind of humor . . . and cartoons were, until then, based on pantomime–we did a lot of jumping about and acting it out with the short cartoons. That doesn't work for this kind of writing. *The Simpsons*, if you watch them, are very low key. We had to learn that in the first year."

Gracie Films brought in some advisors to help train the crew in this new form of animated storytelling. Producer Richard Sakai was especially helpful, dropping by the studio to show clips from classic series like *Taxi*, as a way of illustrating what it was the producers were after. Animator/director Brad Bird, hired as an executive consultant, did boards and character design work–and had a major impact on both the writers and the artists. Many, including Matt Groening, have attributed much of *The Simpsons'* cinematic visual approach to Bird's influence. "He's the one who first helped verbalize the difference in styles," Pipkin says. "One of the big tenets of animation is you act with your whole body . . . you think of the silhouette. That's not what *The Simpsons* is about. Those arms are in, those legs are in . . . it's about facial expression."

It took a while for the crew to get it.

When the first show ["Some Enchanted Evening"] came back from the Korean animation house, Margot describes it as a total disaster. "Gabor Csupo and I took it over to Gracie Films, Jim Brooks looked at it, and he lay down on the floor and said, 'This is un-airable.' And Gabor's and my stomach just went *pfffffffft* . . . because we had worked so hard, such long hours just to get that one done . . . but then, the next one was coming back the following week, and that was David Silverman's–"Bart the Genius"– and David got the kind of humor that it was."

The Simpsons' original lead director, who happened to be the most experienced crew member when it came to producing series animation, helmed that first episode about a bad baby-sitter. He was also the series' first casualty, as Pipkin was asked to let him go. "He directed it very cartoony, and they hated it," Pipkin recalls. "It had a lot of physical gags, so, consequently, you didn't pay attention to the words. And *The Simpsons* wasn't about physical humor. I owe him, because he helped me in how to put together a series. But he couldn't bridge the gap from cartoon comedy to the kind of comedy the executive producers wanted. Whereas David Silverman, Wes Archer, and Rich Moore–they got it. They understood what we were going for."

So embarrassed were the producers by the style, tone, and inconsistencies of that first episode that they delayed the initial airdate with Fox and instead opted to run a *Simpsons* Christmas special, "Simpsons Roasting on an Open Fire." From that point on, things went much smoother. "We began to get what it was that the exec producers were going for, and they, in turn, began to get more familiar with how to view an animatic, how to read a storyboard," Pipkin states. ("Some Enchanted Evening" wound up being redirected by David Silverman, and turned up as the last show of Season One in a much-improved state.)

Through it all, the crew worked feverishly to get the series ready for that first season. And they began in the most sardine-can-tight environment imaginable–legendary animation director Bob Clampett's old building on Seward Street. When Csupo had first rented the space, he'd had no idea who owned the building. "I didn't recognize Bob, because I'd never seen him–but when he said that he's Bob Clampett, I almost fainted! I said, 'Well, guess what? I'm an animator, too.' [He and his wife Sody] said, 'Okay, we want you in this building *because* you're an animator–and we'll give you a discounted rate.' That's how it started."

Layout artist Ken Bruce shoots some home video while fellow artist Tom Copolla works behind him at The Simpsons' *cramped original production offices, circa 1990.*

"In those years when animation really took off, it was all about streamlining facilities, cubicles all nicely in a row, and clean, neat office space, with new buildings for DreamWorks and new buildings for Disney," Ken Bruce muses. "This was a rented little *rat house*, with pigeons that lived outside one of the windows, and people who *smoked* in the room . . . We were, like, twenty-five in a cubicle, literally working back to back. I mean, there were times when I couldn't push my chair back because I would bump into somebody. . . . The pigeon poop was so thick and offensive that everybody was getting sick–the friggin' pigeons would fly into the room! But we had fun. It's so funny, because as the buildings got better and cleaner in this business, the interpersonal dynamics went down the tubes. There was something about that nasty environment, something that we don't get a lot these days . . . we had a good time."

Margot Pipkin also laughs about that first workspace. "In my office–I was the producer–we had two other people. That's how tight it was." Both Paul Germain and the show's production manager shared the tiny space with Pipkin. "It was the most funky, cool kind of place you can ever imagine," Germain adds fondly. "A bunch of artists with dreadlocks and stuff . . . just the greatest atmosphere. I loved working there . . . this was one of the happiest times of my working life."

About two-thirds of the way through the first season, the show moved from Seward to nicer facilities on Highland Avenue. But the atmosphere at *The Simpsons* remained loose and chaotic and nutty. "We still worked our *butts* off," Pipkin roars, "'cause we were doing it so on the cheap! It didn't change much at all."

It's a long-standing tradition on most animated productions for the artists to try sneaking little jokes into the periphery of a film or TV show. This was especially true on *The Simpsons*. Because the crew was asked to adhere strictly to the scripts–without adding their own gags, as was customary on cartoon shows–many of them felt constrained. Animators and board artists in general are a loose, crazy bunch, and their insanity has to come out somewhere. Margot Pipkin found herself policing the artwork on a regular basis, just to avoid disaster later on. "I would go around and tell them, 'You've got to get rid of that.' One of our artists loved to do these funny little X-rated jokes in the background. I *always* had to check his stuff. But they all did it. I had to go through everything with a fine-tooth comb, like some horrible drill sergeant: 'Darlin', you cannot do that.'"

Teale Wang, another artist who joined Klasky Csupo when they went to a half-hour series, painted backgrounds with Gyorgyi Peluce. *The Simpsons'* cels and backgrounds were and still are painted by hand with cel vinyl–the old fashioned way–one of the only series not colorized on computer. "Any changes that had to get made, you had to make those changes by hand . . . it was a really time-consuming thing," Wang says.

Meanwhile, Matt Groening and Jim Brooks were busy making creative decisions for the overall feel of the series, including the all-important opening theme music. Groening decided that he wanted a lush, fully orchestrated, yet irreverent theme that would prime the TV audience for what was coming. The producers found the perfect composer in Danny Elfman, who a few years earlier had created a wildly original score for Tim Burton's first feature, *Pee-wee's Big Adventure* (1985). To give Elfman a better idea of what he was imagining, Groening gave him a sampling tape he'd cobbled together–featuring a nutty mix of material that included a Frank Zappa electric shaver jingle, a "Teach Your Parrot to Talk" recording, some cuts from Nino Rota's *Juliet of the Spirits* soundtrack, and *The Jetsons* theme music. Elfman came back with the now-famous *Simpsons* theme, and Groening and Brooks were ecstatic.

The *Simpsons* creative team had their first clue that the show was a success when they found themselves approached by rabidly enthusiastic fans, who literally wanted a piece of them.

"I knew it was a hit when I was peeing in a urinal, and someone went apeshit over my *Simpsons* jacket," Bruce relates. "Some guy was like, 'Dude, that's the coolest show ever!' while I'm trying to urinate. 'Where'd ya get yer jacket? Where'd ya get yer jacket? I've gotta get yer jacket!' We all wore our jackets with pride." (It's customary in the biz to make up jackets and/or baseball caps for the crew, usually bearing a colorful embroidery of the show's logo.) This was the first piece of *Simpsons* merchandise that tchotchke-starved fans had ever seen, since little was available at that point to the general public.

"When the ratings started coming in on the series, we couldn't believe it," says Pipkin. "We just got more and more amazed . . . because the ratings kept going up and up . . . and we originally thought it was going to be this kind of low-key sort of thing on this new network, Fox, and not that many people would watch it, and then, suddenly, it just became a phenomenon!"

In 1990, *The Simpsons* won an Emmy Award for "Best Animated Program." It would turn out to be just the first in a long list of nominations and awards over the years. In terms of popularity, nothing else even comes close. *The Flintstones*, possibly its only real competition, aired in first run for just four years. Homer, Marge, and family have been on the air for fourteen seasons and counting, maintaining a level of excellence along the way that's rarely wavered–an amazing feat for any television series, animated or live.

A Fish Tale That Changed Everything

How a Tadpole Grew into *The Little Mermaid* and Woke Up Disney Feature Animation

Hans Christian Andersen, in his original fairy-tale "The Little Mermaid," had given the story a grim ending. The mermaid not only fails to marry her handsome prince–she dissolves into "death-cold sea foam," and perishes unhappily ever after. Thankfully, Ron Clements and John Musker chose a different path for the heroine in their version of the story.

When the brass at Disney Feature Animation put *The Little Mermaid* into development, they initially assigned some writers other than Clements and Musker, something that Clements wasn't thrilled about. He felt it was his baby–after all, he was the one who'd written the treatment that got the project going in the first place. Finally, he says, "I don't think they liked what anybody else was doing with it." So head of animation Peter Schneider decided to let Clements and Musker try their hand at a script of *The Little Mermaid*.

Every writing team has their own way of doing things, a method that works for them. Some physically sit together in the same room and write every word *together*. Others work separately, e-mailing scenes back and forth as they rewrite each other's pages. Still, others collaborate over the telephone, wearing headsets and talking things through as both sit in front of their computers.

Clements and Musker–who would continue their successful run as writers/producers/directors of *Aladdin* (1992), *Hercules* (1997), and *Treasure Planet* (2002)–have their own process that they started when writing *The Little Mermaid*, their very first screenplay. It began out of necessity, since both were still finishing directorial chores (along with Dave Michener and Burny Mattinson) on *The Great Mouse Detective* (1986), and were situated in adjacent offices. As they describe the way they work, you can't help but feel the passion and sheer joy they take in the scripting of a project:

"We work out the story together, with boards and thumbnails," Clements begins. "Once we feel like we've got the story outlined, John kind of starts–we do research together, but then John starts–he has a way of writing where he fills pages and pages and pages with ideas, and dialogue, and little bits of business."

Musker jumps in, describing the brainstorming phase of their scripts as total improv–he'll write the same scene eight times in a row, each one different, sometimes with dialogue, sometimes not. "Usually, I go in order of the script. Like, 'Here's the opening scene'–and I write it until I'm all written out and I can't think of anything else. Then I go on to the next bit, and as I'm going, I feed Ron the pages, and I go through the whole movie that way."

Clements then *rewrites*, adding new material without ever showing his partner. "He's seen everything I do," Musker says, "but I don't see anything he does until he's gotten all the way through, so I'm not derailing him with,

'Hey, wait a minute, what are you doing?' Basically, we get a ninety-page script that has some of my stuff, plus things I've never seen, and adaptations of what I've written, and then, we go from there."

At that, Clements laughs: "He reads it, and a lot of times he doesn't even remember what he wrote."

Musker is also grinning now: "I'm like, '*This* is great, but I didn't really like *this* part.' And he says, 'Well, that was in *your* thing,' and I'm like, 'It was?' So then, I sort of do rewrites of what he's written, and then it goes back and forth a few times, and then we turn it in."

The first draft took them a few months to complete. "The big thing with *Mermaid*, and I don't think we've ever gotten this reaction on any other script we've written, is that everybody, especially Jeffrey Katzenberg, loved it. I mean, they went nuts about the script," Clements marvels. *The Little Mermaid* was, in fact, a film of firsts for Clements and Musker: their first screenplay together, their first producing and directing effort as a team, and the first time Disney had ever launched an animated feature utilizing a fully realized script.

But there was another writer/producer who'd joined in on the creative process very early on–long before the script was finished–who influenced *The Little Mermaid* profoundly. His name was Howard Ashman.

Ashman had, at that point in his career, already achieved cult status in musical comedy history as co-creator of the off-Broadway show *Little Shop of Horrors*. In collaboration with composer Alan Menken, not only had he written the lyrics, he'd penned the show's book (based on Roger Corman's 1960 low-budget film of the same name), directed several productions of it, and was even the voice of the opening narration. *Little Shop* was a smash hit, playing for years and years, that then was made into an equally successful feature film directed by Frank Oz in 1986. One of the show's main investors was David Geffen, who also happened to be friends with Jeffrey Katzenberg. "David Geffen was pushing Howard to Jeffrey," John Musker says, "telling him, 'He's a guy you've gotta work with!'"

As it happens, Katzenberg helped run a company that Ashman had always been enamored of. "When he was a kid, Howard had a dream," confides Bill Lauch, Ashman's partner since 1984. "In this dream, the *Mickey Mouse Club* Mouseketeers appeared in his bedroom window and asked him to come join them, and run away. But when it finally happened, it was Jeffrey Katzenberg who came." Katzenberg asked Ashman to take a look at the storyboards they'd been working on. "When Howard saw *The Little Mermaid*, he got very excited," Lauch recalls. "He always loved the original tale, and thought this was something he really wanted to work on."

Musker clearly remembers their first meeting, which took place in New York. He and Ron Clements met Howard Ashman at the Helmsley Hotel, and the three of them went out to lunch. To their surprise, Ashman had already outlined the song slots that had been included in the original treatment, and he'd added a few more himself. He then proceeded to discuss some of his ideas–ideas that were already very fleshed out, Musker recalls.

Clearly, he'd put a lot of thought into the project. In fact, many of the songs that made it into the finished movie were in Howard Ashman's head right from the start. At that first meeting, he suggested inserting a serenade that turned into "Kiss the Girl," as well as the production number "Under the Sea" and Louie the Chef's riotously sadistic "Les Poissons." But his input didn't stop with mere song suggestions. He had some very specific thoughts about the characters, too, like King Triton's right-hand crab, Sebastian.

A lovely model sheet of Ariel's music teacher and guardian: the Caribbean crab, Sebastian. © Disney Enterprises, Inc.

"We had a crab in the original story," explains Clements, "'cause he was a character who could go both under water and on land. But in *our* story he was British–his name was Clarence and he was sort of a stuffed shirt–and Howard said, 'Let's make him Rastafarian.' That was a twist, 'cause first we were thinking that he's so dignified, and such a pompous character . . . how can he be laid-back?" Ashman told them to picture him sounding like Geoffrey Holder, the tall black Caribbean actor–and suddenly, it worked for Clements and Musker.

"Howard was looking for a way to infuse the movie with something a little bit hip, something to rhythmically enliven it in some way," explains Bill Lauch. "So he thought if the crab were Jamaican or Rastafarian, he could use some calypso or reggae music in the film."

The crab grew from a minor supporting character into a major one, becoming the king's distinguished court composer and Ariel's guardian, Horatio Thelonious Ignatius Crustaceous Sebastian. Infectiously voiced by Samuel Wright, he also headlines the movie's Caribbean-flavored show-stopper, "Under the Sea."

As they worked to develop the character of the little mermaid herself, the filmmakers saw her as more than a rebellious teen defying her father to get what she wanted. In Ariel, they strove to create an empowered young woman, even if everyone didn't always perceive her that way. As Clements points out, "We actually felt Ariel is a much more active heroine than Cinderella or Snow White or Sleeping Beauty. She goes out, and she makes things happen, she makes her own choices . . . but still, we did get nailed later on by some people who claimed, 'She just wants to marry this guy.'"

Clements admits that the romantic element of Ariel's story is key to the plot. "It really was about love at first sight," he concedes. "Everything in *Mermaid* totally relied on it–and you kind of had to believe that that was possible. That somehow these two people who'd never really met were destined to be together, 'cause they *couldn't* really meet–or, I should say, know who each other was–until the end of the movie."

The Little Mermaid also happens to boast one of the all-time great cartoon villainesses in the character of Ursula the evil sea witch–right up there, for my money, with Cruella de Vil from Disney's *One Hundred and One Dalmatians* (1962). What ended up in the finished film as a vain, cunning, zaftig octopus actually took many shapes and forms in her development. It was Ron Clements who'd decided from the beginning to push her heavily as the villain of the tale, making her a rival to King Triton, even curiously noting that she'd once lived in the palace.

Early on, Ashman–then a huge fan of the TV show *Dynasty*–had hoped that the role would be spoken and sung by Joan Collins. Clements and Musker, on the other hand, were picturing Beatrice Arthur (of *Maude* and *Golden Girls* fame) in their heads, and even described Ursula that way in the script. Either way, they'd written a very vampy, campy character, and their design crew had a ball devising her look.

"We had designs where she was more like a manta ray," Musker notes, describing a great red manta ray cape. "Bruce Morris, one of the development guys, thought she should be a scorpion fish, with all these needles . . .

but before that, even, Rob Minkoff did a drawing based kind of on [the late drag actor] Divine–this overweight matron as the witch, and Howard said, 'I love it! It's a Miami Beach matron–it's *perfect!*' Ultimately, Matt O'Callahan, a story guy, came up with the idea that if we were going to go with her *heavy*, how about making her an octopus? That way, we could get all that propulsion stuff, and it's a simple shape to draw."

One of many early rough character designs of Ursula, The Little Mermaid's *wicked sea witch. © Disney Enterprises, Inc.*

Though Ursula's appearance continued to evolve, the filmmakers never wavered in how they imagined her voice–husky and low, in contrast to Ariel's: a soprano ingénue and a basso, world-weary, funny, deadpan villain. When they actually went after Bea Arthur for the part, they were–surprisingly–rejected by her agent, who seemed livid at the suggestion that her client could even be thought of as a witch. "Her agent, I guess, read the script, and it described the witch as having a Bea Arthur–type basso voice . . . but she just read it, somehow in her mind, like we were saying Bea Arthur *is* a witch," Musker surmises. "I don't think she even gave it to her."

A lot of actresses auditioned for the role, among them Nancy Marchand, Nancy Wilson, Roseanne, Gretchen Wyler, Charlotte Rae, and Elaine Stritch. "We liked Charlotte Rae, and Howard was totally gung ho for Elaine Stritch. Neither of them had done the song yet ["Poor Unfortunate Soul"], so we held second auditions where Elaine Stritch would do the song, and Charlotte Rae would do the song," says Clements.

After they listened to both recordings, they all finally picked Elaine Stritch. The story department even started sketching out scenes of the character to a test track recorded by Stritch. "She was fantastic as the witch," Roger Allers recalls, who was then working as a story artist on the film. "It was [*in a deep, raspy voice*] this *boozy* kind of witch . . . it was hysterical."

However, Stritch, a pro with years of theatrical experience, didn't take well to Howard Ashman's style of direction. For one thing, "she wouldn't do the song at the tempo he wanted," Musker says. "Howard, with all his songs, he was kind of Svengali-like . . . and he would sing the demo for them. He *was* the witch, and he *was* the crab, and he would shape those performances. He would really channel himself into those people to do performances that he kind of initiated." But Stritch didn't respond to that kind of prompting. She was also fighting a long and now self-admitted battle with the bottle, which didn't help matters. They had to let her go.

Ron Clements heaves a sigh: "So we had these two leading contenders, and then, suddenly, we didn't have *either* of them. And then we had to go through a whole 'nother group of auditions ... " Among them was Pat Carroll, known to TV audiences for her role in Rodgers & Hammerstein's *Cinderella*, as well as her prodigious body of work in the theater. She got the final call to perform Ursula and left an indelible impression as the sea witch, playing her as unctuous, sly, campy, and deliciously evil. "Fortunately, I only look like her a little bit," the actress roars with laughter.

Back then, picking select takes from all the recorded dialogue was a slow process. "There were cassette tapes, and all the actors' lines were transcribed. We would listen to the cassettes in a room, and just go through everything," Musker relates. "So we were doing that with Howard, and he was going nuts. He was like, 'I can't believe you do it this way! Don't they have a computer? Isn't there a way to organize the dialogue so you'd have all this stuff in there?' Actually, what he was predicting is exactly the way we do it today. Now, on an Avid, we *do* input all this stuff–and we can just go *bang, bang*, I didn't like that line–and they've got the five others they've inputted."

Early in the development of *The Little Mermaid*, a transition was brewing that would have a great impact on the film. Howard Ashman had gone on from *Little Shop of Horrors* to collaborate on the 1986 Broadway musical *Smile*–not with Alan Menken, but with award-winning composer Marvin Hamlisch. The play was a flop, closing soon after it opened. At the time, he considered bringing Hamlisch in to compose on his new Disney project, but it wasn't to be. "They had a falling-out of some sorts," John Musker believes. Ashman instead sought out his *Little Shop* partner, Alan Menken, who eagerly agreed to work on the animated film–his first.

And history was made. Ashman and Menken would go on to great acclaim for their collaborations on Disney features, but it all started with this one.

As production heated up, Clements and Musker's film was generating the kind of electricity that hadn't been felt at Disney in years. The song of the mermaid was so strong, many at the studio couldn't resist its pull. Roger Allers, who had worked himself up to the position of head of story on *Oliver & Company* (1988) and really should have seen that film through to the end, claims he had no choice but to leave the project early to work on *The Little Mermaid*.

"I *had* to go work on *Little Mermaid*," he enthuses. "*Oliver & Company* was fun . . . but while I was working on it, my room was situated in such a way that Alan Menken and Howard Ashman's room was two doors down. They were working out the songs on their little portable synthesizer, and the music was pouring down into my office–and I was thinking, 'Oh, this is great! I'm *loving* this!' and getting so excited about it . . . and then I asked Ron and John if I could read their treatment, and the treatment was *fantastic*. I just *had* to work on that project–I felt like the mermaid train was leavin' the station, and God, I just had to get on!"

Sue Nichols, a story artist who worked for Clements and Musker at Disney, says, "I loved working with them. . . . They *listen*. You could be the janitor; if you have a better idea than the producer, they'll listen to the better idea no matter who gives it to them." Thanks to the input of so many talented people, the movie just steadily improved as production continued. Unlike lots of other animated features, which undergo major turmoil along the way–sometimes exploding in the middle of everything and getting reinvented–things went pretty smoothly.

The directors were pleased with their product, but neither had any idea what kind of impact the movie would have. At early test screenings, audience reaction was through the roof–especially from adults, which was the last thing they'd expected. It even caused the studio heads at Disney to rethink the film's marketing campaign. When the picture opened, it became what was then the highest grossing animated film, ever.

More importantly, by fusing Ashman and Menken's musical theater aesthetic with Clements and Musker's solid animation storytelling skills, they came up with something brand new: a sort of animated Broadway musical. This cross-pollination would generate further offspring in time, as several notable Disney features were reconceived as live theatrical productions–with spectacular results. *Beauty and the Beast* and *The Lion King* have been running on stage for years, with no end in sight.

The Little Mermaid also became a sort of unofficial template for many of the studio's subsequent animated musicals, which all featured similar story structure and song placement. Some have argued that *Mermaid* is still the best of these films, but, in any case, it's a formula that served Disney well for years.

Something Silly Is Afin

Putting *SpongeBob SquarePants* Together

The world of TV cartoons is a zany, wacky place. Pretty much anything's possible–the loonier the idea, the more suitable it is for animation. A few

SpongeBob indulging in his favorite pastime: jellyfishing.

years ago, some friends of mine told me to check out a truly bizarre new series on Nickelodeon called *SpongeBob SquarePants* (1999). The first time I watched it, my initial reaction was, "Hmmm . . . I wonder what these guys were smoking when they hatched this one." The show takes place entirely underwater, in an almost hallucinogenic floral Hawaiian setting (the city of Bikini Bottom) somewhere below the Pacific Ocean, and features the adventures of SpongeBob SquarePants, a nerdy sponge who lives inside a pineapple with his pet snail, Gary. He has an ornery next-door neighbor named Squidward and a dim-witted starfish pal named Patrick, works as a fry cook at the Krusty Krab restaurant, and manages to irritate the heck out of everyone with his relentlessly cheery disposition and grating personality.

Oh, and did I mention that the show is laugh-out-loud funny?

SpongeBob SquarePants is the insane brainchild of a rather sane, thoughtful guy named Stephen Hillenburg, whose background revolves chiefly around . . . you guessed it, the ocean. As a self-described "typical kid," he grew up loving cartoons and comics but dreamed of a career as a marine biologist.

"All the while, I'd always been interested in drawing and painting, but not necessarily drawing *fish*–y'know, like scientific illustrations," he says. "I actually could never figure out where the two met, or would meet." So Hillenburg followed his interests, ending up at the Marine Institute (later renamed the Ocean Institute) in Dana Point, California, a marine education center where he worked as a teacher and sort of staff illustrator. In many ways, it was a perfect first stop on the road to *SpongeBob SquarePants*. "The goal there was always how to teach science, but make it fun and easy to swallow for kids," he recalls. "So we did whale watches, touch tanks, a whale skeleton that kids could look at, game shows . . . it was a very creative place."

Meanwhile, some of TV's wackier programs at the time–namely, *The New Adventures of Mighty Mouse* and *Pee-wee's Playhouse*–started the creative wheels turning in Hillenburg's mind. "I think that sparked something in me," he says. "I don't know if this is true for everybody else, but it always seems like, for me, I'll start thinking about something and it takes about ten years to actually have it happen, or have someone else believe in it. . . . It took me a few years to get it together."

Hillenburg decided to go back to school–*art* school–where he began to blossom as an experimental animator and filmmaker. Armed with three short films he made at CalArts, he began to show his work at animation festivals, which is where he met Joe Murray, creator of Nickelodeon's *Rocko's Modern Life* (1993). It turns out that at the time, Murray was looking for people to direct his Rocko cartoons. Talk about destiny: Stephen Hillenburg's very first job in the animation biz was as a director (and, later, creative director) on that wonderfully skewed Nickelodeon series. "Yeah," he laughs, "I have friends that give me a hard time about that. It's funny, but doors opened when I stepped into the animation world." It was also a great education for what would come later.

As *Rocko* was winding down, Hillenburg decided to take some time off to develop an idea that had been slowly starting to form in his head, of an underwater cartoon show. Finally, his past and present skills were about to come together in a big way. "I thought it would be interesting to do one based on all these weird little invertebrates that I liked," he explains. "At the Marine Institute I had done a comic of undersea tide pool animals called 'The Inter-Tidal Zone'–it was a little bit funny, but more importantly, it was supposed to inform." From this notion sprung a plethora of other ideas, taking the theme to a new level: He would explore "the whole tiki/surf culture/nautical imagery . . . just as a backdrop."

Hillenburg rolled up his sleeves and began to work, drawing starfish and other small invertebrates . . . which led him to the idea of a sponge–"being a very weird animal, and a very weird name." The innocuous, nondescript creature seemed the perfect vehicle for his main character: "I'd sort of decided I wanted to do a show about an innocent, and about an optimistic character that can really *annoy* other characters . . . sort of like Laurel and Hardy, or Pee-wee Herman," he explains. "Those were really appealing, and so that became the thesis, the main idea of the show: the story of this innocent, childlike character who you watch go through the trials of life, and we watch other characters try to manipulate him and then they usually get it in the end, and that's what's funny."

In other words, Hillenburg wanted a classic comedy archetype whose film origin dates all the way back to Charlie Chaplin's "Little Tramp."

The marine sponge soon gave way to the SpongeBob we know and love today: "I was drawing the natural ones for a while," recalls Hillenburg, "and then I drew a square one–a sink sponge–and it all synched up, pardon the pun. But it just seemed like . . . y'know, I was looking for this nerdy, optimistic character, and here's this squeaky-clean square . . . I thought the symbol fit the character type."

Just a few of SpongeBob's many silly faces, in this grouping of poses.

And his bizarro name? Where'd *that* come from? Hillenburg chuckles again: "Originally, he was named Sponge Boy. Y'know, you take an inanimate object, like apple, and you put the word 'boy' on it–Apple Boy–and it becomes alive. . . . But Sponge Boy was trademarked by someone. So I decided on an alternate: *SpongeBob*, like Billy Bob. I felt it was important to have his first name be "Sponge" so that when you looked at him you wouldn't think, 'Cheese Man.' And then, having a first name, I thought, 'last name' . . . *SquarePants* just had a nice ring to it, and it also made him square, again referring to the nerdiness. That whole process of figuring out what you're gonna do is kinda hit-and-miss . . . I just write down a lot of things."

Hillenburg brought some trusted friends and colleagues over from *Rocko* to help him develop the new series. Very early on, he hired painter Nicholas R. Jennings (later *SpongeBob SquarePants'* art director) to work on the background styling with him, and Derek Drymon (who became the show's creative director) to help develop content. Steve would toss ideas at Derek, who proved the perfect sounding board for what seemed to be working, and what didn't. "A second brain always helps, I think," Hillenburg says now. "Those two guys were very important in the initial stages of development, along with another writer from *Rocko*, Tim Hill, who helped me develop the bible when we put that together."

As for the overall design of the show, the Hawaiian floral motif felt very natural to Hillenburg. "Personally, I think when you look at the undersea world, it *is* like that," he observes. "It's very surreal and beautiful at the same time. I definitely was hoping that people would see it as a new, kind of unknown world, and be excited by it."

Reusable background of a road in Bikini Bottom, from SpongeBob SquarePants' *stock bible.*

He pitched the series to Nickelodeon's execs–the cast of characters, the theme and look of the show, some story ideas, how it relates to kids, and so on–a few times. They were immediately interested after the first pitch, but wanted to see more, so Hillenburg and crew doubled the length of the bible, adding more info and stories, and pitched that. Then, they were asked to create a storyboard for the seven-minute pilot episode, which he and Drymon wrote and drew together. At that point, the execs *really* liked what they saw. Albie Hecht, president of film and TV at Nickelodeon, said, "Let's make this pilot."

To further develop Hillenburg's main characters, he brought on a few designers to help flesh out the visuals with model sheets and other artwork. "Things became a little more solidified, like how tall is one character compared to another one . . . what are the eye shapes . . . how do you break these characters down so an animator can animate them in 3-D," he elaborates. "I worked with the staff, giving notes, and sometimes drawing things myself, but it's always a back-and-forth process.

"So I went to Korea for a few weeks to oversee it, and then we finished the pilot. They tested it [in front of focus groups], we talked about it for a few months, they had some concerns about a few things, which led to some discussion. It wasn't a horror story at all."

What issues did Nickelodeon have with his show?

Hillenburg explains Nick's philosophy, which is that they're a TV network for children, and always want the key question answered: How will a show relate to kids? After all, SpongeBob–as well as everyone else on the show–was an adult. "They wanted to know if I could make him have parents at his house, and be in school," Hillenburg relates, "and I said, 'Y'know what? I can't do that. This is more like Warner Bros. in the sense that these are adult-like characters. They have their own lives.' What's funny for me, about the show, is an adult character that has the autonomy or freedom of an adult, but he acts like a little kid–and he drives other adults crazy. SpongeBob epitomizes what it's like to be a free-spirited kid, and that was my argument–that this still is about kids . . . it's about being optimistic and naïve and learning things, and he's not jaded. Which is what real kids represent to me."

His stance was effective. Still, Hillenburg did offer to create parents for SpongeBob and have them appear in a couple of shows, and the network was satisfied.

When they officially got the green light, the *SpongeBob* gang kicked production into high gear, taking on a full crew and busying themselves with designing and creating stories for Season One. With a show this quirky, there were bound to be growing pains as they prepared it for airing, plus a certain amount of give-and-take between themselves and the network.

Hillenburg cites a prime example with an early episode called "Ripped Pants": "SpongeBob is at the beach, and he rips his pants and gets a lot of attention. So he keeps running around and ripping his pants, ripping his pants . . . and the joke gets old. It's a very sad story, 'cause he reaches the point where he's sort of ostracized. And the network couldn't understand–the note was, 'Why is SpongeBob ripping his pants and then laughing hysterically? He should be depressed and scared.' Well, that's the point of the whole story–that he does this and then he learns that he went too far. And then he pulls it back with a lament, a song about ripping his pants . . . which is totally silly, but helped solve the story. And they agreed to do it the way we intended, and I think it's a good show."

As on any TV series, the writers and producers learned to pick their battles, giving in on some and fighting for others, especially if they believed something was truly funny. "I think it's been a very positive experience," Hillenburg states of his relationship with Nickelodeon. "I think the show is what it is because they really left us alone . . . gave us notes but kinda knew what was important for them, and let us run with it."

Detail of a lush SpongeBob SquarePants *background from the episode "Wet Painters," designed by Paula Spence and painted by Peter Bennett.*

As things progressed, they settled into a comfort zone with one another. Helen Kalafatic, *SpongeBob*'s producer for several seasons, notes that the tone of the series helped. "We want to appeal to people's sense of humor without being nasty . . . it's not a mean-spirited show, and we don't try to get really dark," she explains. "Everybody wants what they want, but we always find the middle ground and end up agreeing on what works best. . . . It's been good–the best show that I've ever worked on."

In a bit of an old-fashioned touch, *SpongeBob*'s creators decided to open each show with a kicky, graphic musical sequence–sporting lyrics by Hillenburg and Drymon–set to a loud tune that evokes the classic old nautical ditty, "Blow the Man Down." Appropriately, a salty sea captain (voiced by Pat Pinney) sings the song, and a chorus of kids' voices answers each line:

Captain: *Are ya ready, kids?*
Kids: *Aye aye, captain!*
Captain: *I can't hear you!*
Kids: *(louder) AYE AYE, CAPTAIN!*
Captain: *Ohhhh . . . Who lives in a pineapple under the sea?*
Kids: *SpongeBob SquarePants!*
Captain: *Absorbent and yellow and porous is he!*
Kids: *SpongeBob SquarePants!*
Captain: *If nautical nonsense be somethin' you wish,*
Kids: *SpongeBob SquarePants!*
Captain: *Then drop on the deck, and glub like a fish!*
Kids: *SpongeBob SquarePants!*
Captain: *Ready?*
Everyone: *SPONGEBOB SQUAREPANTS, SPONGEBOB SQUAREPANTS, SPONGEBOB SQUAREPANTS!*
Captain: *SpongeBob . . . SquarePants!*

The show premiered in the summer of 1999 and quickly became one of the highest-rated animated series for kids in the history of television. And it's not just children who are rabid fans–*SpongeBob SquarePants* has a huge adult following. Hillenburg attributes the show's success to the fact that "we write what we think is funny, what we think doesn't go over a kid's head but an adult will find amusing. It sort of all goes back to that basic theme, which is that innocence prevails . . . and SpongeBob represents this thing that I think adults *wish* they still had, and their kids can relate to."

In 2002, after creating an initial run of sixty original *SpongeBob* episodes, Stephen Hillenburg decided to take a break. The best thing about the whole experience for him, he says, has been "that the show is . . . surreal and whimsical, but, actually, people aren't put off by it . . . plus, the fact that my staff really enjoyed working on it, and the public seems to really like it. That's the great reward."

CHAPTER 3 AUTEUR! AUTEUR!

Those Creative Geniuses Who Can Do It All

"I invented the whole concept of cartoon violence. Before I came along, all cartoon animals did was play the ukulele. I changed all that."

—Chester J. Lampwick, purported inventor of Itchy the mouse, on *The Simpsons* episode, "The Day the Violence Died" (1996).

There are some creators in the animation industry whose styles are so distinctive, their work is instantly recognizable. They're filmmakers and storytellers who possess many skills–the ability to design, write, storyboard, produce, and direct. A few names immediately spring to mind: Tex Avery, Bob Clampett, Friz Freleng, Chuck Jones, Bob McKimson, and Frank Tashlin, the great Warner Bros. directors who created the funniest cartoons in the history of the world; Bill Hanna and Joe Barbera, for their brilliant MGM *Tom and Jerry* shorts. Jay Ward, for *Rocky and Bullwinkle*, *Dudley Do-Right*, and *George of the Jungle*; the Fleischer brothers, for *Popeye* and *Betty Boop*.

With the passing of Chuck Jones in 2002, the last of the old guard is now all but gone. So who are our modern day auteurs? Where are the energetic, young creators who are carving their niches in animation history by crafting original cartoons–toons that bear their distinctly identifiable stamp?

Here's the good news: They're alive and well and working.

Thanks to the development of cable television, the staggering growth of the motion picture business, and the home video/DVD revolution, the 1990s toon boom was much bigger than anything that ever could have preceded it. In TV, there's a show you can point to that broke down the walls in terms of content and tone, perhaps the edgiest cartoon series ever purportedly created for kids: Nickelodeon's *The Ren & Stimpy Show*.

LET'S GIVE 'EM BOOGERS AND FARTS

John Kricfalusi Finds a Home for *Ren & Stimpy*

Ren & Stimpy's creator made no secret of the fact that he wanted desperately to break the mold–and *scrape off* the mold–of the seventies and eighties, where the whole studio system was "set up to fail," as he puts it. It was while working at Hanna-Barbera that Kricfalusi became particularly frustrated with that system. "It was designed to thwart you at every turn," he remarks. "If you tried to do anything creative, somebody would catch that drawing and take it out. They had a department called the On-Model Department–I call it the 'Yellow Sheet Department'–who would take out any pose that didn't look like a pose on the model sheet, and they would redraw it on a yellow piece of paper. And *that's* what would go to the assistants."

He longed for a return to the old way of creating a cartoon, where a director "follows it through from script to screen. That way, there's at least one guy who knows what the story is all about," as Kricfalusi puts it. "And if he sees something good, like a real funny part of the script, he's gonna make damn sure it makes it to the screen and doesn't get reinterpreted."

What started out as a pet peeve turned into something of a crusade once he got the go-ahead from Nickelodeon's then-V.P. of animation production, Vanessa Coffey, to make *Ren & Stimpy.* She still howls when she recalls his initial pitch:

> *"He came in with an open shirt on, with a tie* underneath *the shirt, and jet black dyed hair. I thought, 'Oh my God, I'm up in this room all by myself . . . but I'll be okay . . . I hope.' It was a lot of fun. He was throwing himself all over the place, and I thought he was out of his fuckin' mind–but I was interested in his stuff.*
>
> *"He pitched me three shows:* Your Gang, Jimmy the Idiot Boy, *and* Atomic Pig. *I flew him into New York to pitch to Gerry Laybourne, and Debbie Beece, and Herb Scannell, and he kinda did the same thing. He threw himself all over the room, had everybody scared to death, his Certs were flying out of his pocket. Gerry said, 'Let's work with him' . . . so John and I talked a little more, and I said, 'Y'know, I really don't like these projects . . . but I do like the cat and the dog in* Your Gang.*' It was a group of kids that lived in a neighborhood, and one of them had a cat and dog, Ren and Stimpy. So we pulled them out of that show, and created another show."*

In truth, John K. wanted to do *Ren & Stimpy* all along–the other characters were just window dressing.

The fledgling network had never produced an animated series before, so they didn't have any preconceived notions of how to make one. If Spumco, Kricfalusi's production company (which even had a naughty name–"Spum means sperm," he confesses), wanted to write their shows by coming up with outlines and then storyboard each cartoon, that was just fine with them. They were impressed with the director's unbridled passion, and decided to give him free reign.

Kricfalusi had a very clear vision for his new show, based on his work with *The Jetsons* in Taipei and *The New Adventures of Mighty Mouse.* Separate storyboard and layout teams would be led by different directors, with Kricfalusi overseeing the entire process. He was also extremely particular about the quality of the drawing and character poses. "I'd do tons of poses on the layouts," he relates. "That, to me, was where we had the most control over the entertainment . . . 'cause you can have the funniest script in the world, but if it's drawn badly and there're no expressions or poses that tell the jokes, it's just mouths reading lines."

Furthermore, Kricfalusi sought to do bizarre character comedy–yet somehow keep his protagonists endearing and accessible. "If it was *just* bizarre, and the characters didn't have any warmth or believability, it wouldn't have worked. I wanted [Ren and Stimpy's relationship] to be so strong that it didn't matter what situation you put 'em in."

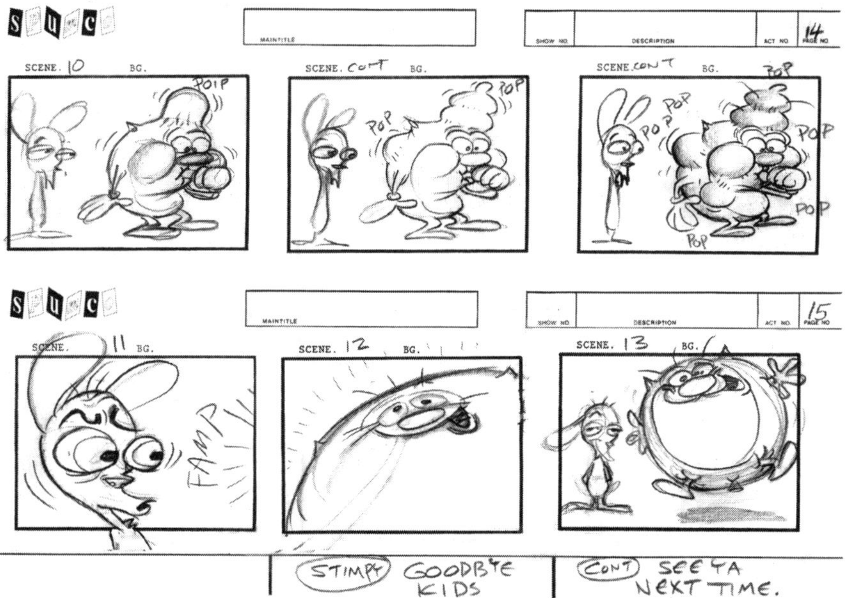

Storyboard detail of a typically demented Ren & Stimpy *sight gag.*

To get this vision on screen, he set out to pull together a staff of artists and writers who may not have had much experience in the business, but possessed tons of raw talent. "People with less experience, but talent, are much easier to work with," he feels, "because they don't have preconceived notions. They have less formula to erase."

Jim Smith, Bob Camp, Lynne Naylor, and Kricfalusi formed the nucleus of Spumco as *Ren & Stimpy* ramped up for production. They went out and hired people they'd worked with before, including Chris Reccardi, Jim Gomez, Bill Wray, and others. Kricfalusi was aggressive in his pursuit of those whom he felt would help realize his vision. One of them was Teale Wang, who'd been doing color styling on the first year of *The Simpsons*. She'd just been laid off, but that's merely the nature of a business wherein large staffs are let go in between seasons. Not the worst situation, as far as Wang was concerned: getting a three-month break while knowing that there's a job to come back to. "But then," recalls Wang, "I got a phone call from a friend of mine named Libby Simon, who was producing this new pilot called *Ren & Stimpy*. She said, 'Can you come over? It's just a mess over here, we need some help color keying.'"

When the artist showed up at the Spumco offices, she was flabbergasted. It was chaotic, and every bit as rough and tumble as the early *Simpsons* work environment–bad lighting, cheap desks, and so forth. Neither John Kricfalusi nor his crew had ever created a show of such enormity from the ground up before, and Wang's weeks of "helping out" were intense. When she was almost done, Kricfalusi asked her to stay as his full-time color-key supervisor. "Now here I am," muses Wang, "going back to *The Simpsons*, which was huge, and I would probably still be there–it was never gonna die–and here was this insane *Ren & Stimpy*, which he couldn't promise me anything on other than it's a really good show. I said, 'I don't know, John, I've got this gig at *The Simpsons*, y'know, it's a sure thing, and as much as I love doing this . . .' And he sat back, he looked at me and rubbed his chin and said, 'I understand.' And I said 'What?' And he pegged me so fast. He said, 'I know the type of person you are. You like it safe, you like the sure bet. I understand, there are people like that.' I went, *'Fuck you! I'll take your fucking job!!'* I was so pissed!" She roars with laughter at the recollection, citing the incident as a perfect example of John Kricfalusi's manipulative skills.

Once he'd assembled most of his crew, Kricfalusi encouraged creative input from them. "Anybody that came up with anything funny, I would use," he states. "Everyone contributed–the more entertainment, the better." But it was their leader who set the tone, and whose voice was the driving force of the show. Quite literally, as it would turn out.

So many animated series at that time sounded alike–their characters spoke in the same exaggerated "cartoon" voices, by then almost a parody of themselves. *Ren & Stimpy* sounded nothing like that. The show's creator decided to continue performing the demented Peter Lorre-esque voice of Ren Hoek himself, just as he'd been doing in countless pitches and meetings. "I didn't really want to, 'cause I hate the sound of my own voice . . . [but] I tried everybody, all kinds of people on it, and none of them could get the intensity I wanted, or the sickness. My performances embarrass the shit outta me, they're so stilted. But the only thing they have is that intensity."

For the voice of Stimpy, Kricfalusi knew exactly whom he wanted. He'd met the versatile voice-over actor Billy West several years earlier, on a short-lived revival of Bob Clampett's old *Beany and Cecil* show. West had been trying out some voices one day in the recording studio, when he happened to imitate Larry Fine of the Three Stooges. Kricfalusi fell off his chair, laughing. "I didn't think *anybody* could do Larry Fine," he says. "When we did *Ren & Stimpy*, I knew I was gonna try to get Billy West, 'cause he's the Mel Blanc of today." Once he had his man, Kricfalusi worked with him to develop a distinct sound for Stimpy. "Billy tried a bunch of different things, and I don't know why, but I said, 'This doesn't even sound like it'll make sense, but why don't you try your Larry Fine voice.' It didn't quite gel in my head right away–but I said, 'Y'know what? It's weird, let's do it, and it'll grow.'"

The Ren & Stimpy Show begot a number of television trends. For one thing, it was the first animated series made for TV that gave director and story credit at the head of each cartoon. Now it's commonplace to see, but back then, it was considered revolutionary. For another, you never saw that much grotesquerie on the tube before. The gross-out factor was something Kricfalusi planned from the get-go, and he knew his audience well.

The artists delighted in creating grotesque close-up paintings like this one of Ren's eyeballs, replete with mucus gobs and engorged veins, from the episode "Dog Show."

"We're making this for kids," he points out. "They *love* gross stuff. So let's give 'em boogers and farts! And I loved [famed grotesque illustrator] Basil Wolverton–so we just said we'll do Wolverton-style drawings for any time we have a close-up, where we wanna show something gross! We'll do it really detailed and it'll be a painting. And we had great painters, like Bill Wray and Scott Wills."

Kricfalusi also adored messing with the visual continuity of the story. When someone first accused him of "destroying the believability of the cartoon, because, all of a sudden, the shot looks totally different," his reaction was a wry, "So?"

Of course, that *was* the joke.

Another TV cartoon innovation *Ren & Stimpy* introduced was its use of old-fashioned music. It added to the show's whole retro style, further setting it apart from anything that was airing then. To a degree, this was done out of necessity. "We couldn't afford an actual composer, and, at the same time, I didn't think anybody would be able to compose anything remotely like what I would want," Kricfalusi believed. A longtime fan of music from the 1930s through the 1950s, he felt that *Ren & Stimpy* should be scored with "old-fashioned TV sitcom music . . . and movie music." He also quickly learned the power of music in storytelling: "You could just set up a mood right away. Y'know, all your scenes didn't always come back looking great–but it didn't matter. Sometimes you could fix it with the music. And that was a great discovery, 'cause I had never had anything to do with music before in a cartoon."

Then there's the subject of color. Kricfalusi had firm ideas when it came to the use of color in his shows, and in cartoons in general. "John was *very* methodical about his palette," affirms Teale Wang, who ended up color styling *Ren & Stimpy* for its entire run. "He's got very intense color theories . . . it was just not anything he could let slide; it was very near and dear to his heart."

Kricfalusi is only too happy to elaborate: "Number one: no pink, no purple, no lime green. 'Cause they're the only three colors that most cartoons use. And it drives me insane." Number two: "I don't like primary colors or secondary colors in big areas. When I say that to painters who work for me, they get really mad 'cause they think that I've left them with no colors. 'Well, if I can't use blue, red, yellow, orange, green, purple, or pink, what other colors are there?' And then I pull out a giant stack of reference, and open up books full of nature photographs that I clipped out of magazines, old illustrations, old paintings from *Playboy* magazine–just tons of stuff, and I say 'Look at all these! Here's earthy colors, here's warm colors, here's cool colors' . . . and generally, the kind of colors I like, they harmonize. Which is something that people just don't seem to know anymore, except for the Cartoon Network stuff."

Kricfalusi admits to being heavily influenced by the sophisticated use of color in Japanese cartoons, and by the work of classic illustrators like Frank Frazetta. "When I first started doing color, it was trial and error, trying to come up with things," he explains. "That's why *Ren & Stimpy* was very different in color than what came before, but wasn't always beautiful, or perfect, or always working really well. Whereas I see stuff in *Powerpuff Girls* and *Dexter's Lab* now where I think the color is the biggest thing–it screams at you, it's so pretty."

Throughout his tenure as producer and director of *Ren & Stimpy*, John K. was known as a perfectionist's perfectionist, obsessing over every single aspect of his show. He knew it didn't always endear him to his crew, who often found themselves redoing work over and over as they tried to please the boss. "A lot of times that was inspiring, and it did take you to a place that did something new," recalls Bill Wray, the show's lead background painter, "but other times, it was an unproductive dead end. And a lot of people cracked under it."

"I had theories about every department, y'know? Sound . . . color . . . no one was safe," Kricfalusi concedes. "I didn't want anyone to do what they'd been doing by rote for the last twenty years. But I had stuff to back it all up–I had lots of examples of what I wanted, and I would explain it real carefully." One early staffer characterized him as "the Charlie Chaplin of animation: no matter what it took, no matter how much time it took, he was determined to get his work perfect."

Kricfalusi admits there were days when he felt overwhelmed by the sheer volume of work and responsibility on his shoulders–much of it brought on by his own drive for perfection. If he found he wasn't thrilled with a particular cartoon, he purposely removed his name from the credits. "Nurse Stimpy" was one such episode: "'Nurse Stimpy,' to me at the time, looked so ugly. In hindsight, I can see that it came out funny . . . but it looked so horrible. It's just sloppy, the way it went through production." He also had his favorites–some of which are regarded as cartoon classics today: episodes like "Space Madness," "The Boy Who Cried Rat," and "Stimpy's Invention," a cartoon that was reworked so many times, it may hold the record for longest ever in production.

The premise of "Stimpy's Invention" was simple enough: In an attempt to help perennially angry Ren cheer up, Stimpy invents the "Happy Helmet," a remote-controlled device that allows him to manipulate his pal's

Ren & Stimpy

Ren & Stimpy :: Acting Reference ::
"Stimpy's Invention" Scene 62

The notorious Happy Helmet has Ren Hoek in hysterics in this sequence of layout drawings from the episode "Stimpy's Invention."

mind, sending the Chihuahua into a state of pure bliss–completely against his will. The cartoon came out convulsively funny, and even featured an original song called "Happy Happy, Joy Joy" that received a lot of airplay. But actually producing it was anything but easy.

When it came to his cartoons' content, Kricfalusi would barter with the network. The way the understanding worked, if he delivered some shows with heart, he'd be allowed to get more outrageous on others, like "Stimpy's Invention." But such was not the case when Nickelodeon saw this episode's storyboard. "They hated it. They said it was about mind control, that it was gonna scare kids–it was too intense, it was too extreme," he says, equally certain at the time that kids would love it. "Look at all the crazy expressions that Ren had, struggling to fight the helmet. Bob Camp did that storyboard, and it was genius." The network flew Vanessa Coffey to L.A., to try to convince the director to toss out the board–but Kricfalusi literally begged: "I got down on my knees and said, 'This is gonna be the best cartoon of the season. You have got to trust me! No kid is going to be scared, they're gonna be pissing themselves with laughter.' To this day, I don't understand what they had against 'Stimpy's Invention.'"

Coffey eventually acquiesced, but asked that some of the more extreme drawings be taken out, which Kricfalusi agreed to in the end. The result was one of the funniest, most twisted cartoons of the series. "Now, a lot of things that we had to struggle for are just taken for granted," he notes.

"For the most part, we got away with murder," says Ken Bruce, who worked on *Ren & Stimpy* as a timing director. "Oftentimes, there'd be a note from Standards [the network watchdogs that keep an eye on content] saying, 'Don't do *this*,' so we *wouldn't* do this. We would do something that in our minds was even more naughty, and, for some reason, get away with it!" As Kricfalusi himself will admit, he was continually prodding and provoking, trying to push the envelope a little further all the time. He tells of how the show's mock superhero, Powdered Toast Man–and his trademark flatulence–was an outgrowth of the fake TV commercials they were creating.

"We wanted to do cereal commercials, and I thought of an idea: not cereal, but powdered toast for breakfast that comes in a can," Kricfalusi explains. "I've got these reels I collect of old commercials from the fifties, and there's one of Superman selling *Wheaties* or something . . . where the kids sit down and they start eating–*'These are so good!'*–and, all of a sudden, you hear the wind whistling and Superman flies through the window–*'It's Superman!'* So, I thought we'll do that with powdered toast, only we'll have to have a superhero character: Powdered Toast Man."

In the *Ren & Stimpy* version, the superhero swoops in, scrapes his toast particles onto the kids' plates, and winks at them. "Then, when he goes to fly out the window and bends down in anticipation, the sound effects guy added a *fart*," Kricfalusi chuckles. "It wasn't written in the story or anything, but we all laughed–and then we thought, 'Man, we're gonna get killed if we put this in here, but it's so funny we've gotta see if we can do it.'"

So he phoned Coffey in New York and told her about the fart. Her reaction was disbelief: "A fart?!" He explained how funny it played, and she finally said, "Okay, put it in." And so, powdered toast in a can (with vitamin *F*–for *fart*, of course) was born on TV. *Ren & Stimpy* even went on to devote an entire episode–the Christmas show, no less–to a *scent*-imental storyline that followed Stimpy as he went in search of his very first fart, which had disappeared and was now lost ("Stimpy's First Fart," renamed "Son of Stimpy" before the show aired).

When the wacky series finally premiered on TV on a Sunday morning in August 1991, the network was flooded with fan mail. The show's crew made an early publicity appearance at a comic book store in L.A. called the Golden Apple, and was greeted by a mob scene. Hundreds of fans were waiting for autographs or to talk to their heroes, the creators of *Ren & Stimpy*. When a TV monitor inside the store began playing the "Space Madness" episode, everybody started chanting along with the dialogue. "They had it all memorized," Kricfalusi recalls. "It was weird. Things became catchphrases that were never intended to be catchphrases. 'Cause I *hated* catchphrases. I would read [another show's] bible, and it would give you five pages of lists of each character's catchphrases: '*This is what this character says every day*.' Oh, okay."

Not to say that Kricfalusi was looking a gift horse in the mouth. The fans' admiration helped to patch up some of the differences and resentment among the crew. "We were all amazed. It was great. All the people that might've been mad at me for working them so hard, they were like, 'Oh, now we get it.' It was a rough time . . . everybody's nerves were frayed. But y'know, that washed all that away right away."

For his part, Kricfalusi admits that he was completely confident from the start, never doubting that his show would be a giant hit. "Because I didn't do anything that wasn't obvious," he notes. "To me, if you're gonna do a show for kids and you put boogers in it and gross drawings, it's gonna be a hit. . . . Everything was so crappy at the time–cartoons were the most boring they'd ever been. All the *cartooniness* had been taken out of them. So I knew that if you did something that had imagination in it, the kids would eat it up. I didn't know *adults* would, though–that was the weird part! Teenagers and college kids and adults. That I didn't expect."

It also spawned a host of imitators. "Since *Ren & Stimpy*, there've been a lot of *Ren & Stimpy*-type shows," Vanessa Coffey notes, but few came close to its originality or sheer in-your-face audacity. The series became a cult sensation: endlessly dissected, worshiped, and fawned over by fans, and–when its creator and the network faced off during Season Two, resulting in Kricfalusi's dismissal–the source of more controversy and Internet chatter, probably, than any other cartoon show in TV history. In 2002, many of those fans had reason to rejoice: Parent company Viacom decided to revive *Ren & Stimpy* as a series, with John Kricfalusi back at the reins–farts, nose goblins, and all.

From Russia, with Glove

Genndy Tartakovsky's *Dexter's Lab* Explodes

As cable TV continued to grow, Nickelodeon soon found itself competing for young viewers' attentions with its first legitimate rival. On October 1, 1992, Turner Broadcasting launched a twenty-four-hour, ad-supported, all-animated channel, and called it Cartoon Network. Turner, which already owned Hanna-Barbera by then, initially culled its programming from what was billed "the world's largest cartoon library." It was only a short time later, however, when they began to roll out their own original programming. Today, it is the widely acknowledged home to some of the brightest, best looking, most imaginative cartoons ever made.

Genndy Tartakovsky, who created two of Cartoon Network's biggest hits, *Dexter's Laboratory* and *Samurai Jack*, is undoubtedly one of the most successful men ever to pull on an animation glove. What makes this auteur's accomplishments all the more startling are his sincere expressions of humility. As you read in chapter 1, Tartakovsky reveals that he didn't start to draw until his family moved from Moscow to the United States when he was already seven years old. So he got a late start, at least compared to his friends and colleagues in the animation world, and claims that his style didn't even begin to evolve until 1993.

"I was horrible," he states flatly–but don't let his humble demeanor mislead you: "I've always been really aggressive. I'm never one to step down from a challenge. . . . I set some goals for myself, and that was that."

Detail from an expressive model sheet of Dexter.

Genndy Tartakovsky's initial goals weren't what anyone would describe as lofty. He'd decided that he wanted to be an animator, and that's the path he followed. While attending CalArts, he created the very first *Dexter's Lab* pencil test–although back then it didn't yet have that name, nor did he even get to finish it. Did he believe that he was on to something–an idea that might be translated into a successful TV series?

"Not at all," he replies. "To come out of school and get your own show was impossible. It almost wasn't even a dream, because it was unheard of. At that point, there was no Cartoon Network, there was no shorts program. Even Nickelodeon was still starting out. My goal was to get a job as an assistant . . . assistant animate under somebody really good, learn for ten years . . . and then become an animator."

It was during his second term at CalArts that Genndy realized he was attracted to more of a 1950s type of look and sensibility. "The thing that influenced me the most was the UPA [United Productions of America] studios' style of animation. It was a *huge* influence," he says. "A lot of people in school were doing full Disney-style animation . . . and for me, I wasn't really interested in that. I wanted to push myself into doing something more original, more different, more making fun of movement than trying to copy it."

After school, Tartakovsky ended up in Spain for a few months, working as an animator on the *Batman* series. His career then took him back to the United States, where stints at Colossal Pictures (animating commercials), Hanna-Barbera (storyboarding *Two Stupid Dogs*) and Film Roman (doing timing for *The Critic*) proved less than satisfying. It was while he was at Film Roman, however, that his old producer Larry Huber called. "He goes, 'Cartoon Network is starting out, and they're gonna be doing these shorts. And I showed 'em your [*Dexter*] pencil test and they really liked it. Do you wanna do a seven-minute storyboard?' And I was like, 'Yeah, okay.'"

So Tartakovsky drew up the storyboard, pitched it to the network, and was given the green light to produce the short film for their new showcase, *World Premiere Toons*. As he developed the cartoon, it was time to give the brother and sister characters some names. "I just kind of started playing around . . . and I knew I needed a scientific name," he recalls. "At first, I actually had Dartmouth, and she was Daisy. *Dartmouth and Daisy*. Then I was kinda thinking, 'Ahhh, that's not that great . . . Dartmouth doesn't exactly roll off the tongue.' And there was already [Walt Disney's] Daisy Duck. I had some name books and I was going through them–and I liked Dee Dee a lot. That was kind of unusual and fun, plus she had two ponytails . . . and then Dexter. 'Yeah, Dexter's kind of cool.' So that came together. But [the title] *Dexter's Laboratory* didn't happen until a little bit later . . . maybe not even until the middle of the short."

A lively rough model sheet that captures Dexter and sister Dee Dee's manic relationship.

His concept came into much sharper focus now: Dexter, a short, redheaded boy genius with a vaguely eastern European accent, lives in a quiet suburban neighborhood with a mom who loves to cook and clean, a dad who's wild for bowling, and a loopy, incredibly annoying big sister named Dee Dee. Dexter frequently slips away to his fully equipped secret lab to solve problems ranging from saving the world to thwarting schoolyard bullies. Dee Dee just wants to dance or eat cookies, and manages to get in Dexter's way–sometimes by happenstance, but often on purpose.

Tartakovsky grew up with an older brother, but says he didn't try to draw from real life for the basis of Dexter's relationship with Dee Dee. "Not too much. I think I was more of a pain in the ass for him . . . but he was a pain in the ass, too, to a degree." He pauses, then laughs before admitting, "There's probably little bits of [our relationship] in there."

The design of *Dexter's Laboratory* was simple and whimsical, a throwback to the highly stylized look of the fifties with its use of thick black lines and bold color. (Ironically, the graphic designers of that decade were also breaking away from common trends of their day; UPA's artists had aimed for a hip and thoroughly modern style–the very same style that we now regard as *retro*.)

As his production moved forward, Tartakovsky had able assistance from collaborators who shared the same influences. "Craig McCracken and Paul Rudish helped me design *Dexter* a lot," he says. The three had gone to school together and were all inspired by that UPA stylization, so they were on the same page. "We kind of helped each other out," Tartakovsky explains. "Everybody did their own thing. When we finished the Dexter short and shipped it off, we worked on Craig's short [*The Whoopass Girls*, soon to be called *Powerpuff Girls*]. And it was the same thing . . . the three of us again, and we just all worked on our strengths." He still wasn't thinking "TV series"–they were just enjoying the shorts that were coming out of the collaboration. Tartakovsky recalls the feeling as something more like, "Ahh, the short turned out great, let's see what else we can do."

But then, he explains, he was struck by an idea for another *Dexter* cartoon: "Dee Dee eats some cookies and she would grow to be huge, and we would see Dexter inside a robot." The team went to work on this after they'd finished the first *Powerpuff* short. And this time, the network asked for six half hours of *Dexter*. As Tartakovsky points out, "The shorts had become incredibly popular on Cartoon Network–*Dexter's Lab* was consistently the highest rated–so the network decided it wanted more. It was really that simple."

When he heard the good news, he claims he got "kind of excited. Everything happened so fast that I didn't really get a chance to [get carried away]. I was just kind of figuring out a plan how to do it." He pulled together a multitalented team, including McCracken to art direct, write, and direct; Rudish and Rob Renzetti to write and direct; and Larry Huber and Sherry Gunther to executive produce the cartoons, along with Genndy, who would also write, direct, and creatively control his show.

In the winter of 1995, *Dexter's Laboratory* premiered as a series on Cartoon Network. Part of the show's mix included two other cartoons, *Dial M for Monkey* and *The Justice Friends*, which would appear from time to time in between *Dexter* toons. The series was popular right away, garnering Annie and Emmy Award nominations over the next several years, and winning two Annies (for writing, and for Christine Cavanaugh's distinctive vocal performance as Dexter).

An intricate layout of Dexter's invention to prevent himself from scratching his chicken pox in the theatrical short, "Chicken Scratch" (2002).

As they were picked up for a second, third, and fourth season, Tartakovsky's confidence in himself as a producer grew even stronger. He learned to lean even more on his team for support, and began delegating additional responsibilities to them. He found that, occasionally, the show would veer down paths that he himself wouldn't have chosen as director–but that it didn't necessarily hurt the cartoons. "Things would go off to left field ... and almost, sometimes, I would *let* it happen and just wait till it comes back, when we could see it as a cartoon, to tell if it works or not." Occasionally, he would just leave it the way it was. "The thing about cartoons is, everybody's gonna do 'em differently," Tartakovsky notes. "As long as I laugh at it, it looks good, and it's entertaining and true to Dexter's character, then it's good."

As for Cartoon Network, they developed a reputation for trusting their creators and allowing them considerable artistic freedom, within the limits of television standards. "They're great to work with," confirms Genndy, before grinning. "We're almost spoiled to a degree, 'cause we don't get a lot of notes, and we have a lot of freedom. So that when we *do* get a note, it's like, 'What the hell is this?!'"

CRAIG McCRACKEN'S MIGHTY MITES
The Powerpuff Girls

While *Dexter's Laboratory* continued to thrive, another Cartoon Network auteur was about to be launched ... and most of the same talents who'd helped turn *Dexter* into a hit would play a huge role in his emergence.

Bubbles, Blossom, and Buttercup, the universe's tiniest and cutest superheroes, burst onto the scene as stars of their own cartoon show in 1997, when *The Powerpuff Girls* premiered on TV. Their creator, Craig McCracken, had waited for what felt like an eternity to him to finally get his animated series on the air: about six years from its inception.

McCracken had always been an unusually ambitious kid. But for the longest time, his dream was to be a comic strip artist, not an animator–to do strips for the newspapers, to do comic books–that's what McCracken craved. When he began to develop his own comics, like "Marty the Mouse" and "CrudPuppy" (an angry, obnoxious dog), he discovered that he wasn't into doing traditional four-panel gags. His creations were becoming elaborate whole pages that needed music, effects, and spoken dialogue ... and that was when he realized he'd better look into filmmaking.

It was in school, along with pals Genndy Tartakovsky and Paul Rudish, that his affinity for the classic UPA style began to click for him. "I always knew there was this graphic style that I liked–I had seen it somewhere," he notes. "But growing up in Southern California, you know, there was no access to UPA cartoons ... you might've seen it somewhere, in some ether world, and your subconscious remembers seeing it, but it wasn't till I got to

When they're not saving Townsville from nefarious villains, Blossom, Buttercup, and Bubbles (left to right) love to color and draw as their teacher, Ms. Keane, looks on approvingly.

CalArts that I really found it and realized *that's* the stuff–that fifties graphic style that I knew I always liked; I just didn't have any reference to it."

Once McCracken completed his freshman project, "The No-Neck Joes," he had to come up with another idea. Inspired by director Joe Horne's weird little animated serial for MTV, *The Adventures of Stevie and Zoya*, he decided to try a superhero/good guy/bad guy narrative story–which is what led him to come up with the girls.

As soon as he began to create *The Whoopass Girls* short film, "A Sticky Situation," he believed that this was the original idea that could put him on the map. That year, he planned to make not one, but *four* different cartoons featuring his pint-sized heroines. "I wrote and storyboarded four of them, recorded all four of them, did the layouts for two, and only finished one. So I felt like I'd screwed up because I didn't get all four films done that year," he says.

To describe Craig McCracken as *driven* is probably an understatement. *Whoopass Girls* took up so much of his time, he admits that he pretty much stopped attending classes or doing his other assignments. "At the end of the year, y'know, all the teachers were like, 'Who's this guy?'" One of his animation instructors, Becky Bristow, was impressed. She was the first one to encourage McCracken, confirming his notion that *Whoopass Girls* had the potential to be a TV series. She also just happened to be friends with Linda Simensky, who was director of development for Nickelodeon back then. Bristow convinced her to drop by and take a look, and the exec liked what she saw–but couldn't do anything with it at the time.

"It really wasn't right for Nick," Simensky says today. "They definitely weren't looking for superheroes or action. . . . With Nickelodeon, it was a lot about characters sort of going through exploration, and finding themselves. *The Powerpuff Girls* were there already. They were just gonna go out on adventures."

The girls first sprang to life as a small thumbnail drawing–so small that McCracken couldn't give them too many distinctly articulated features–and when he tried to enlarge the image to refine it, he realized that some things shouldn't be tampered with. "That's why they don't have fingers or anything," he explains. "Because I drew them so tiny... and when I tried to add fingers, I was like, okay, I'm not gonna screw with it. I stumbled accidentally onto something that works; I'm just gonna leave it."

Once he'd conceived them, with their stylized design and great big peepers (a nod to 1960s artist Margaret Keane's huge-eyed paintings of children–the Powerpuff Girls' teacher is even named Ms. Keane), he basically hatched the whole concept that we know today, including wild supporting characters like simian archfiend Mojo Jojo, whose evil proclamations are hilariously stilted.

Mojo Jojo, evil genius (and a very bad monkey).

For a variety of reasons–not the least of which was McCracken's full-time work on *Dexter's Lab*–it would be over six years before the girls made it to the small screen as stars of their own series. At one point, he was so convinced that *The Powerpuff Girls* wouldn't get picked up by Cartoon Network that he actually shopped it around town to other studios. Most of them claimed to like the idea, but obviously not enough to buy it. "I'm glad that it didn't happen elsewhere," he says, "'cause it would've ended up on the shelf." As Simensky puts it, "If *Powerpuff* had ended up at Nickelodeon, it wouldn't have been *Powerpuff* . . . it would've been completely dissected into something just so different."

Part of the problem was, Cartoon Network had taken the two original *Powerpuff Girls* shorts around to focus groups, where kids would watch and offer their reactions–and the response from those groups was mixed, at best. "I went to one in L.A.," McCracken recalls, "and this group of eleven-year-old boys basically said, 'This is the worst show we've ever seen, this is a terrible cartoon!'" *Dexter's Lab*, on the other hand, usually tested well, so the network felt much more confident putting that one into production. By then, Linda Simensky had joined Cartoon Network and always just assumed that *Powerpuff Girls* would eventually become a full series. She became its staunchest advocate. "The thing that no one was saying was, 'Well, this didn't test well . . . so let's *fix* it,'" she says today.

Simensky wanted to keep the *Dexter* crew together. "It was such a great team of guys. At that point, they were on their third season, and I said to Mike Lazzo, 'Wouldn't it be great to keep them all together, and not have them just leave after their fourth season? If we could get *Powerpuff* fixed, they could segue into another show.'" Lazzo completely agreed, and the two execs began pushing the idea at the network.

McCracken went back to work on *The Powerpuff Girls*. He began by addressing an issue that had repeatedly come up: What was the difference between Bubbles, Blossom, and Buttercup? So the creator worked out a chart that truly explained everything. "When I did the first shorts, I was more focused on weird concepts than developing characters," he observes. "That was my biggest mistake. I knew the characters so well cause *I'd* been working with them for years, but I forgot that I wasn't telling the virgin audience who they were." So this time, he made sure the girls' distinct personalities were evident. He made the backstory–their creation by Professor Utonium out of sugar, spice, and everything nice, plus an accidental dose of Chemical X–play into the main stories more.

Animation rotation model of Professor Utonium, creator and father of The Powerpuff Girls.

He refined their world, added more wacky supporting characters. It became a solid concept . . . and Cartoon Network finally said *yes*.

As post-production work on Season Four of *Dexter's Lab* progressed, the rest of the crew just slid right onto *Powerpuff Girls*, albeit with a shift in leadership. Genndy Tartakovsky stayed on as supervising producer and co-director–his attitude was that Craig had worked on his show, so now he'd work on Craig's show–but this was definitely McCracken's baby. And this time, he was ready. "Craig had learned so much from doing those *Dexters*, that he was like a different person from the shorts to his first series," Simensky offers. "When he did the first board for the redeveloped show, it was brilliant."

Powerpuff Girls is distinguished by clever writing suffused with tongue-in-cheek humor, strong design, and glorious use of color. Creators and designers all through the industry quickly took note. "I look at *Powerpuff Girls* and I see perfect color combinations," gushes John Kricfalusi, who has nothing but admiration for the series. Glen Hanson, designer of MTV's short-lived but strikingly imagined *Spy Groove* (2000), calls *Powerpuff* "one of the most beautifully art directed animated shows ever. The graphic nature . . . the bold lines around the characters–there's such a wonderful, simple, strong sense of design there."

McCracken's creative hand is evident in all aspects of the show. He presides over every story session, supervising the board artists, directors, and writers. "We'll just throw ideas around until we come up with stories that feel good," he says, "and then break it up into beats, structurally." For each episode, a three-to-four-page outline is written based on these story sessions. Once the outline is completed, he proofreads. "And then, what I'll do is write really detailed notes . . . how I want the sequence to be boarded, some inspirational stuff to look at, what the goal of the sequence is, from whose perspective it's supposed to be drawn . . . I'll put those notes on it."

The storyboard artists take it from there, generally getting six weeks to board an eleven-minute cartoon, and adding their own creative input along the way. "Everybody's got a certain voice and a certain style," McCracken observes, "and we try to give shows to people 'cause we know, 'You can do this one amazingly well, this is perfect for you.' So they do their rough board, and then they put it up on the wall and pitch it to the whole crew . . . and we cut stuff and re-board things." The artists then clean up the revised storyboard. Once McCracken gets it back, he'll "go through it, and maybe redraw stuff, or–if they misinterpreted a note I had–I'll re-board a sequence . . . just redo it. It's just the nature of the business, to get the shows right."

The Powerpuff Girls has already produced many standout cartoons, including "Bare Facts" and "Bubblevicious" (both Emmy-nominated), and "Meet the Beat-Alls," a witty pun-filled toon jammed with clever Beatles references in both visuals and dialogue. The plot: Four of the girls' most vanquished (and frustrated) enemies–Mojo Jojo, Fuzzy Lumpkins, Princess Morbucks, and Him–band together to form an unbeatable crime team, dubbing themselves "The Beat-Alls" and unleashing an "eight day's a week" wave of evil carnage on the residents of Townsville. Of course, only our tiny superheroes can halt this "brutish invasion." Slyly pinpointing the Bad Four's one weakness, the girls enlist the aid of seductive Asian monkey Moko Jono (a "performance criminal") to seduce Mojo Jojo and break up the Beat-Alls once and for all. Practically every line of dialogue in the toon is cribbed from Beatles' song lyrics and album titles–and it all works.

Powerpuff quickly became a huge hit for the network, and their first monster marketing success. Before long, there were *Powerpuff Girls* toys, storybooks, activity books, stickers, tattoos, glitter pens, puzzles, CDs, audio and videocassettes, DVDs, posters in stores all over the world, and a feature film spin-off, *The Powerpuff Girls Movie* (2002).

Linda Simensky felt vindicated for her unwavering belief in the series: "It needed time to get out there and kind of percolate. It worked out so perfectly for the show. Even think about all that licensing that was done; Cartoon Network was not ready two years earlier to handle all that. So I think Craig was incredibly lucky. Ultimately, it's the best possible thing that could have happened to the show."

Meanwhile, Genndy Tartakovsky was getting restless to do something else. His involvement on the first two seasons of *Powerpuff* was intense–and he was growing weary of working strictly on comedy. As he puts it: "Sometime toward the middle late half of *Powerpuff Girls*, I was getting tired . . . and I was getting antsy to do another show of mine. So then, I thought, maybe I'll do an action show." That show turned out to be as different from *Dexter's Lab* and *Powerpuff Girls* as anyone could possibly imagine.

YOU DON'T KNOW JACK

Genndy's Stylish Samurai Cuts Loose

"I've always loved samurais, I've always been influenced by samurais–*Seven Samurai,* all that stuff. I really wanted to do that," Tartakovsky reveals. Just one major problem cropped up early on: There's a lot of swordplay in samurai tales. In fact, try making one without any. Standards being what they are in kids' programming these days, that kind of graphic violence is taboo. Not to worry: Genndy's fertile mind found a way around that issue.

"I can't really *cut* anybody," he noted, "and there's no fun in doing samurai action if I can't. . . . So I thought, 'Oh, what if they're all robots? And I can get away with some, y'know, hard-core fighting?' That's where the whole sci-fi element came from. Like, 'Oh, then maybe he's thrown into the future, and there's this wizard, and so on.' I knew that I didn't want it to be bound to one world; I wanted [Jack] to do all this traveling . . . so the story started to come together out of the necessities that I needed to make the show."

Over dinner one night, he pitched the idea to Mike Lazzo, head of programming at the network. Lazzo remembers the pitch well: "He said, 'Hey, remember David Carradine in *Kung Fu*? Wasn't that cool?'"

That was it, the whole pitch. They bought it immediately–and *Samurai Jack* was born. Cartoon Network's faith in Tartakovsky was so strong, he probably could have sold them anything. "Genndy had done such a good job up until that point–if there was anyone we could trust, it was Genndy," is how Linda Simensky puts it. "He had placed enormous pressure on himself. . . . It was basically, 'How can I top everything I've ever done, and how can I top everything I've ever seen?'"

Publicity art created in the vertical style of classic Japanese prints.

His concept and back-story for *Samurai Jack* were simple, yet left room for much layering: Samurai Jack is a proud warrior, a man of few words who's determined to overthrow the evil reign of the shape-shifting wizard Aku. As a young boy, he'd witnessed his society's enslavement at the hands of the wicked sorcerer. Jack's father had sent him away to study with the world's foremost scholars, and to be trained in martial arts. With his mind and body sharply honed, the boy returns home a man, ready to vanquish Aku and end his terrible reign. But before he can strike, the wizard thrusts the warrior through a time portal. Samurai Jack lands in a strange and dark future, with but one goal: to find the portal and return home to liberate his people. But the future is a very bleak place, segregated into tribes and policed by Aku's evil robot warlords. In the course of his quest, Jack encounters exotic civilizations, unusual creatures, and modern urban landscapes with fantastic trappings.

The unique visuals of *Samurai Jack*–lush, painterly backgrounds, and characters drawn as solid colors without any lines–developed slowly. "It kind of evolved," Genndy says. "I definitely wanted the show to have a different feel to it, and then, once I started to work out the idea, I realized that I wanted to make a cartoony action show–a *stylized* action show. I'd been doing black lines all through *Dexter*, all through *Powerpuff*, and I was just kind of sick of it . . . even though I love the black line. And I just said, 'Oh, maybe I'll take out the lines.' And because of computers, you could do it a lot easier. To do it by hand would be almost impossible."

Tartakovsky began to study Disney art from the fifties–which employed minimal line work–and found that he loved the way it felt. Then, someone showed him *The Little Prince and the Eight-headed Dragon*, a sixties Japanese cartoon–and he was amazed to discover that it had *no lines.* Or so he thought. "Well, there were some self-colored lines," he concedes, "but because the print was old, it appeared that it had no lines around it. And it had a great feel to it. I wanted *Samurai Jack* flat and highly stylized . . . a lot of lighting and mood. It would be a show with very little dialogue, [more] about the action, simple stories, and the character. And that's what I wanted."

Jack leaps into battle with evil wizard Aku in this publicity image from Samurai Jack.

Cartoon Network never even asked Tartakovsky for a test. He did one on his own, just to see if his idea was feasible. The footage, created by Genndy and background painter Lou Romano, was simpler-looking than the polished series–but still striking, depicting Samurai Jack battling giant insect robots, and utilizing graphic split-screen wipes and close-ups for dramatic impact. It also confirmed Tartakovsky's hunch: "I storyboarded this little sequence, they animated it overseas, and it came back. And it *worked*. 'Cause I wasn't even sure . . . can they do it? Is it gonna be too hard? Can they do this action? So I did this two-minute thing, and it turned out great."

Not only did the network love it, but Tartakovsky had an easier time hiring talent for his new project, since they could now *see* exactly what he wanted. "Y'know, nobody *envisioned* it. Nobody understood really what I was talking about," he says. "And even when Mike Lazzo and Linda Simensky saw the first half hour when it came back, all silent with no music, they were just like, 'God, I never pictured it being like *this*!'"

The director and his small crew dove into their research on samurai culture, scouring through books and screening films. Says Tartakovsky, "I read about all the history. . . . We tried to stay true to the way of the warrior, the Bushido Code, as much as we could. That's kind of what makes Jack straight as opposed to the crazy world around him." Yet, he claims the show has just as many modern influences. "It's kind of a big meld of everything."

They began outlining story ideas, and showing them to the network. The director remembers that "one of the outlines actually said, 'After Jack builds weapons, 20 minutes of fighting.' That was in the outline that I sent to Cartoon Network. What we talked about when I was pitching the show to them was that [Samurai Jack] was going to have the most amazing fight sequences that anybody's ever seen. And we're not going to cheat the audience and just give them two minutes at the very end after fifteen story plots. We're going to give them one very thin, clear, simple story plot, and then fifteen minutes of action."

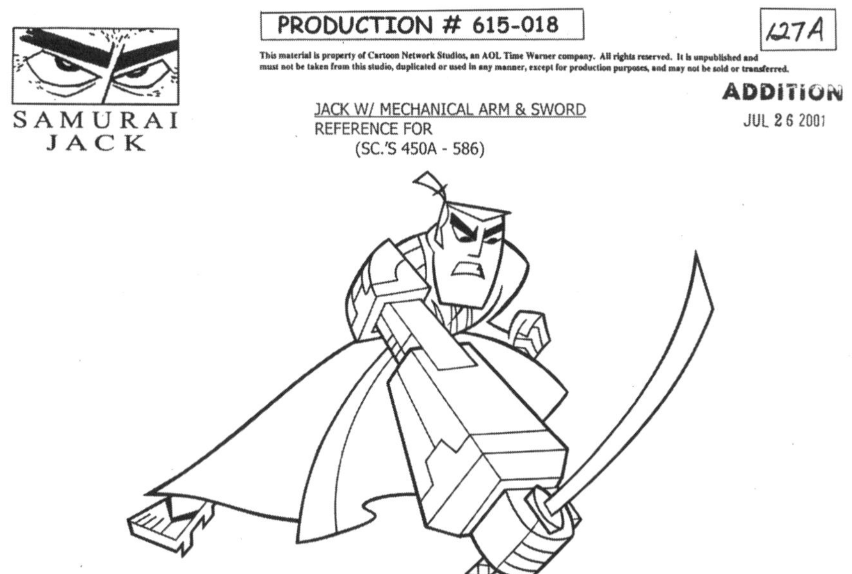

Model sheet of Jack wearing a cybernetic arm in this dramatic pose drawn by Paul Rudish for episode XVIII.

If anyone was worried about possible criticism for depicting too much animated mayhem, they didn't show it. Paul Rudish, who also works on the show, dismisses any such notions. "People never complain about violence," he says. "They complain about sexual references. They complain about innuendo ... but no one really calls in about violence. The thing that Genndy smartly did was, you know, Samurai Jack does not fight humans. He fights robots, he fights demons ... and, you know, the robot lobby is pretty quiet."

From the start, Tartakovsky planned *Samurai Jack* with far more visuals than dialogue, which made the look of this show extremely crucial, even more so than on other projects. When Scott Wills–a brilliant painter who had left television years before to work exclusively on feature films–agreed to join the new series, essentially as its art director, Genndy was thrilled. "It really came together when Scott Wills came aboard," he confirms. "'Cause when Scott started to paint, all of a sudden, we had lighting, we had mood and atmosphere."

Wills admits that the early *Samurai Jack* test they showed him influenced his decision to hop aboard, even though he knew he had his work cut out for him. "That first test that was done by Genndy and Lou Romano had a lot of texture," the painter says today. "Maybe Genndy was thinking *texture . . . crazy texture*, I dunno. It was just a first shot, and good for what it was, but he didn't really have the time I've had to sort of coalesce it into a style."

Tartakovsky figures he initially spent "about three or four months to kind of put [the show] together. Dan Krall, once he finished up on *Powerpuff*, did a bunch of drawings for me, for backgrounds, and we started to develop the kind of environment we wanted."

Then he recruited Rudish to help him storyboard the first episode, which was feature-length at an hour and a half. As they continued working, the show's crew began to grow. "Paul and myself storyboarded the movie," he explains, "so when we were boarding the first half hour, nobody else was working on it. When we started boarding the second half hour, other people began storyboarding the fourth and fifth half hours . . . so then it started to get spread out."

Somewhere along the way, Tartakovsky determined that he wanted the music on *Samurai Jack* to sound different, yet incorporate appropriate Asian and multicultural influences. He decided to combine "old Japanese drums with new techno and hip-hop. And through each episode, each new culture that Jack visits

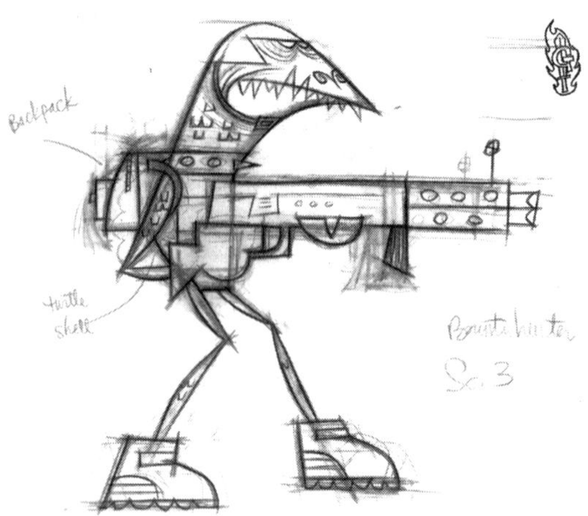

Character design of an alien bounty hunter drawn by Craig Kellman for Samurai Jack *episode XVII.*

or runs across will have its own music. Sometimes, we'll combine old traditional Indian music with hip-hop beats and make kind of a meld . . . and there's this kind of underground movement that really sounds amazing, and we're going to try to give [the show] some of that."

When the finished series first hit the air, the acclaim was almost instantaneous–from critics and viewers alike. "The industry buzz was good, but you never know how people are gonna react to it," Genndy points out. "But yeah, it was all great." Soon after, word spread through the showbiz grapevine that a live-action *Samurai Jack* feature film was in the works, even as the TV series continues in production.

Meanwhile, Tartakovsky strives to keep the show feeling fresh. "From week to week, it's completely different," he says. "We don't have two shows that are the same." While proud of his latest success, he admits that all the years of pulling double and triple duty on various projects at once has him feeling a bit burned out. "I wanna finish the series and work on the theatrical version–on a slower schedule," he sighs.

He Said "Size" . . . Huh Huh Huh

Mike Judge's *Beavis and Butt-Head* Rock On

Most of us have known guys like *Beavis and Butt-Head* (1993). They were our hopelessly immature friends in high school, the horny outcast rock 'n' roll obsessed losers who'd laugh their asses off at all things stupid and infantile. Oh, okay, some of us *were* Beavis and Butt-Head. But it took Mike Judge, creator of MTV's hip cartoon satire, to put the two archetypical bad boys on the map forever.

Beavis and Butt-Head live in a bland, blue-collar, modern suburban American world filled with crappy burger joints, neon-lit shopping malls, and the ever-present TV set as their chief cultural outlet. The pair is also a prime example of a classic comedy team: both dumber than dirt, with one (Beavis) thinking he's smarter than the other. Everything they try to do goes horribly wrong–usually brought on by their own stultifying ineptitude. And then there are the duo's hyperactive hormones, stuck in perpetual overdrive.

"They're great characters–so brilliantly observed," notes Billy Aronson, one of the series' writers. "How truly pathetic it is being a fourteen-year-old boy . . . I mean, your body is a disgusting thing, yet you have incredible desires for sex. And you're a billion miles from getting anywhere with it!"

The landmark MTV series' format consisted of short segments wrapped around music videos, with Beavis and Butt-Head's voices (both performed

Butt-Head and Beavis doing what they do best: sitting on the couch and watching TV.

by Judge) offering wisecracks and dumb comments over the footage. The animation was crude and unevenly drawn, its first season episodes wildly erratic in quality . . . yet viewers were immediately drawn to it. The show's early success was puzzling, even to its creator. "I can't believe it was a hit, when you look at it. I think people just wanted to like it," Judge speculates. "Also, some of the video stuff saved it–the video comments–I think that's what carried it through the bad episodes. In the first season there're a few I think are really good and some that are just horrible. The third season of the show was where it started to get good . . . the third and fourth."

Mike Judge's own huge success in the world of animation was equally unexpected.

"I always had this pipe dream of going into comedy," he relates. "I used to read *National Lampoon* magazine–I was gonna try to write for them. I actually started to write something, and then I was looking for, like, where you can send it and it said, 'We don't take any unsolicited submissions.' And so I just never sent anything. I found out years later that they actually did read stuff that got sent to them . . . but I just thought, 'Oh, I guess you have to *know* somebody, so, well, okay . . . I guess I'll just be an engineer.'"

Judge got a degree in physics at the University of California, San Diego, because he excelled at math, and because–as he admits, almost sheepishly–it was the easy path for him through school. But after working on electronic weapons systems for F-18 fighter jets for about a year, he realized it wasn't the life he wanted.

So he became a musician and made his way to Austin, Texas. "It always ends up in print as [sounding dorky] *Mike played in a band* . . . but I was just a sideman. I was never into the *rock star thing*, it was none of that." Kind of curious, considering how associated with rock music his Beavis and Butt-Head characters later became. "Yeah, well, a lot of that was kinda my playing upright bass and having to look out at people going, '*Play some fuckin' rock 'n' roll!*'" Judge muses.

Meanwhile, his pipe dream never went away. "People would say, 'You should go into comedy.' But I knew that I would not be good as a stand-up comedian . . . and so, when that's out of the picture, what do you do? I just had no idea what the course of action was." All along, Mike Judge loved animation, and always wanted to try his hand at making a cartoon . . . but never put two and two together. "I never made the connection of that being a way to get into comedy," he says. "I'd thought of 'em as two separate things. And then I saw the Animation Celebration in Dallas in '88 or '89–and it just kinda hit me suddenly: There was a guy from Dallas who had a short in there. They had his artwork on display, the cels, and I was just lookin' at 'em and going, 'Man . . . if a guy in Dallas did it, that means there must be a camera. Maybe you can rent time on it' . . . Suddenly, it just hit me, like, 'Wow, *this* is what I'm gonna do!'"

Shooting on a Bolex camera that he had bought for two hundred dollars, he created two short toons–*Office Space* and *Huh?*–even improvising his own lip-synch method to get his characters talking. He then popped them both onto one tape and labeled his creation *Inbred Jed's Homemade Cartoons*. "I wanted to get people's attention, so I made a little sticker of an inbred guy and put it on the tape. 'Cause I knew the return address said "Texas," and maybe people would say, 'What the hell is *this*?'"

A clever ploy–but even so, Judge wasn't quite sure what to do next. So he picked up the phone, called Information, got hold of every relevant address he could find, and mailed out about fifteen tapes. "And then I just started getting calls."

Soon after, the shorts began appearing in animation festivals, on Comedy Central, and even on *Saturday Night Live*. More importantly, people kept asking him to make more–in a hurry. "I was going, 'God, I shoulda done this when I was twenty-two,'" he laughs. His third short was *Inbred Jed* (1991) for Spike and Mike's Sick and Twisted Festival of Animation, but it was the fourth idea–*Frog Baseball* (1992), a short that featured his two idiotic slackers for the first time, playing baseball . . . with a frog–that bought him a spot on MTV's *Liquid Television*, followed by his own series on the same network.

Judge explains how it all began with him doodling in a notebook: "I was trying to draw this guy I had gone to high school with, who wasn't at all like Beavis and Butt-Head, actually, but he laughed like Beavis. He was kind of a *nerdy* spaz . . . he's a nuclear engineer now. Anyway, I was trying to draw him, and I drew something that didn't look anything like him. I tried, like, four or five times . . . and, basically, two of them–one became Beavis, and one became Butt-Head."

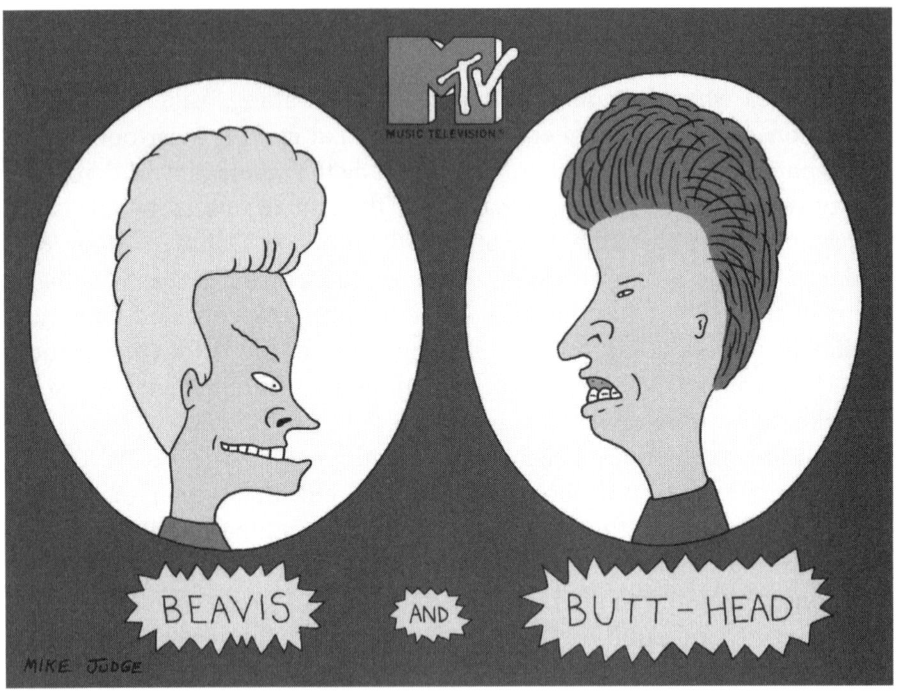

In creating his characters, Mike Judge tends to start with the voice and then draw the faces to match–as is the case, for example, with Milton in *Office Space*, *King of the Hill*'s Hank, and the hippie teacher of *Beavis and Butt-Head*–but this time, he worked in reverse: "Okay, what would these guys talk like, and what would they say? It all came from the drawing," he explains, adding that Beavis got his name from someone Judge went to junior high school with, and Butt-Head was named after . . . "Well, Butt-Head was just . . . Butt-Head."

Judge drew *Frog Baseball* up as a storyboard first, showed it to a few friends, and–when it made them laugh–went ahead and animated it. He's confessed that some of the boys' behavior was based on his own relationship with his older brother when they were younger. Like most immature adolescent guys, Beavis and Butt-Head never cease finding words such as *butt*, *ass-crack*, and *cornhole* a continuing source of hilarity. Nothing tickles their juvenile sensibilities more than finding the "hidden" smut content in everyday conversation. A typical exchange from the series:

Butt-Head: *You should shine your pants so they look like that dude's.*
Beavis: *I do shine my pants.*
Butt-Head: *Huh huh huh . . . you said* douche.

Or this morsel, from Season Four's "They're Coming to Take Me Away, Huh Huh," which Mike Judge has cited as one of his favorite examples:

Psychiatrist: *Beavis and Butt-Head are new here, so let's all try not to be too hard on them, okay?*
Butt-Head: *Huh huh. She said* hard on. *Huh huh.*
Beavis: *Yeah. Huh huh.*

"There's just something funny about how inane and simple they are," Judge says. "There's a part of me that's like that, but I know better. But then, it's funny when you see someone who *doesn't* know better, and they'll just say anything. They're not ashamed of being dumb. It's kinda refreshing."

Recounting his show's early days, Judge recalls a great deal of anxiety. He negotiated the sale of *Beavis and Butt-Head* to MTV without ever meeting with them, or even understanding fully what he was doing. "At the beginning, I was so green . . . I hadn't flown to New York yet–I was just dealing with them over the phone for, like, almost six months. First, I was negotiating with *Liquid Television*, and then I didn't know [*Beavis and Butt-Head*] was gonna be a show . . . I thought it would just be little station IDs or something." He soon realized, however, that this was potentially a career-making decision; yet, he remained unaware of what the proper protocol was. "I had no agent; I had no friends in show business . . . I had no advisors; I had no lawyer," he says. "So I sold it to 'em, retaining a percentage and stuff like that."

When production commenced, it didn't get any easier. MTV had never made an animated series before, so they contracted the work out to an independent producer in New York. "The first season they hired this guy, but all he had done was some commercials . . . he had no idea what he was doing. He kind of ignored the model sheets . . . and basically just said 'Oh, I know how to do this. You just draw *badly* and do sloppy animation and it'll come out looking right,'" Judge groans. "There was no control. He wouldn't let me see anything–it was a chaotic mess. Some episodes, I was hands-on . . . some I never saw until the animation was sent off. There were some happy accidents that looked kind of okay . . . and some of the guys he chose actually made 'em look right, but it was just completely haphazard." The characters began to appear more like Judge's original drawings as the series progressed. "That's the thing. . . . If you look at the way they were by Season Three, that's really close to the first model sheets I drew of them."

Befitting the show's meager budget, its animation style was simple; a lot of it was done with "cycles"–shooting the same few drawings over and over again, back and forth. "Some of it was mine," Judge reveals. "Any time they're talking, that's just a trace-back of all the mouths I did. That's my animation of them talking. Stuff like Beavis doing a fist-shake, I animated. Most of the stuff on the couch is my animation. Them head-banging, I animated. . . . But the first season, it was just all over the place. Some of it was right, and some of it wasn't."

To make things even more difficult, Judge was still living in Dallas at the time, so he found himself flying to New York every other week and checking into a hotel. "There was so much stress at the beginning," he says. "But I just kinda thought, 'Well, I don't want to be difficult and blow this. It's my first shot. I don't wanna start out with a reputation, I wanna be agreeable.'" Of the first twenty-seven episodes, he wrote nine of them. The rest were filtered through his brain, for the most part, even though, he admits, "there's some stuff I'm not proud of."

Nevertheless, once *Beavis and Butt-Head* began running on TV in 1993, Judge recalls that people took note. "The day after it aired, [MTV's animation honcho] Abby Terkuhle came in and said, 'We got a *one* last night.'" When the show's creator confessed his ignorance about rating points, Terkuhle explained that it was significantly higher than MTV's usual numbers back then. "So I said, 'Oh, well, that's good.' And then, the next night, it was a *one point two* . . . even though it was just the same two episodes airing over and over again. [The producer] was supposed to have twenty-two when it went on the air March 8, and he had *two*. And then he had two more coming in at the end of the week, with no time to fix 'em or anything."

The long-distance commute was taking a toll on him, so Judge decided to move his family from Dallas to New York. He remembers riding a train up to Westchester one day while hunting for a place to live, and overhearing two stockbrokers talking about his series. "One was trying to describe *Beavis and Butt-Head* to the other, but he was getting it all wrong. He was going, 'Oh yeah, they've got this cartoon called *Beavis and Butt-Face*, and they play *frog-ball*'–and the other guy wasn't laughing at all. I wanted to come forward and correct him," he laughs, adding that he managed to restrain himself. "I was going, 'Wow, that's kinda cool . . .' but I thought the first five episodes were such a disaster that I didn't think it was gonna be a hit."

In fact, the series' early success left him feeling both pride and discomfort at once.

"At that point, I was so unhappy with those episodes, I almost didn't *want* it to be big," he says. Judge was able to console himself with the knowledge that better episodes would soon air–and the warm glow of the media spotlight was soothing. Hearing David Letterman quote lines of *Beavis and Butt-Head* dialogue on his nightly show and seeing his creation on the cover of *Rolling Stone* didn't hurt: "It's like, every day I'd hear something new about somebody using it as a sort of cultural reference. Things started happening pretty quickly once it became a hit. And I'd signed with management like a month before it went on the air, so things started to get better. . . . Y'know, I guess you always hear this about people who have a success, but it didn't really hit me till much later."

He claims it truly sank in that his two dysfunctional characters had hit the big time when he began hearing senators mention their names in Congress, and Arnold Schwarzenegger utter a line in James Cameron's *True Lies* (1994): "*I've got Beavis and Butt-Head after me*."

But with all the new attention came criticism. Suddenly, Judge found his work being knocked by "all kinds of weird little groups, and 'Morality in Media' types. I mean, that year, the whole thing of violence in the media being the main problem in the country was at a fever pitch, and *Beavis and Butt-Head* was right there on a silver platter as a scapegoat."

Thankfully, the series had vocal–and eloquent–defenders, who *got* the joke. Noted conservative columnist William F. Buckley's *National Review* rode to Mike Judge's defense, along with the *Washington Post*, *Time* magazine, the *Los Angeles Times*, and many other esteemed publications, critics, and celebrities. "It was great to have some of these more respected people–more respected than myself–like *Beavis and Butt-Head*, because there's a lot of people that don't form their own opinion," says Judge. "It's like Einstein said: 'Few people think with their own minds and feel with their own hearts.' But yeah, David Letterman, Bernardo Bertolucci, Stephen King, and Jerry Seinfeld . . . that was really nice."

Whether people loved it or hated it, *Beavis and Butt-Head* is one of a handful of shows that helped change the tone of what we were used to hearing and seeing on television.

"Y'know, it's weird," Judge offers, thoughtfully measuring his words. "I'm really not the type that's, like, trying to push the envelope or do something foul on TV . . . and I actually don't like it when something is just foul for no reason. Sometimes, *Beavis and Butt-Head* slipped into that . . . but on the whole, I don't think it did. It wasn't the intention. To me, it's right when it's satire and it's not right when it's not satire."

"I think some of the time Beavis and Butt-Head did make fun of other people in a way that you weren't sure you were supposed to laugh *at* them," Billy Aronson observes. "When it's great, of course, is when they're making fun of people and you know it's 'cause they're so powerless, and their insults turn back on themselves. They end up making fun of themselves, showing off their stupidity–*that's* brilliant."

The original conception of Bobby, Hank, and Peggy, drawn by creator Mike Judge for his second hit toon series, King of the Hill.

Judge was able to build on his first success, going on to co-create Fox's long-running animated sitcom, *King of the Hill*. Having hit shows on two different networks has provided him with an interesting view of contrasting management styles. "The good thing about being on MTV was that there was very little creative interference," Judge remarks. "I could sit there and improvise over the videos, say anything I wanted. The problem was, it was really disorganized and we did way too much too fast. It wasn't protected the way you protect a show. They were rerunning them in such an erratic way–people would see the same ones over and over again. But then, the downside of that is the way a network will, y'know, make you do table reads, and everyone thinks they have to get a laugh every ten seconds. . . . It makes for this kinda stilted dialogue that doesn't sound natural." Judge feels that, most of the time, *King of the Hill* doesn't suffer from that, "but that's the battle."

As for the dysfunctional duo, we may not have seen the last of them. "I think I might have another *Beavis and Butt-Head* movie in me," Mike Judge says. "There's renewed interest in doing a sequel. Plus, they did some market research . . . and found that a lot of people want them on the air again." He pretty much rules out doing another series featuring *Beavis and Butt-Head*, however. "Maybe a TV special . . . but it was wearing thin on me there towards the end. I actually wanted to stop it even earlier. It's not like I don't like doing the characters anymore . . . it's just having to crank out a bunch of them. I feel if it were, like, twelve episodes a year it would be fun."

Huh huh huh . . . cool.

CHAPTER 4
AND THEN I WROTE . . .
How Screenwriters and Story Artists Get Toons Moving

"There has to be a brain. The humor rarely comes from the animation. It has to be on the boards. . . . For a feature to hold together as a drama and have a continuity with personalities, it has to be very carefully worked out."

— Bill Peet, longtime Disney story man (1994)

It may be a hoary old Hollywood cliché, but it's certainly true: It all starts with the writer. Unlike their counterparts in the world of live-action TV or filmmaking, however, animation writers fall into several different categories: those who write with words, those who write with images, and those who are skilled at both.

For years, storyboard artists were traditionally the real writers of cartoons, before television came into the picture. Remember, until the 1950s, toons were either theatrical shorts or full-length feature films. Board artists were–and still are–story people and gag people. In animated features, they work with the producers, directors, visual development artists, and other writers to discern who the main and supporting characters are, and why they want what they want.

The traditional way of starting an animated feature film has often been with no more than an idea or outline, moving right into visual development, and then boarding and scripting simultaneously. Over time–usually *a lot* of time–the film's story comes together. If your movie is based on an already existing book or fairy tale, it's a bit easier: you've got a general structure to help guide you. With an original story, the filmmakers must start from square one–and that can take even longer. Some producers and directors prefer to begin with a fully realized script, using it as a blueprint for the visuals and boarding.

But any way you tackle it, the process still begins with characters and a story–and that's where the writer comes in.

On animated TV series, the typewritten script was the standard for a long time. In recent years, there's been a movement by many creators–especially those of gag-driven shorts like *Ren & Stimpy* and *Dexter's Laboratory*–to go back to the way cartoons used to be written in the old days. Animation is so visual, they reason, that it just makes more sense to write a story with images and words all at once. Others still choose to begin with the written word and *then* move to storyboards, "plussing" the script–that is, adding jokes and comedic bits later on. It truly is a matter of preference, as both methods work. With long-form, more dramatic cartoon shows, such as *Justice League* and *Batman*, structure and storytelling are paramount–absolutely necessitating a strong script.

Then, we've got prime-time comedy series like *The Simpsons* and *King of the Hill*, where the written word is indisputably king. These shows are created the same way as sitcoms–by a team of writers seated around a table, tossing ideas at one another before someone goes off and actually starts typing. Ultimately, only one or two of the writers will take the screen credit, but there's a reason for this:

"It's an open secret in TV–there are some shows where maybe one person writes almost everything," longtime *Simpsons* writer and story editor Al Jean has said. "I know David Kelly, I think, writes most of the shows he's responsible for, but on a show like *The Simpsons*, the writing credit is used to pay royalties. So, if you think of the idea, and you did the first draft, you get all of the royalties. But in terms of whose lines are which, I would say in no episode does any one person have more than 40 percent of the lines."[1]

Ultimately, however one approaches the creation of an animated project, writers and artists must work together as a cohesive unit. Acclaimed toon scribe and author Paul Dini (*Batman: The Animated Series*, *Superman*, *Batman Beyond*) likens good animation writing to being part of a band, where writers, artists, directors, and animators contribute equally.

"If the writers insist the artists have to render their scripts to the letter with little or no involvement to the stories' creation, they run the risk of creating a faithful, but potentially lifeless, cartoon," Dini maintains. "It's like a composer telling a musician to play his notes exactly as written, with no chance of harmony or improvisation. Likewise, if artists are allowed to throw out all characterization and story structure and make up the cartoon as they go along, they may create a piece that amuses themselves, but could leave the audience confused, or worse, bored. It doesn't matter how cool the poses are or how accomplished the animation; if you don't engage the viewers, you've got no show. The best animation story creation comes when both artists and writers share a united vision of what their film is about, and work to each other's strengths."

With that in mind, let's take a closer look at a few different toon writers and the projects they helped bring to life: some who did it with words, others with pictures, and some who used both.

SPOONING WITH TOONS

Penning *The Tick* for the Tube

Ben Edlund, creator of *The Tick*, was a self-confessed TV animation junkie as a child of the seventies. "Yes, I was an addict," he admits. "Saturday morning represented to me . . . a very *high pressure* morning, where you had to be on top of whatever cartoon was coming on the three networks. Y'know, like, you had to make sure you caught *Scooby-Doo*, but then you had to get over to watch *Space Ghost* or whatever. It was a lot of scheduling. From about 8:00 in the morning till about 12:00, my brother and I were in, watching . . . it was important to keep abreast of all of them. And that was mainly terrible animation," Edlund chuckles. "With really dumb storylines."

Not that we're actually aware of any of that when we're kids.

"Not really, no. We were in television's thrall. So we would watch *The Amazing Chan and the Chan Clan* [which featured Jodie Foster's voice as one of the tykes!], and *Hong Kong Phooey* . . . and it all made the same sense. But it was more, I think, an automatic response; it wasn't an infatuation, it was just what you did as a kid."

In Edlund's case, of course, it was also feeding his fertile, twisted imagination. Like most others who end up in the cartoon biz, he was drawing at an early age, and already running his own comic strips in the junior high and high school papers–anthropomorphic superhero strips with titles like "Maximilian, Warrior Pig," "Ex-Men," and "Combat Wombat." It was then, at about age seventeen, with comedy and sci-fi swirling through his noggin, that an early incarnation of *The Tick* first occurred to him.

"I played a lot of *Dungeons and Dragons* and *Marvel Super Heroes*, which was another role-playing game. In that situation, you have a small, tight group of socially stunted males which functions as a captive audience for whatever crosses your transom," he muses. "*The Tick* was just an, 'Oh, wouldn't it be funny if there was a superhero named the Tick?' kind of thing. And y'know, the initial take was that he would be dropping out of the sky and sticking his nose in your head and drinking your blood. A primitive version of what he became. It was almost just always a single panel or a couple of panels, and some kind of caption emblazoned across the bottom, and that's it."

How closely did it resemble the big, blue, antennaed galoot with the absurd battle cry of "*SPOON!!!*" that we came to know and love?

"Not so much. A little bit–a muscular, large guy, still had no pupils. Still had that kind of cutaway face mask . . . but otherwise different in that his proboscis was really long and pointed and he was covered with fur, as if you were looking at an electron microscope picture of a tick. And that became too hard to draw," he laughs. "A lot of work. And he was black and white . . . in fact, for the entirety of the comic book run that I did, he was in black and white. It was reprinted in color, but I wasn't really involved."

Ben Edlund's creation followed a quirky path on its way to wide audience recognition.

A friend of his, the manager of a local retail comic book chain, had been posting some of those single panel *Tick* gags on a wall of the store–around the same time that the owner decided to get into publishing. George Suarez started up New England Comics Press, hired the teenager to draw for him, and ultimately offered to print a two-page *Tick* story in his newsletter-catalog.

"That went, and then I did another installment . . . and it seemed to get good response," Edlund recounts. "From there, [Suarez] said, 'If you do a book-length story of this character, I'll publish it.' So that's what I did for the first year and a half of my life at the Massachusetts College of Art. A lot of my scholastic energy went into developing this comic book after hours. By about issue 3 or 4, I started to get the impression that people were reading it."

Along the way, *The Tick* evolved into a clever parody of superhero comics. "Over the course of the twelve issues I did, it got to a place where they did almost nothing. It started with comedy, and really didn't have a super villain until issue 6. So, in a way, it was always light on action–but by issue 10, it was mainly about a road trip, and about living together, and about different ways of approaching the world. It started to become the *antithesis* of a superhero comic book . . . although I still wanted a fight or two, and some cool gadgets and so forth."

Edlund's career goal all along was to write and create for TV and film, so he abruptly halted the comic book to begin developing pitches for an animated version of *The Tick*. "That's why the comic ends in such a lurch. I was sort of drawn away to do what I always wanted to do. So I said, 'Screw comics!'" he cracks.

Tick and his nebbishy accountant sidekick, Arthur, try to rest up for their big road trip in this splash page from Ben Edlund's cult fave comic book, The Tick.

Over time, the property began attracting potential suitors. "There were offers from people in California who wanted to turn *The Tick* into a feature or a cartoon. A number of offers . . . very lowball, strange, buy-out-the-rights, kind of bizarre contracts . . . but it signaled the beginning of speculative interest on the part of outside people."

A few years went by, with *The Tick* passing through several hands along the way and not much happening. While every TV network turned it down, its cynical creator (by then all of twenty-one) looked at most of the meetings and negotiating as "more like taking some elective courses at school, 'cause I really didn't think it was gonna go anywhere. It was *The Tick*. It was weird, and stupid."

The turning point came in 1992, when a development exec named Nina Hahn from New York-based Sunbow Entertainment expressed an interest in producing it as a TV series. "They [Sunbow] had a personal connection with one of the people at Fox Kids, Karen Barnes. So they were able to get it in onto her desk and make her read it. Nina Hahn was, like, *The Tick*'s champion. *It's who you know!*" Edlund blusters mockingly.

Sunbow paired him up with Richard Liebmann-Smith–a scribe who'd also never written an animated TV series before–to develop the show together. Liebmann-Smith had worked for years as an editor and writer for various science publications, but had always dabbled in comedy. "In a way that you couldn't make a living, I was writing funny stuff," he explains. "I wrote for the *New Yorker*, I wrote for *Playboy*, I wrote short pieces, humorous stuff."

Hahn, in pairing Edlund and Liebmann-Smith–virtual strangers to one another–had made an interesting decision in not hiring an experienced animation writer. "It was a bold and, I think, intelligent decision," opines Liebmann-Smith. "Intelligent because it was a very unusual project, and I think she was worried that full-time animation writers are too 'smoothed over.'"

The two were thrown together, basically, to try and figure out how to turn *The Tick* into a cartoon–and had a difficult time of it for many months. "Animation scripts, as we learned–and which was fine with Ben–are written for the storyboard artists," explains Liebmann-Smith. "So you're giving all this direction that would normally be the work of a director. We had to learn how you actually put an animation script together. It took us a number of months, and a number of drafts, and a number of story lines, to come up with the pilot episode."

In *The Tick* comic books, the big joke was that these were not-so-super superheroes who sat around and did nothing. Yes, there were villains, and there were evil plots afoot . . . but they were always tangential to the Tick and Arthur sitting around and having domestic squabbles of various sorts. The two scribes began to realize that this was *not* going to work for Saturday morning animation.

"Eventually, we got so frustrated," Liebmann-Smith remembers. "And [Fox and Sunbow] got frustrated. . . . We couldn't figure out how to satisfy them and make something that would be true to Ben's vision of *The Tick*, and to what we could do in a cartoon."

Fox was quickly losing patience, and both writers knew they were in trouble. "We were about to get dropped, because the script still hadn't worked itself out," Edlund recalls. "There were too many people [at the network and production company] saying, 'I like this but I don't like *that*' . . . and, 'This is good but *this* is a problem.' Everything in television, if you're not careful, is a committee problem. Even crossing the street can become a committee problem. The *chicken* doesn't even wanna get to the other side."

So Fox issued an ultimatum to Sunbow, says Edlund. On a Friday, they were told they'd have three days to come up with a brand-new script, or they'd be scrapped. "And that was actually perfect, because then Richard and I just said, 'Okay, *we'll* do it.' And there was no time for any kind of discourse. Sunbow had to sit back; everybody who had been involved up to this point, not in a way that was cataclysmically wrong or anything–just too many people–had to sit back. And we took the pieces that made sense from the original versions, and *slammed* through a script. In forty-eight hours. And I had a cold at the time!"

"We essentially tore up everything we had done," Liebmann-Smith adds. "This was after, like, three months of premise and script, then back to premise . . . then outline . . . back to premise–nobody was happy. So we said, 'Look. We'll write it our way, just to amuse ourselves!'"

As promised, they handed in their new script on Monday. The network had a markedly different reaction this time: "It blew their doors off," relates Edlund. "They *loved* it. They called back and said, 'Okay, you're back in the running, and you're a front-runner. This is exactly what we thought it could be.' And so, if there was a committee problem in the beginning, this was the kind of perfect, almost cinematic situation where you go, 'Okay. Everybody shut up. It works now!' Everyone had advice for various aspects of production, but as far as the tone and the vision of it, it was like, 'Let's sit back, we're gonna succeed if Richard and Ben are allowed to proceed.'"

"We also created a bible, which was very well received," Liebmann-Smith offers. "They wanted a bible for their own internal discussions, and, ultimately, for giving out to other writers. Ours was pretty long . . . and because we had not seen [other show's] bibles, it's a very bizarre document–written in *Tick*-ese, in big, purple, screaming tones. And it doesn't exactly follow the form of a bible . . . it's just, 'BEHOLD: THE TICK!' And then it goes on about The Tick for a long time. It *does* cover what a bible should . . . some sample stories, et cetera, but I don't know how useful it was for writers. And it was never a pitch document–I mean, bibles usually have that dual purpose."

Fox Kids initially decided to pick up the series for six episodes, and allowed Ben Edlund and Richard Liebmann-Smith to write five of the six scripts. But the network, still not confident that the pair could do it all themselves, hired a talented West Coast story editor named Marty Pasko. Although Pasko was well versed in both comic book and screenwriting, he didn't last long on *The Tick*.

"He bounced off of the bubble through no fault of his own in particular," Edlund explains. "It's just that the big, heavy lifting of where the show was going was happening in New York. So it was difficult for anyone else to get in at that stage. Pasko wrote one episode, but we rewrote it. Eventually, it was determined that his position was unnecessary–not that *he* was, but *we* became the story editors by the end of the first season."

As production continued and *The Tick* found its way onto Fox Kids' Saturday morning lineup in 1994, the duo hatched most of the story ideas themselves, and ended up shouldering most of the scriptwriting chores, as well–which made complete sense, according to Liebmann-Smith: "It turns out to be very true of most shows that the story editor–or team–really ends up writing most of the thing. And there are good reasons for that. One of them is that it's those people who are ultimately responsible. It's those people who have the best sense of the continuity of a series beyond episode-to-episode, and it's those people who are most sensitive to the needs and demands of the production entities or the broadcast entities."

Edlund and Liebmann-Smith found that it took more effort to *unwrite* a script than it did to just sit down, start from scratch, and do it themselves–which happened time and again on *The Tick*. "So we ended up doing most of it," says Liebmann-Smith. Eventually, Pippin Parker [Sarah Jessica's brother] and Andy Yerkes did some writing, and, toward the end, Chris McCulloch–who had worked on *The Tick* comic book–and Randolph Heard came aboard for the third season.

From the start, *The Tick* boasted a satiric, skewed sensibility that probably went over the heads of most kids watching on Saturday mornings. Its supposed target audience–eight-to-twelve-year-old boys–tend not to find lampooning superheroism particularly funny. "There was an eight-year-old

The big blue guy–"Iconic Tick," as Ben Edlund describes him–as he appeared on his animated TV series. © ABC Children's Productions

boy that I knew who once looked at us and said, 'You guys don't like superheroes much, do you?'" Liebmann-Smith recalls. "They really want to believe . . . and they have a great investment in the fantasy of superpowers. So to just show these guys as jerks–they really didn't like it that much."

On the other hand, in the non-target audience–college kids and teens–*The Tick* turned out to have a huge cult following. The cable network Comedy Central took note and began running the series during its third season, airing episodes one week after they debuted on Fox. "On Comedy Central, we were finally hitting the audience we were intended for," says Edlund.

"It ran for years on Comedy Central," confirms Liebmann-Smith. "And *a lot*. They used to run 'Tick-a-thons' . . . and here's the fascinating thing about it: This show was written to, and for, Saturday morning standards. We were not allowed to show lots of violence. No guns, except ray guns. Very constrained physical fighting. Language was certainly constrained. It's quite unusual that a show that was written to those standards could then transfer over to Comedy Central. Because if we had been writing it for them to begin with, we would have had much more freedom to do the kinds of things that amused *us*. It always impressed me that this show could be so hip as to appeal to that audience, when it was targeted to–not written for, but marketed to–children!"

And, finally, where exactly did the Tick's buffoonish war cry, "SPOON!" come from?

"It comes from the comic, but it has no 'origin' there," grins Liebmann-Smith. "In the animated version, the Tick decides that they've gotta become more superheroic. And among the things they have to do is come up with battle cries. So there's a moment in episode 13–which is pretty late–where the Tick holds up a spoon, looks at it, and 'SPOON!' becomes his battle cry. Arthur's is like, 'Okay. You mean, like, 'Not in the face! Not in the face!'"

Ben Edlund and Richard Liebmann-Smith moved on from *The Tick* to considerable success as TV and film scribes, in both toons and live action. The duo worked together on Fox's short-lived live-action version of *The Tick* (2001), and Liebmann-Smith lists Disney's animated TV series, *Hercules* (1998), and HBO's *George and Martha* (1999) among his writing projects. Edlund, one of the screenwriters of Twentieth Century Fox's ambitious animated flop feature, *Titan A.E.* (2000) (apparently, they *can't* hear you scream in space if no one is listening or watching), has gone on to write for TV series like Joss Whedon's sci-fi western, *Firefly* (2002). Not surprisingly, both still look back at their animated *Tick* days with great fondness.

"It was a *very* good experience. In retrospect, we had a great, great deal of power–that I've never had since, on any show," says Liebmann-Smith.

"Probably the best working arrangement I'll ever have, apart from being the king of a small country," Edlund admits, a goal he can still aspire to. "Sure. I'm working on my cessation papers even as we speak. But yeah. A really good situation. Didn't know it at the time. I was shocked by how much work it required . . . but as far as control, it couldn't really be beat."

The Vis Dev of Beau, Bea, and Al

Writing Some Animated Disney Classics—with Pictures

Sue C. Nichols is what's known in the industry as a *vis dev* person–short for *visual development*–which can be a misleading job description. Their skills are so much more than merely visual; they're also writers and problem solvers, absolutely indispensable to the creative process. You won't find their names near the head of the credit crawl, nor will they get much press when an animated film breaks all box office records. But just try making a toon without them.

For years, Nichols has been one of the best vis dev and storyboard people in the business, having helped to create some of Disney's greatest animated motion pictures of the 1990s: *Beauty and the Beast*, *The Lion King*, *Aladdin*, and *Hercules*.

So, just what does a vis dev person actually do? They sketch, paint, scribble, doodle, draw, and think–imagining characters, props, locations, key story points, the staging of a scene or piece of business, major and minor plot twists–in short, much of what goes into creating a story. "For animation you really need to do that," Nichols explains, "because it's such a visual medium. You have to say, 'Okay, how can we tell the story with visuals?' On most projects I'd start off when it's all just basic *pitch art* and developing designs for characters, 'cause they're not even far enough yet on story to start boarding. Then, when they [finally begin] storyboarding, I'd do, like, the first initial pass . . . which could go for six to eight months. And by then, when it came time to finessing the boards and just doing the niggling details, another project was getting started–so they'd usually pull me off onto the *starting* project. I usually didn't hang around to finish the boarding."

Her role on *Beauty and the Beast* also began very early on in its development. She started off by designing "people and costumes and situations," while her colleague Hans Bacher worked on environments and styling. "We would sit in on story sessions, and they'd say, 'Okay, the Beast's house is enchanted.' It was our job to come up with why, what, all of that . . . so you're just as much a story person as the storyboard people," she explains. "If someone said, 'We need a character who fulfills *this* function,' then we could throw out several designs for them."

While Bacher experimented with the look and feel of the Beast's foreboding castle, Nichols focused on realizing some of the castle's servants–once mortals, but now transformed by a spell into living candlesticks, clocks, dust mops, dishes, and other enchanted household objects. "I came onto the film at a time when there were just *male* sidekicks . . . and I was the person who said, 'Beauty needs a female confidant to calm her down, and make her feel welcome and protected. Because she's gotta go from being petrified and scared, to liking this guy, to falling in love with him, and then kissing him and wanting to stay with him for the rest of her life . . . in just *how* many minutes?!" she chuckles. That confidant came about eventually in the character of Mrs. Potts, the motherly teapot voiced by Angela Lansbury. But it didn't start out that way.

First, Nichols came up with Madame Armoire, a giant wardrobe cabinet. "She was written into the script, and she was boarded. And it wasn't until we got thick into the boarding that we all realized she's too big to run up and down the stairs! Now, Chris Sanders had drawn Mrs. Potts, thinking, 'Wouldn't that be a fun little Angela Lansbury *Upstairs Downstairs*-type maid character?' She was in little bits here and there, and we realized that she would be the perfect mobile character to take over Madame Armoire's role–so the two got combined."

An early Sue Nichols concept drawing of Mrs. Armoire, Belle's large confidant who was eventually supplanted by Mrs. Potts in Beauty and the Beast. *© Disney Enterprises, Inc.*

Mrs. Potts' importance in the story grew and grew, with the character even singing the film's memorable title tune, the ballad "Beauty and the Beast." (Madame Armoire did end up in the final film but in a much less significant role, simply named Wardrobe and voiced by comedienne Jo Anne Worley.)

Nichols enjoys this early phase of a project, as it usually happens without the kinds of constraints or pressures that can sometimes inhibit the creative process. "What I like about development," she notes, "is that it's a small group of people working together to come up with something new and different. . . . Y'know, what can we bring to animation that live action can't do? And if you do it right off the bat, and not later, when the story's locked, it's so much easier."

In all, *Beauty and the Beast* was in development for about five years, beginning in 1988. Early on, co-directors Richard and Jill Purdum worked on the story along with screenwriter Linda Woolverton, taking it off in a very artistic but dark direction. "Then Disney finally said, 'Uh, that's *too* out there. We want something a little different, yes, but we still need to do something a little more commercial,'" Nichols says, believing that "it was a good call. Because up until then cartoons were for kids, and to do *Beauty and the Beast*–which was more dramatic a story than anything we'd ever done before–people were very scared. We thought this wouldn't sell at all. . . . It's funny, looking back at the story now, it's, like, *fluffy*, not all that scary, but at the time . . ."

About nine months into her stint on *Beauty and the Beast*, Nichols found herself reassigned to *Aladdin*. It actually marked a return to that project for her–she'd done visual development on it for about two years before being pulled off and assigned to *Beauty and the Beast*. During Nichols' first *Aladdin* stint, the story focused mainly on the relationship between the street urchin and his mother, depicting Aladdin's attempts to make his mother proud of him. "But things were so disorganized," Nichols recalls. "Linda Woolverton was doing a script . . . and we were supposed to be developing it *with* her."

Instead, Nichols recounts, she and production designer Richard Vander Wende were asked by management not to bother Woolverton. So she and Vander Wende found themselves sitting around and working in a vacuum, asking each other who the characters were, and what they were about. "It was crazy," she muses. "We spent so much wasted time there. It was the chaos before the organization." There were about a dozen scripts written along the way, and too many disparate elements being kicked around. Nichols wanted to drop the character of Aladdin's mother but was told to keep plugging away, even though nothing seemed to be jelling.

It was at that point that Ron Clements and John Musker came aboard as producers/directors of the movie. "Eventually, when Ron and John tried to organize things, it was just too difficult to tell the Aladdin/Genie story–which everybody wanted to see in animation–*and* tell this mother story," Nichols relates. "It was too long a film."

In her second tour of duty on *Aladdin*, Sue Nichols left vis dev behind and began storyboarding. By then, she says, "all the board people at the studio were still working on *Beauty*, so we didn't have very many board artists . . . that's why I got pulled out of just doing visual design, into doing boarding. And we just started boarding like crazy, getting the story up.

"Ron and John took over, and stripped it down. . . . They took the script, had it rewritten, and we brought in other writers to come in and help pursue Ron and John's direction. When we finally got all the boards up on reels, that's when Jeffrey [Katzenberg] finally agreed, 'Okay, you can change it. Get rid of the mother, and make it simpler.'"

Then, as now, the board artists were all an integral part of the collaborative storytelling. Everyone sketches and draws out their assigned sequences on paper, then mounts each drawing one after the other on an enormous bulletin board–until each board resembles a huge comic strip. They're then placed up on a wall for viewing purposes, and each storyboard person gets to stand in front of the film's crew and ham it up while pitching his or her sequence as animatedly as possible.

Sue Nichols further describes the process: "The way we liked working was to have your designers and your board people all in the story sessions together. You'd pitch to the whole group–not just the directors–and everybody would say, 'Well, I think this isn't working,' or, 'This is working,' or, 'Hey, that's a good idea, but it would work better in my sequence. My sequence is doing *this*, so maybe you should do this in yours' . . . and it was a very hands-on, draw-things-as-you're-talking, put-it-up-on-the-board session. That's where most of the structure writing is done . . . and the writers are there, too, so they're adding their input, saying, 'Well, how 'bout tweaking the dialogue this way, it would be a funnier gag if we tried this' . . . It was very much a group collaborative writing effort." The writers would then go off and rewrite, and the board artists would draw the newly revised scenes. "Back then, we had about two weeks to do a sequence, then come in with it. Nowadays, they want two-day turnarounds. *It's crazy*," she laughs.

When the story crew began to focus on *Aladdin* as more of an adventure yarn, things moved faster. "Once you get the story approved, everything just speeds up," Nichols says. Because she only stayed around on projects long enough to solve the major initial problems, other artists would take over and re-board her work. On *Aladdin*, she claims, "by the final reels none of my stuff was left in the film. The inspiration and the ideas were there, they were just restaged differently . . . just because everything was *constantly* changing."

She insists that the process has never left her feeling slighted, or with a bruised ego. "Oh, no. 'Cause your ideas are there, they're just redrawn for staging purposes, or whatever. That's what I like about being at the very front of it. You're getting the concepts and the ideas down, you're coming up with that. It's fun to see what they do with it. . . . By the time the finished project comes out, there may be nothing that you can point to and say, 'That is 100 percent mine,' 'cause it never works that way. But that's what I love about it: coming up with the concept, and then seeing what people do with it. Y'know, give it *legs*, see where it runs to!"

Chairwoman of the Boards

Getting the Story of *The Lion King* Up and Running

Brenda Chapman will always have a place in film history. When she co-directed DreamWorks' *The Prince of Egypt* (1998), she broke down a wall that had been standing in place for many decades, becoming the very first female director to helm a major studio's animated motion picture. Chapman–now married to animation and live-action Disney director Kevin Lima (*Tarzan, 102 Dalmatians*)–had worked her way up the ladder, starting as a board artist on *The Little Mermaid* and cleanup animator on *Who Framed Roger Rabbit*. When she was approached to work on *King of the Jungle*, however, her reaction was grim. She really didn't want to; no one did.

"I thought, 'Oh, God . . .' But it was one of those things where, if I'd said *no*, they probably wouldn't offer me another one. George Scribner was directing, and Roger Allers had just come on as co-director, and he was the one who wanted me as head of story." Chapman and Allers had a history of working together–at that time, most recently on *Beauty and the Beast*–with Allers invariably in the role of mentor. By that point, she admits, she was ready to assert her independence–but couldn't resist his offer. Problem was, head of story on *King of the Jungle* wasn't her idea of a dream job, despite the promotion: "It was hard, because the story wasn't very good," she says. Of course, back then, no one knew that *The Lion King*, as it came to be known, would end up one of the most popular toons of all time.

The film tells the epic story of Simba, a lion cub struggling to find his place in the *circle of life*, that delicate balance of nature that bonds all living creatures. Heir apparent to his father, King Mufasa, Simba falls prey to the treachery of his scheming uncle, Scar, who has designs on his brother's throne. Scar lures the cub to a remote canyon, where his henchmen set off a wildebeest stampede–and then cold-bloodedly orchestrates Mufasa's death by trampling as the king attempts to rescue his son. Simba, believing that he caused his own father to be killed, wanders off into the jungle to hide in shame. Two carefree but warmhearted pals, Timon and Pumbaa (an acerbically funny meerkat and flatulent warthog), eventually befriend him, and as the young lion grows up he adopts his buddies' motto, *hakuna matata* ("no worries"). Years later, with the help of the mystical baboon shaman Rafiki, and Nala, a lioness pal from his childhood, Simba comes to understand that he must accept the responsibility of his destiny. He returns home an adult, defeating Scar and assuming the throne that is rightfully his.

The story is simple and cleanly told, but it took a *long* time to get that way, Chapman remembers. "Back then, we had more characters at the beginning . . . and the basic plot was similar . . . except that Simba didn't go away," she notes. "He stayed, and became this lazy, slovenly, horrible character that Scar was trying to *make* that way, so that when Simba came of age to take his kingdom, Scar could overthrow him. Because Scar was running the kingdom, anyway, in lieu of this cub–and when the cub came of age, Scar was going to stage a coup. In that version, Timon and Pumbaa were Simba's childhood buddies, and there were a couple of other characters that we eventually axed–but the real problem was, you never, ever were able to *like* Simba through the whole film."

Brenda Chapman and the rest of the crew labored intensively to make the story work, boarding and reboarding scenes, but it remained a titanic struggle. Thomas Schumacher, who was essentially producing the film at the time, figured that an inspirational trip to Africa would help creatively–he'd set one up to Australia for the crew of *Rescuers Down Under*, and the studio had sent crew to the Loire Valley for *Beauty and the Beast*–so, in October of 1991, Chapman, co-directors George Scribner and Roger Allers, designers Chris Sanders and Lisa Keene, and Jeff Albert (then associate producer of the movie) went off on a two-week safari to Kenya. Chapman recalls the excursion as "incredible": "We were there to observe and sketch, and listen to stories, and take photographs," she recounts. "It was one of the most amazing experiences of my life . . . and it created a bond . . . it created a chemistry" among the crew.

Disney's original Lion King *creative team gathered in front of their guide's Range Rover in Africa (left to right): Roger Allers, Jeff Albert, Lisa Keene, Brenda Chapman, Chris Sanders, and George Scribner.*

The trip benefited the film in a profoundly creative way. Chapman and the rest of the crew took note of everything around them, down to the tiniest detail; the sounds of Africa . . . the songs . . . even the natural *light* felt new and different–a mood they managed to recreate in some of *The Lion King*'s visuals. "Storywise, we got *hakuna matata*, that whole concept," she reveals. "It was Kenya's motto: 'No problems here! You don't have to worry about us!' Because there's so much violence in the neighboring countries, they were just trying to say, 'Hey, tourists, it's safe to come here. *Hakuna matata*.'"

Chapman's journal notes ended up in the hands of the songwriters, Elton John and Tim Rice . . . and the phrase became not only the film's signature tune, but familiar to millions of people around the world.

Some charming touches in *The Lion King* came from unexpected sources. When Rafiki shows up to retrieve Simba late in Act Two, he chants a nonsense rhyme: *Asante sana. Squash banana. We we nugu. Mi mi apana*. "The Rafiki thing, we got that from our guide over there, 'cause he would say that all the time. It was just a silly little thing, a schoolyard chant that he made up as a child. Robert Carr-Hartley . . . he was like third generation Kenyan but his family was Scottish, and he had this great sort of Crocodile Dundee approach to everything. He'd just do that to be silly . . . so I wrote it down and said, 'Okay, translate that for me.' It meant, 'Thank you very much, squashed banana, you're a baboon, and I'm not,'" she laughs. "It just sort of worked."

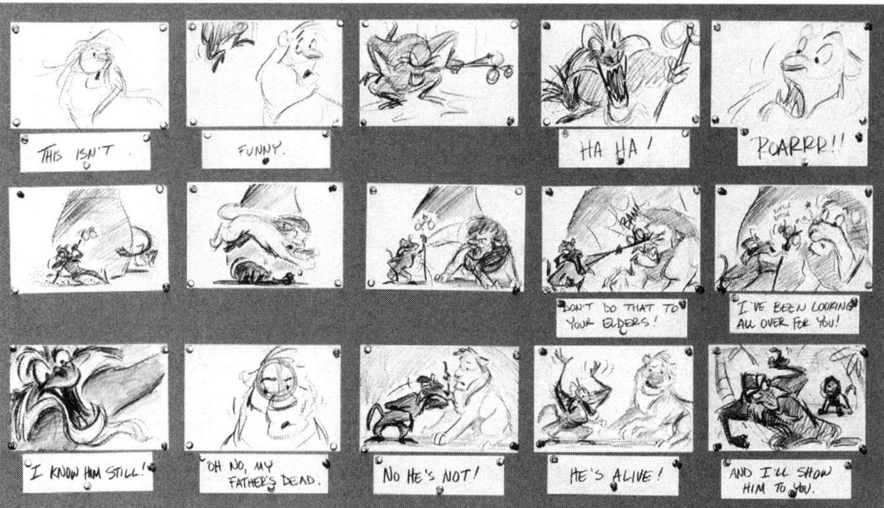

Detail from a 1992 Brenda Chapman board for The Lion King, *depicting an early conception of Rafiki's attempt to lure Simba back to the Pride Lands. © Disney Enterprises, Inc.*

The group returned from Africa newly energized and bursting with passion for the project. But they still couldn't get the overall story to come together. Talented people came and went; George Scribner was let go, Linda Woolverton left, and Rob Minkoff was assigned to co-direct with Roger Allers. The final turning point for the film came when the crew sequestered themselves in a room together for as long as it would take to solve *The Lion King*'s mostly second- and third-act problems, with producer Don Hahn presiding over the meetings.

"We all sat in that room . . . Rob and Roger, and Kirk Wise and Gary Trousdale, and Don and myself," recalls Chapman. "We just sat in that room for two weeks and kicked it around and around and around, and came out with what eventually turned into the version we know now." (See chapter 6.) Within a few months' time two new screenwriters, Irene Mecchi and Jonathan Roberts, had joined the team. They helped to resolve some lingering problems with the story, and *The Lion King* steadily progressed.

When the picture was finally finished, Chapman was stunned at its resounding box office success. Before it had ever opened, she was "very proud of it. I loved it–I was just shell-shocked. By the end, I was devastated . . . so tired, it was such a struggle . . . but I hadn't a clue what it was gonna do. It was the 'B' movie; nobody wanted to work on it. *Pocahontas* was the big 'A' movie, and we got all the 'B' players, the people who didn't have an opportunity because all the five-hundred-pound gorillas were getting the lead roles [on *Pocahontas*]. *Lion King* was a chance for the underlings . . . the passion to prove yourself, and make it work. I think that had a lot to do with it."

Schumacher, who ultimately wound up as the film's executive producer, can't say enough about Chapman's work on the story. "Brenda Chapman is the least talked about, most ignored key player on *The Lion King*," he states. "I think Brenda's contributions to this movie are enormous . . . and she always gets lost in the shuffle of the testosterone tale of where this movie came from. I just think she's brilliant–and she's a *huge* piece of this film."

Chapman's role in *The Lion King*'s creation is also a perfect example of how diverse the writing process can be on an animated feature's story.

TO INFINITIVES AND BEYOND

Scripting Pixar's *Toy Story* and *Toy Story 2*

Pixar Studios' 3D animated features are known not only for their visual artistry, but for their superior storytelling, as well. Andrew Stanton gets top billing as the writer of just about every Pixar screenplay–*Toy Story*, *Toy Story 2*, *A Bug's Life*, and *Monsters, Inc.* "I know. I didn't mean to do that, but I'll take it," he chuckles, before pausing to consider the matter. "No, I think that's truly been my strongest contribution to all the movies."

To Stanton, writing an animated film is very different than writing a live-action feature. And, then again, it isn't. "A big difference is that you are writing for a medium that is much more dependent on visuals–not that film itself isn't a very visual medium, I don't want to shortchange that–but there is definitely an understanding of what the strengths are in animation for your entertainment dollar. . . . The biggest thing is that it's a lot of pantomime . . . a lot of visual metaphors," he explains.

Stanton cites a perfect example in Pixar's own award-winning short film, *Luxo Jr.*, which depicts inanimate objects–in this case, a drafting-table lamp–brought to life and given human characteristics. Not something we see in live action every day. "Or the idea of toys having to treat their playtime as a job," he adds, before nailing it: "It's the juxtaposition of the *fantasy* and the *extraordinary* against everyday truths. That's something that's very much at the core of animation storytelling."

Stanton feels that even the fantastic should be rooted in some form of inherent logic or reality. "Matter of fact, even more so. The hardest movie we had to prepare for was *Monsters, Inc.* because everything was fantasy. And so, you have to be that much more clear about the rules of the world . . . whether you state them in the movie itself to the viewer, or whether you just happen to know them as the creator. I think fantasy films tend to break down when you don't stick to the rules. When you just let magic happen for its own sake at any old time, it doesn't work in a movie."

Andrew Stanton was the very first creative talent hired by John Lasseter, way back in the early days of Pixar. "Pete Docter and I were hired almost in the same week, but he was still in school, so he didn't come for another six months. It's a very small world. . . . I'm only three, maybe four years ahead of him in school, so we knew of each other pretty well. CalArts mafia," he cracks. "But I get the technicality of being the first hire."

Lasseter brought him aboard because he was a talented young animation filmmaker, not because of a particular strength with story or any other specialized area. When he joined the company, it never dawned on Stanton that he'd be considered a writer. "It was not something I even knew I could do or wanted to do," he notes. It also doesn't come as a total shock; most animators write and direct several short films in school–so they're all learning to tell stories cinematically, even if they're not calling themselves *writers* per se, or mastering the fundamentals of perfect writing technique.

"My grasp of grammar and vocabulary is very, very low," Stanton admits. "A lot of other people save my ass and make me look good by the time something is published."

Stanton noticed that as he, Docter, and Lasseter delved deeper and deeper into the creation of *Toy Story*, they developed an almost belligerent confidence on what would and wouldn't work. They began to trust their gut instincts as storytellers. "After a while, you start to realize, 'Well, what I wanna watch on screen *is* what writing is.' They're one and the same thing," he says. "And it isn't about *dialogue* . . . dialogue is driven by what you wanna see on the screen. Once we kind of came to that reality about it, we just started to find more confidence in writing our own stories."

At the heart of Toy Story *is the relationship between Buzz Lightyear and Woody, here seen amused at the stoic space ranger's insistence that he's not a toy. © Disney Enterprises, Inc.*

Stanton found that he learned a lot from TV and film scribe Joss Whedon (creator of *Buffy the Vampire Slayer*), whom he got to work with for about six months. Whedon was the first outside writer brought into Pixar to lend a hand on *Toy Story*–and helped Stanton realize how important good writing was to the making of a feature: "I got, firsthand, to see somebody who was really great at their craft . . . and the mystique, how it was done. Whedon would go into his room and come back with pages the same day, and we'd go over them. But then he had to go. Writers aren't used to being on something for years . . . they're used to being on something for months, and then they have other commitments. And he became this hot ticket during the first year we were working on the movie."

They suddenly found themselves without a screenwriter, and had to begin searching for someone to replace Whedon–a process that can take time. "Pete and I were getting very impatient," Stanton relates. "I just kinda said, 'You know what? I feel like I understand these characters enough. Let's write the scenes we wanna see.' The whole mystique had kinda been dispelled . . . so I just turned on the word processor and started typing. I knew what I wanted to see, and basically said, 'I'm just gonna keep doing this until somebody tells me to stop!' And enough of the spaghetti stuck to the wall, so that after a while [I realized], 'Oh, I guess I can do this.' And that's truly how it happened."

Pete Docter agrees: "That was kind of the fun of doing *Toy Story*," he says. "Y'know how you read about story structure, and it's like, 'Okay, and then you have your *inciting incident* eighteen minutes in?' Well, we didn't know *any* of this stuff! We were just shootin' from the hip, and we didn't know what we were doing. Really, we just kind of gutted our way through it."

"So much of *Toy Story*, from the writing to the execution of an effect, was driven by sheer desire to see something we had not seen in a long time: an animated movie that we were dying to see!" Andrew Stanton continues. "Whenever we would set our bar, we would set it for the favorite movies we had, not the favorite *animated* movies. We just said we're gonna take that label off. And I think the desire was so palpable to just want to break that mold, to just make something better. There *had* to be room to make something better."

Since they were feeling their way through the process, mistakes were inevitable. *Toy Story* went through a seemingly endless series of revisions and rewrites. When the creative team got their first look at the opening section of the film on story reels, they were distressed to find that the characters weren't coming across at all the way they'd hoped. Among many other problems, Woody, the story's protagonist (voiced by Tom Hanks), seemed like a completely self-absorbed jerk, and, even worse, there didn't appear to be any kind of bond between him and Andy, the little boy who owned him. That bond had to be there from the start, Stanton felt, or the audience wouldn't care when something came along to upset it.

He characterizes another of their early problems as "sequence-itis"–expending too much effort concentrating on one scene at a time, and polishing each one out of order–which resulted in many gags but no story flow. It meant heading back to the drawing board, and completely reworking that entire section of the film.

"It was frustrating," Stanton recalls. "But when I look back, it was always eclipsed by how exciting it was to just do it. Because it was our first. I'm sure somebody else has already used this analogy, but we always equated it to the guys at NASA who put men on the moon. They were just these engineers that were too young and stupid to know you *can't* do it. And that's exactly how it felt. Even when we were at our lowest low–which, when I look at it in comparison to some of our other low points on later films, was actually lower than points we hit later–we acted *half* as depressed . . . because we were still just jazzed that we got to make a movie! Since we were so new at it, we were already coming in with a sense of humility . . . and we just wanted it to be better. What happened later in the process was, we got more confident in our choices."

As Pixar strives to create something new and different each time, Stanton has tried his best to avoid falling into formulaic storytelling. "As a matter of fact, I'm very afraid of formula. I mean, that's part of the risk. By going into new territory, you don't have the confidence that it's going to be just as successful or just as enjoyable as the other ones, but there's another kind of confidence that comes: that you're not gonna fall into the trap of being a formula."

Stanton feels the fact that San Francisco–based Pixar is three hundred miles north of the Disney Studios–their partners on each and every animated feature–played a huge role in the making of *Toy Story*. They've had the best of both worlds that way: They could avail themselves of Disney's experience and expertise in how to craft an animated movie, yet maintain a degree of independence at the same time. "We would get their notes, we would fly back, and we would only address the notes that we felt applied. Or we would reinterpret the notes to be what we thought they were saying even though they didn't say it that way. And then, y'know, time heals all wounds. You come back about three months later, and as long as it worked better, as far as they were concerned you [followed] their notes. After a while, if you can keep that pattern going and you keep meeting their expectations–or, in our case, we would exceed them–you just start to gain trust. So by the last year of *Toy Story*, they just got out of our way."

Things were quite different for Stanton and gang on Pixar's subsequent productions, starting with *A Bug's Life* (1998) and continuing on through the present day. "It was different in the sense that we were now self-aware of what we did," he observes. "Fortunately, we were already starting it before *Toy Story* came out, so we didn't have huge heads at the time. The writing [of *Toy Story*] was pretty much close to being done by mid-spring of 1995, and so I jumped off to start *A Bug's Life* while John finished up the production of *Toy Story*."

Ever since then, Stanton's role has been on the front end. "It's been kicking the movie off, it's been giving it its structure, it's been finding our way through ideas and theories, and being able to chart a course when there's nothing tangible to work from. So, pretty much, *writing*. But the thing that's different for me from other writers, in some instances, is that other writers get to think of an idea, work on it, let it sit and stew, and don't have to show it to anybody until they're ready. I don't get that luxury. We come up with the idea, and then Day One I gotta start writing ideas and I've gotta show my ugly work to everybody, a whole crew of people . . . and basically let the dirty laundry show for almost a year, sometimes two years, before it starts to turn into something good."

They deviated from this routine with the creation of *Toy Story*'s sequel. The way things were supposed to happen, a separate crew working in another building would write *Toy Story 2* while Pixar's A-team concentrated on *A Bug's Life*. The problem, according to Andrew Stanton, was that the sequel "was executed almost 90 percent by people that had not worked on *Toy Story*–it was originally going to be a direct-to-video, if you remember. There was just no history there behind the staff making the second one, and it showed. . . . To put it very simply, [the problem] was the story. It was not going to be good, and it just became an *all hands on deck* thing–the entire old team that did *Toy Story* was asked to come and save it."

So they did. Their familiarity with the characters enabled them to turn it around much faster than anyone expected. "So much of writing is about developing character, not about developing plot and story," Stanton points out. Even so, they had to make major adjustments to the plot and story structure–but it came very rapidly. And although *Toy Story 2* had some new toys in it–a cowgirl named Jessie (voiced by Joan Cusack), her delightfully funny but mute horse Bullseye, and Stinky Pete, an old western prospector [illegible]oiced by Kelsey Grammer)–there were only three, not nearly as overwhe[illegible]lming a task as having to develop the entire cast of a movie.

Somewhere along the way, *Toy Story 2* turned into a full-fledged the[illegible]ical release. One of Stanton's collaborators, animation screenwriter [illegible]ve Reynolds (*A Bug's Life*, *Mulan*, *Tarzan*, *The Emperor's New Groove*) [illegible]tes how he was in the recording booth one day to pen some new lines [illegible] Woody when Tom Hanks quipped theatrically, "I *love* it! Why the *hell* [illegible] this gonna be a movie? This should be in theaters! Who do I have to [illegible] make this a major motion picture?!"

Woody, Bullseye, and Jessie, riding to the "Woody's Roundup" theme song on the record player in Toy Story 2. *© Disney Enterprises, Inc./Pixar Animation Studios.*

"He was very funny about it," Reynolds recounts. "Well, [ADR mixer] Doc Kane is so fast on the boards, he loops it back into the sound so that Tom Hanks, within a second, hears, 'Who do I have to call'–and then he puts a big echo reverb on it–'to make this into a major motion *picture picture picture? Who who who who?* . . . ' It was the funniest damn thing, and Tom was laughing, 'Yes. Get Eisner on the phone!'"

Toy Story 2 turned out so well, that's exactly what happened–with many critics even finding the film superior to *Toy Story*.

While they're working on a movie, it's not uncommon for Stanton and his writing team to find themselves revising and tweaking scenes or dialogue almost throughout the entire length of production. "You're rewriting till the bitter end," he affirms, "so you truly are always going, 'Oh, that's a better line. Let's just swap that out, [this one's] funnier.' And they come from all over the place. I wish I could take credit for every funny line that's written, but I can't. I can only take credit for being smart enough to know when a better line comes, and getting rid of one that I might have written to let another one in."

Surprisingly, Pixar's animated films following the original *Toy Story* were initially hatched, for the most part, at one meeting not long before their first feature was almost completed. According to Andrew Stanton, it all hails back to a fateful lunch shared by John Lasseter, Pete Docter, Joe Ranft, and Stanton in 1994: "We said, 'Jesus, guys. We're actually gonna finish this thing. We have this wonderful problem of *what do we do next*? And if we wanna have our jobs and pay people to stay working with us, we need to come up with something now.'"

So they started brainstorming ideas right then and there . . . and those ideas have fueled Pixar's output, says Stanton: *A Bug's Life, Toy Story 2* (filled with many ideas that didn't make it into the original *Toy Story*), *Finding Nemo* . . . "and a couple others which still might be made," he adds. "Which would be very ironic if that happens. Not to say that we haven't had another idea since . . . but it was kind of funny how we just said, 'Alright, let's put a couple things on the wall,' and then, one by one, they kinda get knocked off." It's that belligerent confidence of theirs at work again. "There are no extra ideas hanging out there–we never have any! We just sit there and go, 'We're gonna stay on this until it works!'"

So far, it's served them well. Pixar's animated features are densely packed with visual and verbal ingenuity, and with technical brilliance . . . yet each has that audience-pleasing quality that comes from telling a simple story populated by characters we can all identify with–the heart of solid screenwriting.

CHAPTER 5
AIN'T THAT A PRETTY PICTURE
Creating the Stunning Visuals of TV and Film Cartoons

"The characters are flat, designed characters. They're satire, they're fun to look at . . . so I thought the backgrounds should fit in with that—be designed elements, fun elements. But there's a very fine line between design and rapport with your audience. In other words, you can have a very designed element, and *lose* your audience—so all my design is based on supporting the character and the action that they're involved with."

—Maurice Noble, layout and background designer
of Warner Bros.' and Disney's classic shorts

We talked a lot about writing in the previous chapter–and without good writing, history has proven that it's hard for a project to succeed–but let's face it: Animation is an art form, and one of the most expressive visual mediums in the world.

When you're born with painting or drawing ability, you can choose to apply that talent in so many different ways. Some people become fine artists or sculptors; others become illustrators and designers. Live-action TV and film, theater, publishing, advertising, marketing, and even the corporate world appeal to many artists who choose to make a living at their craft. But it's hard to imagine an industry that attracts as diverse a group of talents as animation.

In the toon world, you can become an animator (which we'll cover in greater depth later on). Or you can work as a story artist, contributing images and ideas to a film or TV series by drawing storyboards. You can become an inspirational sketch artist, unleashing your imagination to dream up the overall look and feel of a project in its very early stages. You can be an art director, production designer, or character designer, if you choose . . . or focus on painting backgrounds, or even drawing props and costumes. There are specialists who concentrate solely on color and mood. Others draw layouts, showing how the scenes will animate and where the camera will move; sculptors, who create maquettes (small figurines of the characters) and miniature sets. The list goes on and on.

Whatever facet of the creative process animation artists choose to apply their unique talents and natural abilities to, they make enormous contributions to help shape every project they work on.

STANDING OUT IN THE BACKGROUND

The Brilliant Art Direction of *Samurai Jack*

Scott Wills, one of today's finest background painters and designers, got his start in the industry on *Ren & Stimpy*. That show's lead background painter, Bill Wray, essentially gave Scott his first big career break by hiring him toward the end of the first season. "That was the best thing I've ever worked on," Wills states without hesitation, "even to this day. I was watching *Ren & Stimpy* just recently–I go through periods where I haven't seen one for, like, three years, and then I'll sit down and watch a bunch of them–and I go, 'God, some of them are so good. . . . I'm, like, so proud to have my name on it.' [Especially] when it's on a great episode."

Wray was the painter who established the look of those wildly funny, insanely grotesque close-up shots that *Ren & Stimpy* was so famous for, and Scott Wills was the lucky artist who got to paint many of them. "I just learned so much from Bill Wray, so much theory that I was able to translate later onto my feature work," notes Wills.

The close-up shots and their medium were gags that the show's creator adored. "It was kind of a joke of his," Wills says of John Kricfalusi. "They would do that, actually, in older cartoons, where they would cut in close and you'd see it would be a painting. He just took the idea a step further. . . . John would always joke that humans are so gross up close–with nature, the closer you look at it, the *grosser* it is, the more disgusting. That was one of his themes. He really liked to put in a good gross-out gag whenever he could. And I just loved painting them! They were easier for me than the regular background stuff."

Wills worked on *Ren & Stimpy* for the rest of its run, honing his craft on that series before moving on to paint backgrounds for animated features, something he did for over six years at Warner Bros. and

DreamWorks. These days, he says he enjoys working on TV more than films. Many of the background artists working on features, he feels, are striving for too much reality in their paintings. And real isn't necessarily better, he says: "I like *design*. I like reducing things to their essence, and simplifying things–stylization and design. That's what I love. For me, it's so much more rewarding. I'm so much more proud of that work."

When Genndy Tartakovsky began his hunt for a background painter for *Samurai Jack*, he knew it had to be someone extraordinary. Bill Wray was approached, but he was busy at the time with another project–so, once again, he was responsible for recruiting Wills onto a show. "I basically got Scott Wills to come in and do the job," Wray says today. "He did a better job than I would have ever done. Scott was at DreamWorks then, and I just said, 'You're gonna go over there and do this!' He kinda wanted to, anyway."

Samurai Jack travels through this verdant jungle to get to the Woolie city in the episode, "The Woolies." Background drawn by Dan Krall and painted by Scott Wills.

"I was really dying to work on TV again," Wills concedes. "But then, my experience with TV was *Ren & Stimpy*. Most people don't have such a good experience. Whether you're a painter or an animator, *no one* leaves features to go to TV–it's unheard of. But I asked Genndy, 'What's the show about?' . . . and the main thing for me was, can I do what I wanna do? And not only that, I didn't want to be locked into one look. I didn't wanna go onto a show where every episode looks the same, and it's so formula. I would've gotten bored in a month. So Genndy said to me, 'This is the perfect show for you, because Jack travels, and goes from place to place, and you can change the look of it–you can change the style.'" Tartakovsky showed Wills the short *Samurai Jack* test they'd shot, and it blew him away. After six years in features, Scott Wills made the move back, joining the creative staff of *Samurai Jack*.

Genndy had wanted Scott on the show very badly. Afterwards, he even admitted to him that he'd had trouble sleeping, so sure was he that he'd receive a phone call from the painter turning him down. The backgrounds were such a key point of Tartakovsky's vision–after all, it's about a guy who travels from place to place; in many ways, it's all *about* environment–that the art direction and painting were absolutely crucial.

Once he began working in earnest on the design of *Samurai Jack*, Wills' goal was to emulate the rich texture and lushness of a feature film. He cites a diverse group of influences on his *Samurai* work, including early Hanna-Barbera cartoons and Japanese posters and prints. "There's an elegance to them, which is something I wanted–weird, I know, 'cause then you have Hanna-Barbera, which isn't exactly elegant . . . but I like things about both, so I try to put those together."

A beautiful vision of Jack's home with stylized lotus blossoms, from "Memories of Home," drawn by Krall and painted by Wills.

Tartakovsky is always there to push Scott Wills further creatively–an atmosphere the painter admits he thrives in, and had sorely missed during his years working on animated films. "*That's* the thing I like," Wills explains. "See, I always usually want to do something with much more inventive color. And being slapped back [like I was in features] and being told, 'That's too crazy, that's too cartoony,' I hated that . . . 'cause I thought, *that's* what's good! And then to come here, and have Genndy push me the other way–like, 'No, be crazier.' Oh, that's so great!"

According to Wills, the look of *Samurai Jack* has also been heavily influenced by the graphic designs of acclaimed painter Charlie Harper, known for his playful yet graphic treatment of animals and nature. "What I love about Harper's work is the ultra-stylization. . . . Even the character design here has been influenced by him–how we draw birds, for example. We've a lot of influences, I have to say, but when I feel like I've done a painting that's very *Samurai Jack*, the way I want it, it's mostly Harper's kind of feeling."

Wills has found that *Samurai Jack* allows him to mix and match approaches and styles–including influences such as Charlie Harper's designs–to create something that feels new and fresh. "The thing about this show . . . what I try to do is, I can paint totally realistically, like photographically–and then, totally on the opposite side, is full-blown UPA-type stylization. I try to combine everything that's good about realistic painting and feature painting, and everything that's good about stylization, and bring it together," he says. "And that's pretty much what *Samurai Jack* is, to the extent that I have the time. It's trying to do all of that–have cinematic lighting, with mood and depth, but at the same time have it feel stylized . . . and do it all in a TV schedule, which can be a fucking nightmare."

Such attention to detail can be a crushing amount of work, and one man simply can't handle that load all by himself. Other painters have contributed to the show, with Wills art directing and overseeing their contributions. He's even managed to bring in his mentor, Bill Wray, to freelance on some episodes. "The pupil has exceeded the master now," Wray says of Wills. "He's a brilliant artist. And he's also just so *clean*. His work looks like it was done by this perfect machine–but it's not machine-like, it's beautiful."

Although their credits read "Background Design Supervisor: Dan Krall" and "Background Paint Supervisor: Scott Wills," *Samurai Jack* is technically art directed by Krall and Wills, working in tandem. First, Dan creates the backgrounds as line drawings; then, Scott figures out the color, lighting and shading, and paints "color keys"–small, highly detailed, full-color versions of what he wants the full-size backgrounds to look like for each scene–and scans them into the computer. "I want them color-corrected," he says, "so I scan them myself. I want the finished paintings to look exactly like the keys." He remains very hands-on, mostly in order to protect his work. Since the actual backgrounds are painted by artists at the production company overseas, Wills makes sure that the painters there follow his color selections exactly, by literally matching them up to the computer files.

His color keys are *so* detailed that there've been occasions where he's caught the overseas painters trying to "cheat." For example, instead of painting new backgrounds based on Wills' work, he claims, "they just took pieces of my one key and 'Frankensteined' them together into all the other paintings, 'cause they didn't wanna paint any of it. You can do that, but you get a lot of problems . . . things start looking blurry, textures get blown up, it starts looking bad."

It means having to redo and tweak everything electronically. Sometimes, he lets them take these shortcuts (it keeps his color choices absolutely true), other times not. "But I have a lot of control, and I've been smart enough to keep them from ruining what I did."

The only downside to striving for perfection on every episode of *Samurai Jack*, says Wills, "is time. I think that's the frustrating thing about this show . . . it's set up in such a feature way–the way it's boarded, y'know–that you watch it almost expecting feature quality. I just wish we had more time. I have a lot of friends in features, and you wanna tell them

Jack is making his way across this mountainside when he happens upon a fierce battle in "The Spartans," drawn by Krall and painted by Wills.

when they see it, 'I didn't spend a *month* on a painting, like you do.'" Yet, despite the brisk production pace bemoaned by Wills, the quality of painting on the show is consistently outstanding, fine enough to merit the creation of a coffee-table book depicting its designs. "Ugh . . . That would be a dream for me," he sighs.

Other professionals in the toon industry have taken note—"Pretty much every show just knocks me away visually," raves writer Paul Dini, echoing the sentiments of most everyone I spoke to—but does the average viewer watching at home notice the difference?

"It's not a conscious thing. . . . Even if they're not looking at details, there's a sense of quality that people totally feel," Scott Wills offers. "Something about it just feels full, and rich, and well done. . . . You watch it, and almost just automatically enter another level of expectations. You almost don't realize it's TV—*This is TV, man!*"

TURNING THE LIGHTS DOWN ON THE DARK KNIGHT

Painter Eric Radomski Cloaks *Batman* in Shadows

In 1992, from out of the abyss known as children's afternoon TV programming, a startling new animated series swooped onto the air. It featured a familiar old hero by the name of Batman, but boasted cartoony, stylized character designs set inside a dark, moodily art-directed, film noir-ish urban environment. It was a look that reminded many of the Fleischers' theatrical *Superman* toons of the 1940s, but had certainly never been seen on an animated TV series. What's more, the show's writing was spare, literate, and packed a mean punch. It all felt totally fresh—yet, at the same time, like a throwback to the old days of cartoon making, when the creators weren't particularly targeting a specific age group, or aiming to please any audience other than themselves.

After several decades of hibernation, Warner Bros. Animation was up and cooking again by the early nineties. Steven Spielberg—always a huge fan—produced a new series called *Tiny Toon Adventures*, that in many ways, harkened back to the classic *Merrie Melodies* and *Looney Tunes* cartoons. The show attracted some brilliant talents, among them Bruce Timm, a character designer and storyboard artist, and Eric Radomski, a background painter with broad experience in animation production.

"It was a very cool family on *Tiny Toons*, and we would have these meetings out in the big open space part of the building on, maybe, a monthly basis," Radomski recalls. "Just to get an update . . . y'know, 'Warner Bros.

Eric Radomski plays with blurred motion in this dramatic sketch of a Ninja, inspired by the short story, "Sarutobi."

is happy, Steven Spielberg is happy, you guys are doing great.'" As the crew got closer to the end of *Tiny Toons*' run, executive producer Jean MacCurdy announced that the company was looking to develop some properties, things that Warner Bros. already had in their library. Anyone who cared to submit ideas for consideration was welcome, she added. *Batman* was certainly one of those properties–Tim Burton's live-action feature had come out already and caused quite a stir. Eric Radomski immediately thought to himself, "Yeah, I've got an idea for the way I would approach it."

Radomski, one of the few artists among his peers who'd never really gotten into comic books as a kid, had found himself enthralled with the stylish, brooding quality of the 1989 feature film–and, notably, its return to the original concept of Batman as an avenging crime fighter driven by his tragic past.

"I just was inspired by the dark approach to the character, 'cause I had only known him from the campy sixties TV version," he explains. "I didn't know until then that Batman had as psychologically twisted a beginning as he did. But I had some overall production design ideas, and basically went off and did a few paintings. I was inspired by some of the illustrators that were hot in the seventies and eighties–Bernie Fuchs and Bob Peak. Those guys were all bringing this minimalist approach to their illustrations . . . and I thought it was really cool. And I had liked a lot of the impressionist painters. Those kinds of ideas–of light allowing things to be just suggested and not fully realized–was kind of the hook for me. I thought, 'Nighttime is basically the environment of *Batman*.'"

As he began to conceptualize, Radomski recalled a painting he had done many years ago while still living in Cleveland, Ohio. "It was a corner of my street on 55th and Broadway, looking down on a slightly drizzly night–my mom still has the painting–and wherever the light was, it sort of lit edges of buildings. You could see some distant cars by way of their headlights and a little bit of reflection on the vehicles. . . . And, as I was putting together my pieces, I thought, 'Wouldn't it be cool to do a city [like that], one that basically starts in complete darkness, and plays into the whole mystique of Batman being able to blend into the shadows?'"

Radomski threw together a few loose paintings, along with a couple of other studies done in colored pencil on board, and submitted them for review to Jean MacCurdy and Tom Ruegger, the senior producer at the studio.

What happened next caught Radomski by surprise. "They came back about a week or two later and called Bruce Timm and me together–he had done some character design. We were both equally dumbfounded, because Jean said, 'We really like what you guys did. We'd like you to produce a little film so you could show us how this might work together.' Bruce and I just kind of looked at each other and went, 'Well, that's cool.'"

So, matched together by MacCurdy, they gamely set out as a team to create a two-minute *Batman* film blending both their visions together as co-directors. Because of Radomski's background in hands-on animation production, he assumed more of a producer/director role, with Bruce Timm more the designer/director.

"I put together sort of the scheme of what we needed to do, while Bruce boarded out a good chunk of it. I also contributed some to the board with a few shots that I thought were pretty cool," says Radomski. "And from that, we did layout at the studio, basically working Bruce's boards up. Background-wise, we pulled in a guy, Ted Blackman, who eventually became the senior designer for the background style of Gotham, and truly defined that art deco look. He really just nailed the city."

While Bruce Timm continued to focus on boards, Eric Radomski busied himself painting all the backgrounds for the short. "There's an original pan-down of the city that was the first painting that I did. . . . It panned down to a jewel heist that was taking place on top of a building. There was a neon thing going on. It got down to the docks, where you saw a boat and reflections. . . . I painted that in multi-layers, which was kinda cool, working over black with frisket and airbrush."

A friend of the painter's, Greg Duffel at Lightbox Animation in Canada, then did the animation and assembled the two-minute test. When it came back, says Radomski, "We added some effects–a moon-glow and some reflections in the water–and basically re-purposed Danny Elfman's music from the Tim Burton movie. Bruce and I contributed the voices 'cause there was no dialogue, more impacts and fight sounds. So we pulled that together, delivered the piece, and thought, 'This was great.' We had a blast, made a cool little film, and expected truly nothing more beyond that."

It had taken them a mere month and a half from start to finish–blinding speed in the animation world. The final product so dazzled the execs at Warner Bros. that they decided to go right to series, with Timm and Radomski on board as creators/producers. The two artists were both thrilled and flabbergasted.

"Not only was it a show, but it was sixty-five episodes up front! An absolute mountain," Radomski muses. "You're just lookin' at it and going, 'How the hell are we gonna get all these done? And who're we gonna hire?' But we basically just never looked back. We moved forward based on that two-minute trailer, which was a great compliment to all of us involved in putting it together. People were coming to us . . . and they were like, 'I just wanna work on the show. I think it's a really cool adaptation of the character.'"

Thanks to the care and attention that they'd lavished on the short film, the creators already had a fully realized design template to work off of once the series began production. "We were basically just building on that," confirms Radomski. "Once we were under the pressure of putting together a staff, putting together a scheme for the sixty-five episodes, and searching for writers and writer/producers, it became apparent that we were not gonna veer too far from what we had established."

Even their color palette was set. "We knew that we wanted to stay in kind of a muted range, and try and measure how far out we could go. At the time, Warner Bros. had a pretty nice-sized palette of color to work with–but it's not like it is today with digital, where you've got a million colors. We were limited to probably a couple hundred that the studio was using both for *Tiny Toons* and every other production. We were able to add in probably twenty additional colors that were all on the deep or muted side of things . . . but the general overall tone we knew we were gonna stick with was almost predominantly all the shows taking place at nighttime, and keeping it very dark. That was the edict for anything we designed, and we tried to light it in a way so that it would instigate shadows and more muted tones."

Radomski admits that the bad boys of *Batman: The Animated Series* were breaking the rules, in particular with their extensive use of black and other very dark colors. "There was definitely, in a purely visual sense, a concern about the overall darkness . . . that people would be looking at their set and kinda saying, 'What the hell's going on?' The point we had to prove was: *That's the point*. He's a mysterious figure that floats in the shadows, and we don't have to be so on-the-nose with every point we're trying to make. We wanted the audience to discover things along with Batman, because he's 'the world's greatest detective.' So let your imagination fill in a lot of the gaps."

It took some time for the network execs to believe that such a dark series would work. And not only from a technical standpoint–the overall tone of the show was equally a concern. "We had to wait until we got the first couple episodes back till they really embraced it, and went, 'Okay, these guys know what they're doing. This looks pretty damn cool.' That's when the floodgates opened," Radomski relates. "I don't know that I'll ever have it as good as I did then. Because we produced that show with next to no interference at all. Fox was in their heyday–Fox Afternoon was just kickin' ass in the ratings–and we were certainly contributing to that. They were totally supportive of us, and we just went our merry way and continued to make shows that we really enjoyed making. That whole first season of sixty-five [episodes] ended up being a terrific experience for everybody that worked on the show."

As for Eric Radomski and Bruce Timm, their creative partnership turned out to be one made in cartoon heaven.

"We didn't even know each other on *Tiny Toons*," says Radomski. "I mean, I was aware of him 'cause he's such a brilliant talent. You couldn't help but see all of his great stuff around the studio . . . but we didn't know one another prior to that. Thrust together, we got along just fine and sort of set up our shop, knew where our strengths and weaknesses were, and basically decided that's the way we would approach this thing. So *character* was absolutely all Bruce. He was much more skilled than I at character design. Background-wise, environment, and sort of overall tone–and managing the crew of artists that were coming in–was gonna be a challenge in itself."

Radomski, naturally adept at dealing with people, took on the task of keeping the artists and crew an integral part of the process while at the same time ensuring that Bruce Timm, who had a very specific vision for *Batman*, was insulated from "all the bullshit so that he wouldn't get distracted. When you've got fifty people working for you, all of them can't think the way that *you* think," notes Radomski, who found himself acting as liaison. "If there were concerns, I would get them first. I'd bring 'em into Bruce. I would give him a practical application of these ideas and thoughts, and it was an easy way for him to take some of 'em and be able to manipulate them in without feeling like he was being forced upon by anybody. That was my big mission and goal: to keep the overall consistency that we intended by keeping everybody generally happy, and trying to make it a very collaborative effort instead of a bunch of egomaniacs going at each other, 'No, fuck you, your ideas are not as good as mine!' That can easily happen, especially on an action show where you've got all the testosterone flying through the studio. And we managed to pull it off well. Everybody got along fine."

Through all of it, Radomski continued to design and paint for the show–including some stunningly beautiful title cards for each episode. "It actually was just sort of a bonus, in the midst of everything. . . . I was like a kid in a candy store with that stuff. Between looking at boards, giving notes, and approving designs, I'd find time to doodle ideas," he says. "Sometimes I'd come up with a few different designs, and then I'd take 'em into Bruce and we'd bounce ideas off each other, and then basically hand them off to our background artists to really push 'em to the next level. For the first sixty-five [shows], they were all traditional designs and paintings. On the last twenty (we picked up another twenty episodes), those were actually the very early days of Warner Bros. embracing Photoshop. So some of 'em got a little bit more involved and elaborate, and introduced the digital process into the *Batman* world. Those title cards were a blast . . . they were dessert on top of everything else."

A heartfelt sketch from Radomski's personal artwork, part of a larger collage depicting the horrors of Auschwitz.

Once all eighty-five episodes of *Batman: The Animated Series* were in the can, and a 1993 theatrical feature spin-off, *Batman: Mask of the Phantasm*, was completed, Radomski decided to work off the last few months of his contract at Warner Bros. and move on to other challenges.

"I wanted to try some different things," he explains. "Be a little avant-garde, a little out of the box." He went on to produce and direct the first several seasons of Todd McFarlane's *Spawn* (1997) for HBO Animation, among other projects–but still looks back fondly on his *Batman* days, and considers the impact it had on his life and career.

"It was the absolute turning point for me . . . in the broadest sense. The friends and talent that I worked with, [I have] absolute respect for, and maintain to this day. From the animation side of it, the films speak for themselves. *Batman* [was] a labor of love, and an education beyond belief. . . . It was truly the closest thing to the good old days that you read about, at Disney and at Warner Bros. Animation with the 'Termite Terrace' group. This was sort of our generation's version. If anything–if it does continue to be a reference point for people to kinda go, 'Wow, we'd like to do something *like* that, not just for style but we wanna put a group together like that'–if that's inspired anyone else to support quality products, like they're doing at Cartoon Network, I think that's the greatest thing that we could've contributed."

PAINTING WITH THE COLORS OF THE WIND

Giaimo's Distinctive Designs for *Pocahontas*

Walt Disney animated feature films have long been heralded not only for their superlative animation, but for their magnificent art direction and styling. Some of the finest painters and illustrators in the world–Eyvind Earle, Gustaf Tenggren, Kay Nielsen, Mary Blair, Gerald Scarfe, and even Salvador Dalí in a brief 1946 stint–have lent their visual skills to the studio's projects. Although Disney fell into a "house style" from the mid-sixties through the early eighties, where every picture's art direction generally looked the same, things began picking up considerably in more recent years.

A remarkable amount of precision and attention is paid to even the tiniest detail on a Disney cartoon feature these days. Every element is orchestrated within a particular design style–the sets, the characters, their costumes and props, the way shadows are cast on the ground, the way smoke rises and billows, the way fire burns or sparks. They all help unify the entire world that the filmmakers seek to create for a story.

Of the many fine films to come out of the studio in the past few decades, *Pocahontas* (1995) stands out as perhaps the most beautifully designed of all. Its angular, stylized, color-saturated art direction brings to mind the studio's own *Sleeping Beauty*, so strikingly imagined by Eyvind Earle back in 1959. Maybe that's not such a coincidence.

"The very first film I remember, when I was five years old, would be *Sleeping Beauty*," says *Pocahontas'* art director, Michael Giaimo. "Actually, I didn't remember the story, but it absolutely stuck with me visually, even more than the other animated theatrical films." And though Earle clearly had a profound influence on the young artist, Giaimo also cites the great illustrator Ronald Searle, *Peanuts* cartoonist Charles Schulz, Dr. Seuss, *Rocky and Bullwinkle*, and the Warner Bros. shorts as equally significant to his developing sensibilities. "I loved [Warner's background designer] Maurice Noble's visual giddiness . . . you could just see in his designs that probably, as he was drawing them, he was tickled by them!"

When Giaimo was invited to art direct *Pocahontas*, it marked a return to the studio for him. He'd worked there earlier in his career as an assistant animator and story artist–"Including nine months on *Black Cauldron*, of all things," he groans. "I hated every minute of it"–but had decided to leave after a few years to pursue his own painting, freelance production design, and a teaching position at CalArts. It was the teaching post that truly helped him become an art director, he feels. "In order to communicate to students, I started to develop theories about design and color. . . . In order to teach, you have to know what you're teaching. So I began to educate myself. I always wondered, why do I like the things I like . . . why are things appealing to me?"

Giaimo taught himself to look at animated films and illustrations and classic picture books, and pull them apart–analyzing what the individual elements were that made up the whole. "I'm more intuitive than that . . . but I could start to see that there was some rhyme or reason to it. There's always the X factor with any piece of art that goes beyond explanation, that makes it great. And I definitely believe in that . . . you have to let intuition take over. But it's kind of a balancing act."

It was *Pocahontas* director Mike Gabriel who asked Giaimo if he'd like to do some development paintings for the film, which was just starting up at Disney. Giaimo's personal work–his own whimsically eccentric paintings, with their bold graphic imagery and heightened sense of color–was what drew Gabriel to him for the job. "Mike said, 'I think you could really offer something to a Native American tale. There's an elegant, primitive quality to your work that I think would dovetail nicely with this film,'" Giaimo recalls. He was flattered to be invited to create something poetic

Pencil sketches of Polynesian-inspired tikis by Giaimo which show how markedly his personal style is influenced by primitive art and cultures.

rather than humorous (a quality that described most of his prior work in animation), and knew that he was ready for the challenge. So he accepted, painting on a freelance basis for a few months–until Eric Goldberg came aboard as Gabriel's co-director, and the two asked Giaimo to join them on staff.

Not everyone was thrilled at first with Michael Giaimo's arrival as art director, however. "I got a lot of criticism. Jeffrey Katzenberg was very apprehensive about my take on the movie . . . because I was known for a strong sense of design, and people thought, 'Well, *Pocahontas* is going to be very naturalistic, with lots of rendered tones and shadows and this and that.' I think some people were surprised at what I was going for: a more reductive, minimalist style."

Early on, Giaimo made a conscious decision to mute the backgrounds in the film in order to bring the characters out more clearly. "That was one of my theories that I really wanted to employ," he explains. "I guess I felt some of the recent Disney movies, as beautiful as they all are, lacked the crispness and illuminative quality that some of the older films had–particularly the fifties films–in which the characters were so brightly illuminated against a background . . . so rich and sumptuous. And I wanted to bring that back. I thought *Pocahontas* was a wonderful vehicle to do that with, and Mike and Eric were really supportive of it. What that meant was, being very selective not with the background elements–because the backgrounds were lush–but with the treatment of them, in which the color palette was so controlled . . . often, I used one overriding hue so that the characters could just pop." Because the bulk of *Pocahontas'* story took place in a forest or glade setting, which had a natural density to begin with, it further enabled Giaimo's dramatic approach to sing.

"We also used very minimal shading on the characters," Eric Goldberg notes. "One thing we didn't do was anything soft-edged in the movie. We kept everything hard and crisp. For example, there are no rack-focus shots in *Pocahontas*. It was a conscious decision to keep a clarity and crispness of style–we wanted to define a fresh world . . . a brand-new, pristine, untouched new world. This was a Mike Giaimo decision."

Giaimo admits it was hard not to think about *Sleeping Beauty* while he was art-directing *Pocahontas*. "Both are set in a forest. . . . Actually, until we took field trips to Virginia to look at the landscape of Jamestown, I didn't think I would do the whole vertical tree thing as much as I did . . . and, of course, that's what Eyvind Earle did with *Sleeping Beauty*. But when I saw what the terrain looked like naturally, I thought, 'Well, I can't avoid it, I just have to go with it.'"

This concept painting for Pocahontas' *"Colors of the Wind" sequence is a perfect example of how Michael Giaimo pushed his designs toward a more stylized, enchanted environment. © Disney Enterprises, Inc.*

When Jeffrey Katzenberg saw some of the first color dailies, he was skeptical. "He kinda looked at me," Giaimo smiles. "Because Jeffrey really loves rendering, and realism. Literalism. And I was so *not* a literalist . . . never will be. My deal was to make a Disney film look artful. We weren't afraid to make it look like art; that was our credo. Ironically, *Lion King* had talking animals in a very real world. I thought, '*Pocahontas* is a very real story; it needs an enchanted look, almost a fantasy look, to counterpoint the realism of the story.'"

Perhaps luckily for Giaimo, Katzenberg–who was alarmed at the flatness of the characters, even though they were beautifully drawn–left Disney at just around that time in order to found DreamWorks with Steven Spielberg and David Geffen. "I fought so hard not to have tones" on those characters, Giaimo stresses, "and he was very apprehensive about that. I often wonder, if he had stayed, would I have gotten the graphic look that I wanted . . . so that was rather serendipitous. When he left, I was kind of home free."

One of Giaimo's few lamentations was the cutting of a favorite song and sequence: John Smith has been captured, tied up, and held in a tent for execution when Pocahontas sneaks in to see him for one last time. The two sing a duet, "If I Never Knew You," which was a declaration of their love. "There was some beautiful imagery in there that ties the movie together," Giaimo reveals: After Pocahontas exits the tent and paddles away in her canoe, she sees Smith reflected in the water. She reaches out to him and he dissolves–which mirrors an earlier scene, when Pocahontas [during the song "Just Around the Riverbend"] saw an image of her then-fiancé Kocoum in the water, and *he* dissolved. "It's what really cinches the song," says the artist.

Thanks in large part to Michael Giaimo's contributions, *Pocahontas* stands as a throwback, artistically, to the heyday of the great Disney features produced at the studio when Walt was still actively running things.

Rhapsody in Aqua, Cobalt, and Periwinkle

Susan Goldberg's *Fantasia/2000* Art Direction

Making a different kind of history altogether several years later, the Disney studio finally credited their first female art director for her work on a cartoon feature film, *Fantasia/2000*.

For all her acclaim and accomplishments at Disney throughout her career, and despite her status as one of Walt's most cherished color stylists and inspirational sketch artists, Mary Blair was never accorded art director credit on screen. Under the old studio system, seldom, if ever, was one artist–male, female, or otherwise–allowed that kind of control on a Disney feature. Ken Anderson was the first, when he was billed in 1961 for art direction and production design of the original *One Hundred and One Dalmatians*, an animated film whose highly graphic, black-line-oriented styling had actually upset Walt Disney tremendously at the time.

Nevertheless, in recent years, many fine designers have been credited for their art direction, including Michael A. Peraza Jr. and Donald A. Towns (*The Little Mermaid*); Bill Perkins (*Aladdin*); Brian McEntee (*Beauty and the Beast*); Andy Gaskill (*The Lion King* and *Hercules*); Daniel St. Pierre (*Tarzan*); Ric Sluiter (*Mulan* and *Lilo & Stitch*); and Susan McKinsey Goldberg, for her award-winning work on several standout segments of *Fantasia/2000*.

Like many others who ended up at the studio, Susan McKinsey Goldberg dreamed about all things Disney as a child growing up in Florida. "When Disney World opened, my parents took me to 'It's a Small World,' and I made them ride on it fourteen times in a row," she remembers. "I used to create paper dolls based on Mary Blair's designs of the three-dimensional figures . . . so, very early on, Disney was already an influence on me."

She also found herself enchanted as a little girl by *Sleeping Beauty*. "I remember wanting to be Princess Aurora. My mother bought me the record album when I had the measles . . . and the house had to be kept dark . . . so I would waltz through the dark house, singing–and I'm tone-deaf. She got really sick of it all," Goldberg chortles. She watched little to no TV, she confesses, choosing instead to read voraciously. "I read *everything*. After I finished all the children's books in the library, I started with 'A' and worked my way all the way to 'Z' in the adult section."

Her love of animals led her to flirt with a career in veterinary medicine, yet she continued to paint and illustrate throughout, eventually ending up at CalArts. "That changed everything. I never knew there was a Disney program at the school–the idea of doing animation had never even occurred to me. But it seemed like such a great way to focus all the things you love in art . . . the idea of a *moving* painting was great." In school, Goldberg became friendly with John Lasseter, Michael Giaimo, Hendel Butoy, John Musker, Tim Burton, and others who would move on to prominence in the toon and film world.

Though she could only afford to attend one year of college, it proved an educational experience in unexpected ways for Goldberg; she began to get a sense of how hard it was for a woman to compete in the male-dominated animation business. "It's a tough field for women," she believes. "Very much an old boys' network. Women, I don't think, have been terribly comfortable with animation . . . it's changing, but I don't think a lot of us grew up on animation like the boys did." One of her instructors kept assuring her that she'd make "a great assistant one day," she recalls with disdain. "When you keep getting told that, you kind of start to fall into that idea . . . you won't aim for the top, because you're not supposed to."

Goldberg–whimsically accompanied to her classes every day by a pet cockatiel named Merlin–also received some strong encouragement at CalArts. Bill Moore, who held a well-deserved reputation as one of the toughest but finest instructors in the program, was impressed with his talented pupil. "You'll make a great art director one day . . . you have an eye for color like I've never seen before," he told her, comparing her abilities, interestingly, with those of another student of his: Michael Giaimo.

Her path eventually led her to animation work in New York City, where she rented an apartment owned by cartoonist Walt Kelly ("It was like living in *Pogo* Land") and met her husband, director/animator Eric Goldberg. The couple lived mostly in London for the better part of a decade before moving to L.A. in the early nineties, where they set about raising their daughters while tackling their own individual assignments–Eric animating and directing features for Disney while Susan did animation cleanup for *Ferngully . . . The Last Rainforest* (1992), the Chuck Jones–directed toon opening for *Mrs. Doubtfire* (1993), and other gigs. Although they teamed up occasionally on various projects (she cleaned up his work on Phil in *Hercules*), the Goldbergs finally got a chance to collaborate most significantly on George Gershwin's "Rhapsody in Blue" and Camille Saint-Saëns' "Carnival of the Animals" for *Fantasia/2000*, each bringing their respective skills to the table.

They tackled the three-minute Saint-Saëns piece first, and spent about a year creating the fanciful segment about a daffy, yo-yo twirling flamingo based on an original idea from ageless Disney story artist Joe Grant.

To achieve the soft watercolor appearance that she wanted on the pink flamingos, Susan and her six-person crew hand-painted each cel, while Eric animated the entire segment himself. "It was great fun," she offers, noting that she not only art directed the piece, but supervised cleanup, as well. "I did a lot of things on 'Carnival' . . . *some* painting–not as much as I would've liked to–because of the two departments I was running. And I was also helping set up to do 'Rhapsody' next."

Although the great illustrator Al Hirschfeld's style had been such a strong influence on the character design in *Aladdin*, he'd had nothing to do with the production of that film. This time, he was approached to design 'Rhapsody in Blue'–an offer he passed on, choosing instead to consult on the segment while giving his blessings to the Goldbergs to again channel his style.

Accordingly, Susan Goldberg's approach to art-directing the musical number was largely influenced by a book Hirschfeld had done with S. J. Perelman, "where he'd used one flat tone mixed underneath other tones, that very thirties and forties look that we were going for." Since it was, after all, 'Rhapsody in *Blue*,' Goldberg literally started out with shades of blue and expanded her palette from there into purples, lavenders, and greens–colors with a significant blue content. This allowed her to then select an occasional warm color from another family, such as red for a little girl's ball, and have it truly stand out on screen. Even so, despite the care and thought that went into many of her selections, Goldberg contends that most of her decisions are made "out of instinct, not out of going, 'Oh, yes, these two colors go together and this creates this.' It's completely instinctive."

Fantasia/2000*'s clever "Rhapsody in Blue" sequence not only boasted award-winning art direction, but satiric jabs at twentieth-century urban life, as well. © Disney Enterprises, Inc.*

To further achieve the stylized, flat color that they were after on 'Rhapsody,' she suggested that they paint all the backgrounds digitally, unlike today's usual method on animated features, which combines computer-colored characters set against traditionally hand-painted scenery. Thanks to that decision, "those backgrounds flew through . . . that production went so fast Disney didn't know what hit 'em," she laughs.

At first, the studio was planning to credit Susan McKinsey Goldberg's contribution only as a cleanup artist on *Fantasia/2000*, until Roy Disney stepped in. "He said, 'She's doing the job, she gets the credit,'" Goldberg states. "Tom Schumacher and [producer] Don Ernst supported it, too." It may have taken until the year 2000 for it to finally happen, but she broke down that wall–one that's down for good, now. "I'm the first credited woman art director [on a Disney cartoon feature]," she proudly affirms.

Her fine work was further acknowledged at the twenty-eighth annual Annie Awards later that year, when Goldberg won the prestigious industry award for Outstanding Production Design in an Animated Feature. "I was totally stunned," she admits. "I didn't even hear my name. Eric said, 'Susan, they just called *you*.' There was a dead silence as the audience waited for me to get off my butt and walk up there . . . but the thing I'm proudest of the most is that Al Hirschfeld liked it. If he hadn't, they could have given me all the awards in the world; I'd still feel like I failed."

Though the entire film itself was uneven–with some segments more distinctive than others–the design throughout was nothing short of spectacular, thanks to the talent of Goldberg and her fellow art directors.

Amazing Feats of Clay

Mr. Melton's Marvelous Maquettes

The art of model-making is a creative component of animation that most people never think of when they consider how a toon gets made. The fact is, animators have long been relying on maquettes–small, three-dimensional sculptures of a film or TV show's characters–to help them realize how those characters can be drawn from every conceivable angle. Of the handful of sculptors who design and create these meticulously crafted figurines, Kent Melton is widely acknowledged as one of the finest in the world.

"I got into animation kind of from the side door, really," he relates. "I was at a music convention, and I had sculpted the Beatles' Saturday morning cartoon characters. I just did 'em because I wanted to; they were nostalgic for me. And an individual who worked in the animation industry was there . . . he saw the sculptures that I had done, and he persuaded me to go out to southern California to try to get in where he was working at the time."

Melton was earning his living as a freelance wood sculptor in the Midwest, but had long thought about working in animation. So he followed the man's advice and headed west for a meeting at the Disney Studios, where someone basically promised him a job if he relocated to Burbank. The artist and his wife, Martha, decided to take that leap, and made the move . . . only to discover a pot of sludge waiting at the end of the rainbow. "Unfortunately, as kind of a baptism into Hollywood, they wouldn't return my calls," Melton remembers, noting that he struggled for a time after that, finding occasional sculpting work where he could. Meanwhile, Don Dougherty (the Disney story artist whose advice he had followed in the first

Kent Melton's very first maquettes: Paul, George, Ringo, and John, as depicted on the animated series The Beatles *(1965). He did the sculpts for fun, but they helped launch his career.*

place) felt somewhat responsible for the sculptor's plight and helped arrange another meeting, this time at Hanna-Barbera–who instantly fell in love with Kent Melton's work.

"That day I ended up meeting Joe Barbera. They weren't really sure how they could utilize a sculptor–they'd never *had* a sculptor at Hanna-Barbera–but I remember Joe essentially saying, 'Yeah, hire the kid. We'll figure out something.' I ended up working there for about four years."

Melton created a lot of sculptures for pitches to the networks–mostly novelty items like a radio-controlled car with Yogi Bear and sidekick Boo Boo riding in a picnic basket racer for *Wacky Racers*. When producer/director Art Leonardi left Hanna-Barbera to work for Warner Bros. on Steven Spielberg's *Tiny Toons*, Melton was asked to freelance on the new series' development. "They decided they were gonna do it like traditional animation, which included having maquettes made," he says. "So this was my first real job sculpting maquettes for animation. I had to sign all these disclosure forms, and, y'know, take the blood oath not to tell anyone about what I'd seen. So I ended up doing the main lineup for *Tiny Toons*–one pose of each character, trying to capture the essence of who they were."

Despite his progress, the sculptor still found himself struggling to make ends meet. It was around this time that a Warner Bros. executive who'd seen the *Tiny Toons* maquettes called him in for a meeting . . . which led Kent Melton's career toward an unexpectedly rewarding detour. "They had a new live-action film they were gonna do–the Tim Burton movie, *Batman* (1989). There were photographs of the actors, and they had sketches of the outfits . . . but they didn't have anything complete. And they wanted me to fuse these different elements together to help kind of realize what the finished image would be like."

Melton's work on the film attracted the eye of another Warner Bros. exec, who happened to be overseeing the start of a new WB catalog. He was asked to create several thousand figurines for the premiere edition, as collectibles. "It was funny, because they were talking to me over the phone–they had no idea that they were talking to some guy in a bungalow in Burbank. I said, 'No, I can't do that. It's just me and my wife, there's just no way. . . .' 'Well, how many *can* you do?' I thought for a minute, and said, 'Well, I dunno, maybe fifty of each or something,' thinking they'd never go for that. He says, 'Okay, that's good!'"

Since the sculptures were to be the most expensive items in the new catalog, everyone figured they'd sell slowly and there'd be plenty of time to create them. Instead, as soon as the catalogs were distributed, the figurines sold out. "I mean, they were still in the casting phase at that point! I remember being so stressed, and working so hard, that my equilibrium would actually go out. I'd be sitting down, and all of a sudden I couldn't tell if I was horizontal or vertical. It was a nightmare, but I did get through it."

Kent Melton's hotly sought-after collectible sculptures catapulted him to instant acclaim–suddenly, his work was appearing in *People* magazine. "Overnight, I was *the guy*. Literally the week before, I was scrounging for a crumb of bread . . . it was dismal. And then, all of a sudden, the phone was just ringin' off the hook."

Melton's fortunes improved considerably from that point. He continued creating collectibles for Warner Bros., and took a staff position as an art director at Universal. But it was a birthday party for his young son that ended up playing the most significant role in his future: As the guests began arriving that day, one of the kids' fathers happened to pass through the kitchen and did a double take at all of Melton's work in progress. That guy turned out to be Thom Enriquez, an artist at Disney . . . who apparently passed the sculptor's name along to Richard Vander Wende, production designer of *Aladdin* . . . who phoned Melton out of the blue and asked him to drop by the studio. "It really surprised me," Melton says, still wide-eyed about it to this day. "'Cause I'd been banging my head against the outside of the place for years, and couldn't get in. I guess the fact that I'd had no formal art training at all had worked against me getting in the door. So anyway . . . I kinda grabbed what I had available, whatever things were in the room, threw 'em into a cardboard box, and drove over there."

Melton was shown into a small office, where he proceeded to display a group of his sculptures on a table. What followed was an almost comical procession of animators and designers filing in and out of the room to see his work. "All they kept saying to me was, 'Wait just a minute, we'll be right back,'" he chuckles. "So then, I'm in there by myself for a while, sittin' there thinking, 'Well, should I just put my stuff away, or what . . .' Eventually, Richard Vander Wende comes back in and he goes, 'We've been doing a cattle call for sculptors because our regular sculptor, Ruben Procopio, is still working on *Beauty and the Beast*, and we want to get going.'"

Vander Wende offered Melton a job on the spot, bypassing the usual tests that people had been asked to submit. He began sculpting the Tiger's Head entrance to the Cave of Wonders in *Aladdin* during his evenings and weekends, while still putting in his art director chores at Universal. "They had me cut right to the chase and do the full-scale, two-and-a-half-foot by three-foot open-mouth version and closed-mouth version, which they digitized and scanned. . . . That was also my first venture into computer animation. Literally, what we saw on the screen was my sculpt, only it could talk and move around. It was very cool."

When he brought in the last Tiger's Head, they merely announced, "Well, guess we're ready to move onto the Genie." He still grins at the recollection. "I didn't say anything–I just thought, 'Cool, if they don't notice, I'll go ahead and do the Genie, too.'"

Melton ended up sculpting *all* the characters for *Aladdin*. "From there it tumbled right into the next film, and just kept going. After the second film, I just decided to quit Universal." He sculpted maquettes for *The Lion King* next, followed by *Pocahontas*, *The Hunchback of Notre Dame*, *Hercules*, *Mulan*, *Tarzan*, *Atlantis*, and *Treasure Planet*.

The first character he got to work on in *The Lion King* was Mufasa, still in its early design stages by Tony Fucile. Melton's first impression was that the lion's head looked perfect– but the body seemed ordinary, with nothing to suggest his personality. As the sculptor set to work, he thought of Mufasa's position as a patriarch . . . and he recalled Michelangelo's sculptures of old warriors. "Y'know, you could tell they were really buff when they were young, and svelte . . . but had kinda started puttin' on the weight, bulking out and getting heavy. So without asking anybody–at the time I was

The sculpt of Mufasa for The Lion King *that Melton innocently took liberties on. They ultimately contributed to the character's final design.* *© Disney Enterprises, Inc.*

pretty naïve–I thought, 'I'm just gonna start bulking him up a little,'" Melton relates.

He retained Mufasa's broad face and strong chin, but beefed up the lion's body to match the head. When Fucile saw what Melton had done, he loved it–so much so that he had photos shot of the sculpture, and then worked off of them. "He said to me, at the end of the film, 'Man, you should get co-design credit on this,' which was very flattering to me."

Kent Melton continued mixing movie maquette assignments with the creation of collectible classics figurines for various studios, including the Disney line. Melton's meticulously modeled and painted figurines are considered to be the finest available by many collectors. In addition to his work for the Disney Studios, he sculpted maquettes for DreamWorks' animated features, *The Prince of Egypt*, *Road to El Dorado*, and *Spirit: Stallion of the Cimarron,* several of Don Bluth's films for Fox–*Troll in Central Park* and *Thumbelina*–and Pixar's *The Incredibles* for director Brad Bird.

Maquettes are far more commonly utilized by animators who work on feature films than on TV series, Melton explains. "In feature animation, they do a lot of things that they don't do in television ... I mean, there are exceptions, but, in general, television's pretty straightforward left-to-right animation, whereas in feature films, you've got some pretty creative camera angle stuff going on ... a lot of foreshortening ... things that require some major thought to move 'em around. And I think that's when the maquettes come in really handy."

The sculptor takes us through a bit of his process on a typical assignment: At first, he explains, he knows little about the characters, so the animators share whatever materials they have–verbal information, thumbnails on a martini napkin, maybe a few animation drawings, and, on rare occasions, a short pencil test. As he gets further into his job–perhaps by the fifth of the dozen or so sculpts he'll create–he might even get some model sheets. Toward his *last* sculpt for a film, there might be cleanup animation. "Ultimately, my goal is to please the animators," he says. "I do also have to please the directors and everybody else, but I feel like my first goal is to get the animator won over, because then I've got somebody in my corner when I face the other people."

Melton's maquettes are less important to the supervising animator than they are to that animator's assistants. "Really, a maquette–for an animator–is just a point of departure," he feels. "It's not the gospel. What's really *The Word* on their character is in their head. So the crew truly does utilize them most. It's a way of making it a little bit more possible to see inside the mind of the lead animator. It's also kind of a security thing for the crew, because they know that the animator's gone over every inch of this thing. If they can't get their question answered by looking at it, well, then, it's okay to go to the animator at that point–but generally, you don't wanna be a pest. They're in the same boat as me: We have a lot of people to answer to."

Given the public's ever-growing mania for collectibles these days, it comes as no surprise that the more popular films' maquettes have become hotly coveted auction items in recent years. And though their sales bring him no financial compensation, Melton admits that he feels satisfaction just the same: "I'm very flattered by the fact that somebody is so touched by a film that they'd wanna lay down that kind of money for my sculpture of a character. I keep it in perspective. . . . I know that the sculpture's part of it, but at the base of the collector is the love of the character and of the film. So I get a little bit of fame by association. At the same time, I realize that if the sculpt wasn't any good at all, they are discerning–they have good taste, most of these people. They know the characters because they're fanatical about it, and if it's not right, they'll know. So, to me, it's an honor."

By now, Kent Melton has gained a measure of acclaim in the industry, and finds himself approached from time to time for advice. "So many people wanna sculpt nowadays, I have a lot of people asking me, 'How can I sculpt like you?' and 'What are your secrets?' I used to always say, 'Well, I don't have any secrets. I just sculpt it to look correctly . . . and then, I realized one day, I *do* have a secret. It's not a big one, but it's real important: My secret of sculpting for animation is to never, ever sculpt a *drawing* of a character. Think of them as being alive–don't fall into the trap of becoming too religious to a specific drawing. One drawing can't capture a character–they're too complex. . . . The beauty of a sculpture is that you can turn it around, and it actually becomes a series of drawings that you can rotate. If you want to sculpt in three dimensions, you have to see the character in three dimensions."

CHAPTER 6
BUT WHAT I REALLY WANNA DO IS . . .
The All-Consuming Task of Directing Toons

"I think people don't really understand what directors do in animation. Having worked with some pretty amazing directors, I get a very clear sense of what they do. And I can tell you for a fact, I can't do it."

—Aron Warner, producer of *Shrek* (2001)

Directing a cartoon TV series or feature film is, hands down, one of the most challenging yet ultimately satisfying jobs in the business. Interestingly, many of the biggest hits of the 1980s, 1990s, and 2000s were helmed by first-time directors . . . who didn't fully grasp the enormity of the task that lay before them. What they may have lacked in experience, though, they more than made up for with talent, enthusiasm, raw energy, and a tireless drive to make their projects as good as they could possibly be. And, without exception, they were all fast learners.

Directing toons is just as much work as directing live-action, but there are some fundamental differences. For one thing, in animation, everything is predetermined and pre-edited in great detail (the movie or TV show is first built in storyboard form), allowing directors to clearly envision their shots–exactly how long they want them to be; which will be close-ups, medium, or wide; and precisely which angles and compositions will be employed in literally each and every sequence. By putting them up on *story reels*–filming the boards in order, and synching them up to a rough soundtrack–they get a solid idea of how it'll all play once the finished product is created. (Some live-action directors, like Steven Spielberg, have adopted this process, enjoying the added control it affords them . . . but it largely remains a technique unique to animation.)

Then there's the issue of *coverage*. Unlike a live shoot–where a scene is often filmed from various different angles to allow more freedom in the editing process–animation is created precisely, with scene length timed exactly to frame. If a director decides he needs another shot, or a longer shot, or a different angle, it has to be planned and created from scratch.

Of course, it helps if an animation director can draw–it's practically essential–since that makes it much easier to express one's ideas to the artists and crew. Directors of the classic cartoon shorts were always traditionally the ones to sketch the key poses for their animators, capturing a character's attitude from scene to scene. And because *everything*–environments, characters, lighting, effects, and so on–is literally created from the ground up, directing an animated film is a process that can take between three and five years; a single half-hour episode of a TV toon can take about nine months. It's all a much slower process than live action, demanding a very particular type of temperament from its leader.

Directing a Film That Nobody Wanted to Work On

The Lion King

Roger Allers feels he got his first taste of directing, unofficially, when he worked as head of story on the Disney feature *Beauty and the Beast*. "I was working with the directors, I was working with the composers, working with the story people . . . it was really involving," he says. "And a lot of people kept saying to me, 'Ya know, you ought to direct.' I kept getting that from everybody . . . but always sort of thought, 'Boy, I don't want to be a director,' because from what I had witnessed, their lives were eaten up. They never got to see their families. I had two small kids–I wanted to be able to go home in the evening and see my kids."

For some reason that even he can't explain, Allers eventually started listening to all those people around him, and began to seriously consider directing a film. "My experience on *Beauty and the Beast* had elements of being a director . . . and I enjoyed it so much that I thought maybe I should give it a try. So I asked Peter Schneider, 'Do you think I could try to direct sometime?'" Schneider's response was, "Well, if you really want to, then we'll see."

That opportunity presented itself within the year–but not the way Allers hoped it would. *Aladdin*–in production at the time–had gotten into the kind of trouble that almost every picture seems to hit at the midway point. During these inevitable crises, the filmmakers lose faith in the project, at least temporarily, and they want to throw everything out. This time it was *Aladdin*'s turn.

So Allers was helping out for about six months on that film when he got an unexpected call from Schneider. "Peter asked me if I would go and co-direct with George Scribner on *King of the Jungle*," Allers recalls. "And I remember telling him that I didn't really want to do that . . . it didn't excite me . . . I dunno, there was something about the approach. It all felt just a little serious, and not very character-driven. Well, a few weeks later, I got a phone call from Jeffrey [Katzenberg], saying 'Rog, y'know, I really want you to jump into this thing. Go in there, help out, be a part of it'–and I'm fighting him all the way–'No, Jeffrey, I really don't wanna do it.' Anyway, he basically wore me down. It took a couple of phone calls . . . but it was hard to say no to Jeffrey. So I went onto the project, and started working with George."

Roger Allers' first challenge was to try and recruit the right talent to work on the movie. "*No one* wanted to work on this project," he says. "So I went around and tried to get everybody to come work with me. I went and got [story artist] Brenda Chapman and said, 'Oh, come on, Brenda, if we're working on it together we'll have fun!'–and Chris Sanders: 'C'mon, Chris, you're really such a great designer, y'know, it'll be fun!' We'd all worked together on *Beauty and the Beast*. It was such a great experience, there was such camaraderie, and we'd all had such a sense of accomplishment. They're all great people."

Once Allers had convinced the crew to hop aboard, he, Scribner, and the others began working on trying to solve the story. About five months later they were sent to Kenya on a photographic safari, to absorb as much of Africa as they could. The trip inspired them enormously, and not only gave them many new insights on the animals and the environment, but some unique touches that profoundly influenced the story (see Brenda Chapman's account in chapter 4).

About a month or two after they returned home, however, *King of the Jungle* experienced a tumultuous upheaval. The studio made a hard decision they felt was in the best interests of the film: They replaced George Scribner with Rob Minkoff as co-director–a move that was difficult emotionally for everyone back then, but which makes sense to Allers in retrospect. "I have to admit, George and I have very different tastes . . . he wanted a story that was more kinda rough–kind of a tooth and claw movie, and characters with really sarcastic attitude. But the biggest difference in our tastes was that he wanted a realistic, photographic look . . . and I was always drawn to things a little more stylized. We used to talk about it, and

I'd say, 'Well, one of my favorite movies was *Peter Pan*.' And he went, 'Oh, that's the movie, style-wise, that I hate the most.' So we were always trying to kind of compromise somewhere in the middle. . . . I don't know where that would've wound up, but probably no place that either of us would've been happy with. And, obviously, the execs weren't happy, either."

Unsettling as it all was, the director is pleased that he and Scribner remain friends to this day, which might not have been the case–even though the switch wasn't something Allers was privy to until it was a fait accompli. Nevertheless, it helped the project. "Rob Minkoff and I were of very similar sensibilities," he says. "We shared a similar sense of humor, we liked a lot of the same music, the same stylization of color . . . I have to say, it was a *really* good partnership."

As they were starting over so radically, everyone felt it would make sense to stop and assess where they were, where the picture was headed, and to make whatever changes were needed. Allers recounts the 1992 brainstorming sessions that helped galvanize the production: "We got together with Don Hahn, who was the producer, and called in Brenda, and Kirk Wise and Gary Trousdale, who were finished with *Beauty and the Beast*, and sort of locked ourselves in a room for about two weeks and just talked about it." The team thoroughly reexamined what the movie was about. "If you're going to do a story about a cub who becomes a king . . . well, what does it *mean* to become a king?" Allers asks. "What does it mean to *be* a king? Does a king have any meaning to us as twentieth century Americans?"

As they delved deeper, an overriding theme kept emerging: *assuming responsibility for those around you*. "It was a story of maturity," the director observes. "And then, on a spiritual level, understanding who you were in connection with the *whole* of everything . . . and coming into an understanding of the individual's relationship to the whole."

They took the story apart structurally, piece by piece, and put it back together. At the time, *King of the Jungle* was starting off with Simba as a young cub, cavorting with all his childhood friends–the warthog, the meerkat, and others. That had to change. They decided that if the story was going to say something about the succession of generations, the audience should be there for the actual beginning: the birth of the new king. "It all sounds so logical, but sometimes, when you're in the middle of it, it's hard to see," adds Allers.

They determined that since the most traumatic event in the story was Simba losing his father, *that* should be the catalyst for all the major changes that happen in his life. Therefore, in their revamped version, when his father is killed, Simba is driven away. And if he's driven away, he's an outcast–so they took those childhood characters away, and made them outcast characters who adopt him. "[This way] you feel the sense of who's coming in to replace the family structure," says Allers. "And so, *all* the structure started changing like that."

As they continued their revisions, how aware were they of similarities to Shakespeare's *Hamlet*? "It was brought up, certainly, because you've got the story of the uncle killing the prince's father. That's an obvious Hamlet relation," Allers offers. "You have the indecision of the prince–well, in this case, to be or not to be *king*. In Hamlet's story, it was more about existence, whether to go on living or not. Yes, we were conscious of it."

Apparently, the director reveals, at one point, Jeffrey Katzenberg even asked them to put as much *Hamlet* in as they could. "As if it were salami that you could just stack on a hero sandwich," Allers laughs. They did go ahead and try, he admits, but it felt forced. The story needed to grow organically, and if there were parallels, great. But if not . . . "There were *other* models that were coming in," he notes. "Like, Joseph and his brothers . . . Joseph was driven into the desert, and was then picked up by another tribe. . . . We were certainly considering the archetypes of *all* those major heroes' journeys."

Allers, Minkoff and Hahn knew better than to assert any kind of leadership role during the think tank sessions. "It was truly a mutual brainstorm

King Mufasa's treacherous brother and assassin, Scar. Their relationship led to inevitable comparisons with the story of Shakespeare's Hamlet. *© Disney Enterprises, Inc.*

. . . [Those sessions are] most effective when there's no hierarchy. When they're uncensored, everyone is allowed to say *whatever* comes to their mind–even if it's the stupidest thing. You have to allow that to happen, because within it might be the germ of a great idea. Or the *reaction* to it may be a great idea! When creative people get together and allow each other to be free, the energy can just spiral through the roof. . . . And folding the writers in, and pulling the story people in, there was a circular soup that just swirled around, everybody feeding off of everybody else. That's why, I think, ultimately, that picture just sprang ahead. We were so far behind schedule, we were *making* it while we were *developing* it," Allers marvels.

As a result of their intensive discussions, Roger Allers and his co-creators felt they were basically starting again from scratch: a lot of new story, new character designs, even a new title–*The Lion King*. "Once we developed the new beat outline and story progression, we didn't stray from it. We felt good about it," he says. "We got the blessings of Michael and Jeffrey and Roy [Disney], and I think we also, to a large extent, were given a bit more autonomy."

The Lion King's music and songs required a lot of the directors' attention, and ultimately underwent a profound transformation, as well. Tim Rice, the film's lyricist, had been in on the process quite early. It was his idea, in fact, to try and get Elton John to collaborate with him. When the famed singer and composer agreed, everyone was thrilled. Of the five songs that John and Rice contributed to *The Lion King*, the most important and thematically resonant was its opening number, "Circle of Life." Composer/arranger Hans Zimmer then took what was essentially a great pop song and imbued it (as well as the film's entire score) with the flavor of Africa, adding choral arrangements, haunting rhythms, and authentic Zulu chants and lyrics courtesy of Zimmer's collaborator on the project, African-born singer/arranger Lebo M.

"When Hans played his version of 'Circle of Life,' we just fell off our chairs. We were stunned! What I had stuck behind that sequence in a very, very early version was [African group] Ladysmith Black Mambazo doing their chants . . . 'cause that's sort of the feeling that I was hoping for," Allers explains. "We actually had *dialogue* in that sequence originally. . . . And when we saw [the opening]–you know, Hans was projecting it at his studio–we said, 'Oh no, this music's too good! Let's get rid of all the dialogue! Let's just do it!' We had to change Rafiki's entrance, everything had to be changed . . . so we simplified it and did it all pantomime. And the power of it just went through the roof!"

As the movie progressed further along, the studio ran a test screening to gauge the reactions of a typical audience–those of the man on the street, the housewives, the kids. "You go to a theater, and then you sit in there, and you just feel the vibes," Allers relates. "You can feel when people lose their focus on a movie, you can feel when people are being entertained . . . you can sense it. Then they ask people questions. *Those* I find less helpful. . . . 'Cause a lot of times, the questions get a little funny. A lot of people said, 'We don't think Mufasa should die,' or, 'I don't like it that the father dies, you shouldn't do that.' Well, you take that out and the *story's gone!* Someone might say, 'Oh, this makes me feel sad. I don't like it.' Well, some things are *supposed* to make you feel sad."

The filmmakers took note of which sequences needed trimming or fleshing out; Michael Eisner felt there wasn't enough of Rafiki–and Allers agreed. "It was really a very personal character for me. I sorta came up with this crazy guy, a crazy monk–he's crazy and he's wise. He's the spiritual center, the one who's aware. In the archetype of the classical hero's journey, he's the wise man . . . who gives the gift of whatever key it is that helps the hero. That was Rafiki." In *The Lion King*, the gift was of a purely psychological nature: Rafiki leads Simba back to experience the lost part of himself, to reconnect with his own identity, with his father and his past. "That was another major addition we made," says the director. "We decided to bring Mufasa back, 'cause that wasn't there originally. We felt, for Simba to truly become whole, the strongest thing would be to have him have an encounter with his father."

This chance for the hero's encounter with what he's lost was unprecedented for Disney. They'd had characters die in films before–Bambi's mother, for example–but had never brought a deceased character back for an encore. Allers feels that Mufasa's mystical reappearance can be interpreted on whatever level one chooses: "Whether this was purely an interior experience of Simba's, or whether it was an exterior experience. I mean, we kind of tried to point that up with Rafiki saying, 'Hoo, the weather! Whoa, what about that weather?!' The whole journey where he leads Simba through the brambles and the twisted roots, that was actually supposed to symbolize–basically, Simba has suppressed and blocked things. Rafiki was taking him back through his *mind*, in a way. That was a pathway leading him back into himself," he concludes, "so he could . . . become whole again."

A difficult and, at times, painful path–under, over, around, and *through* obstacles on the way to completion–not a bad metaphor for Roger Allers' journey through the production of *The Lion King*. When he first reluctantly agreed to co-direct, there was no way for him to know what a far-reaching impact the project would have on his life. As of this writing, there are also at least eight stage productions of *The Lion King* running around the world–a play whose book Allers co-wrote with Irene Mecchi. And although he eventually moved on–in 2000, Allers co-directed his second animated feature for Disney, *The Emperor's New Groove*–his name will always be associated with a royal legacy called *The Lion King*.

IT'S ALL IN THE TIMING

Directing Toons for Cartoon Network

The animation world is filled with multitalented individuals–people who not only design, or write and storyboard, but who can also direct and produce. Some come by their abilities easily and naturally, seemingly born to do it–while others, like Chris Savino, work for years to hone their craft. When he was a kid in Michigan, he dreamt of one day having his own comic strip. The *Mad* magazines and comics that his older brothers brought into the house were more than just diversions to him–they helped shape his sense of humor and drawing style, serving as primers for the budding cartoonist.

"I'd always get the Sunday comics page, and draw every single eye set in there, and all the noses out of the comics, and all of the mouths," Savino recalls. "And then I'd, like, take one set of eyes, and one nose from here and one mouth from there, and make my *own* characters. I did that for years, just kinda copied comics. Old strips were all I ever looked at . . . *Krazy Kat*, *Polly and her Pals*, *Peanuts*, *Pogo* . . . In *Mad*, I dug Sergio Aragonés' cool, loose style."

Like most other kids, Savino watched cartoons on TV, but he never considered them as a possible career until his senior year of high school. "That's when I went, 'Wait a minute . . . there's something happening here' . . . . I knew that [getting a syndicated strip] was a really difficult thing. Looking at the comic artists then, it was all older guys in their fifties. I figured they must've done something before this. And *Ren & Stimpy* had piqued my interest. So I thought, 'Well, the next best step is to probably try to get a job in animation, and learn that way.'"

At that point, *Ren & Stimpy* wasn't on the air as a series yet. Savino had seen John Kricfalusi's pilot episode ("Big House Blues") at the Detroit Institute of Arts, and loved it–so much that it inspired him to mail Kricfalusi a drawing he'd done, along with "a slightly butt-kissing letter." To the artist's shock, John K. responded, asked to see some more work, and ended up offering Savino a position on his new show . . . as an assistant animator.

"Which I'd totally lied about," Savino admits. "I'd said I knew what I was doing, but I didn't." He managed to pick it up pretty quickly, despite the intimidating realization that he was suddenly surrounded by "probably *the* most talented people in the industry at the time." Savino assisted at Spumco for about a year, gradually moving up the animation food chain by doing storyboard revisions and eventually designing character layouts and storyboards for shows like *Rocko's Modern Life*, *Baby Huey*, *Hey Arnold*, and *The Angry Beavers*. Through it all, he never stopped asking questions and absorbing details–information that would serve him well one day as a director and producer.

"I think at every studio I've worked at, I kinda nosed my way into, 'Hey, what's goin' on over in *this* area of production?' and kind of needed to know why people were doing what they were doing and how. . . . Maybe [I was] subconsciously collecting data for later. I learned a lot from everybody. Probably some people thought I was being nosy, who knows?"

Eventually, it all led to an invitation from the crew at Cartoon Network's *Dexter's Laboratory* to come in and show his work. He didn't know it yet, but Chris Savino was about to meet his new home and family. "I met Genndy Tartakovsky for the first time and showed him some of the things I had done," Savino says. "And I think he saw a certain kind of looseness, as well as design, to my drawings, that he said, 'Why not.'"

Savino aced his freelance storyboard assignment for a *Dexter's Lab* cartoon, 'Dee Dee Be Deep,' sweated out his very first pitch there ("I got some laughs, and they liked it!"), and was offered a staff position as a board artist. "I was lucky that they actually needed an in-house position filled," he notes. "So I was finally at a point where I wanted to be–doing storyboards. Because you get to do everything: you get to write, and write jokes, and do the drawings, and do the staging, and tell the story the way that you wanna tell it."

When *Dexter's Laboratory* wrapped, Savino moved onto *Powerpuff Girls* along with everyone else, by then having worked his way into the weekly story meetings as a regular participant. His only frustration: as yet, he still hadn't gotten to direct. That leap–from storyboard to animation–required a developed sense of timing. "Genndy's philosophy was, if you've never really animated, then timing isn't gonna come really easy for you, because you don't appreciate the value of one frame–you don't know what one frame can do for you," Savino explains. "It can make or break a movement. So I was afraid. But I did ask questions all the time, like, 'Why did you choose to make this four frames . . . ?' and Genndy would answer. He was very helpful in that sense. Again, I was socking away little tidbits for later on, whether I knew it or not."

Savino finally attained his long sought-after break when he came up with an idea for an original short, and pitched it to Cartoon Network for their *Cartoon Cartoon* show. They gave him a green light. "The short had many different names, but it ended up being called *Foe Paws* (2000) . . . all about a lonely, old, kind of batty Italian woman who adopts a cat and dog to replace her children. She dresses them up like kids, and forces them to *act* like kids–to stand on two feet, and use silverware and stuff," he relates. "It was my first chance at creating, producing, directing, and designing an entire short."

The dog and cat trying to eat their dinner at the table, in this video clip from Chris Savino's short, Foe Paws.

He still hadn't mastered the art of timing out the sequences–the technical side of directing a toon–but Savino felt that he'd storyboarded it tight enough for anyone to understand how long he wanted specific shots to last, or where a pause would be necessary. Just to be sure, he asked Genndy Tartakovsky to do the timing for *Foe Paws*. "I knew that he understood my sensibilities," notes Savino.

The fledgling director was also keenly aware that his classic comic strip influences showed through loud and clear. "You see the Cliff Sterrett rip-offs, totally, in the staging and the backgrounds . . . the *Polly and her Pals* stuff is very obvious, and anyone who's a fan of his will recognize it. But that's the kind of cartoon I wanted to do–[one that] feels like you're watching a comic strip *moving*. I don't consider myself an animation innovator in any sense. . . . I've always considered myself a *purveyor* of what I liked about cartoons, and want to perpetuate those ideas. 'Cause that's what made *me* laugh, that's what made *me* feel good about the business."

He admits he felt some pressure directing his first toon. "There *was* a nervousness about it . . . but it was more like, 'Am I gonna make my peers laugh?' than, 'Is the audience going to like this?' We do our pitches up on the wall, and nine times out of ten we're writing to make the *guys in the room* laugh. So *that's* the sweat factor! If the audience laughs, then we win double."

Cartoon Network opted not to pick up his short as a series, but now knew what Chris Savino could do: helm a project from start to finish. As they began to wind down the fourth season of *Powerpuff Girls*, some of the crew went off to work on *Samurai Jack*, while others segued into *Powerpuff Girls: The Movie*. That left a whole other group of talented people–including Savino–with time on their hands. So, the network approached him with the notion of directing a long-form project, and asked for suggestions. "I jumped all over that," Savino enthuses. "I said, 'How 'bout a long format *Flintstones*?' and they said, 'Well, pitch us an idea.'"

Savino got in touch with Dave Smith, who'd been his partner for work on *Powerpuff Girls*. "So we came up with *Flintstones on the Rocks*, pitched it to Mike [Lazzo] and Linda [Simensky] . . . and they liked the idea. And before we knew it, we were in production! And this was our foray into actually directing a long-format on our own–we didn't have Craig, we didn't have Genndy. It was all *us*."

The co-directors had hit on an exceedingly cool notion: to go back to Ed Benedict's original character and production designs from when *The Flintstones* began in 1960. "What we wanted to do was pretend that this movie was made right after you saw the very first episode, with its more rough-looking, thick-lined characters and backgrounds. And we took *The Honeymooners'* angle–an adult sitcom about married life. We dropped Pebbles and Bam-Bam altogether, didn't mention who they were, that they were off to college or something. . . . It was just like, maybe this was before they were born, maybe it was after; *you* decide."

The Flintstones' marriage is clearly in trouble, as evidenced from Wilma's impending attack in this scene from Savino and Smith's smart and funny Flintstones on the Rocks.

Once storyboarding on *Flintstones on the Rocks* was almost done, the network ordered another season of *Dexter's Laboratory*. Since Genndy Tartakovsky was too immersed in *Samurai Jack* to take an active hand in it, he turned to Chris Savino to take over as creative director of the series–and Savino leapt at the offer: "Of course I'd do it! Y'know, we had not worked on it long enough to where there wasn't excitement for it. For us, it was like, 'Yeah! Let's do some more, that'll be great!'"

Not only did Savino find a way to juggle both projects at once, he decided it was time to finally assert himself as a fully rounded cartoon director. So he set out to prove, on the new *Dexter's Lab* shorts, that he could do it once and for all. Savino sat down with a stopwatch and started slugging boards . . . and everything he'd absorbed over the years just poured out of him. Instinctively, he knew what he was doing. What's more, he found he was *loving it*.

When the *Dexter's Lab* cartoons started coming back from overseas, and *Flintstones on the Rocks* footage began coming in at the same time, Savino dove in to direct post-production on both. "Genndy's got his own style of how he'll spot music or cues, so I had to emulate what he'd do in certain sequences. Fortunately, Chase Rucker Productions was doing the music again . . . and we had a huge library of *Dexter's Lab* music from the past three seasons. Same with *The Flintstones*: We had a ton of [the old] music cues to go off of, so it made it a little bit easier. And the editing is even more fun than doing the pre-production. It was like, 'Okay, now I can really cut these things and make the timing work.' Cutting a frame here and a frame there really does help. Or if a cartoon is running two minutes long, how do I cut two minutes out of this thing and still make a coherent cartoon that's funny? So it's a very creative process, more than most people realize."

Savino was almost done with post on the third season of *Dexter's Laboratory* when he began wondering what to do next. "It went right down to the wire, and then they said, 'Okay, we're gonna do another season of *Dexter*.' This time I got promoted to producer. I'm doing a lot of the same things I did as creative director last season, but I'm more involved in the budget this time . . . how much people are getting paid, where the money's being spent, creatively shifting money around to pay for things–robbing Peter to pay Paul, that sort of thing."

These days a proficient artist, writer, director, *and* producer, he does it all ("I know what you can call this section," Savino offers: "Animation Whore!"), but he remains proudest of his work on *Dexter's Laboratory*. When he began boarding for the series, "that's when I slowly became involved with every aspect of production. And the freedom that Cartoon Network, as well as Genndy, allowed the artists to express themselves, was basically like the Bugs Bunny cartoons. You can automatically pick out a Chuck Jones . . . or a Friz Freleng . . . or Bob Clampett, just because their styles come through. And we've been allowed to let *our own* styles come through. We had that opportunity to create for ourselves, not having to think about, 'What's this eleven-year-old kid gonna say about this joke?' And the individual styles, as far as even the drawing, the staging, and the acting, all [reflect] the personalities of the people working on the shows."

Still, Savino considers himself to be a *cartoonist*, above all else. His heart is still set on the old print cartoons that first enticed him when he was young. When his work on *Dexter's Lab* is done, he just might follow that path: "I may finally take some time and develop a comic strip to try and sell to the syndicates. I hope I've learned enough to tell good little jokes every day, in character. Y'know, not just stupid knock-knock jokes. Hopefully, what I've learned over the past twelve years in animation will apply to my ultimate goal."

LIGHTS . . . CAMERA . . . SIMULATION

Helming the Computer-Generated *Monsters, Inc.*

We knew for sure that the 3D boom was in full bloom when not one, but *four* computer-animated films–from four different studios–were released one after the other in a short span of time from mid-2001 through early 2002. PDI/DreamWorks' *Shrek* came first; followed by Pixar/Disney's *Monsters, Inc.*; followed by Nickelodeon Films' *Jimmy Neutron: Boy Genius*; followed by Blue Sky/Twentieth Century Fox's *Ice Age*. All four were entertaining movies, with not a dud in the group, and all did remarkable business at the box office. They also had another trait in common: All of them were helmed by first-time feature directors.

Pete Docter, director of *Monsters, Inc.*, learned his craft at the feet of the master. In 1990, John Lasseter lured him fresh out of CalArts to Pixar, where the traditional cel animator got his first taste of 3D computer work on a Listerine TV commercial. There was an enormous learning curve for Docter to bridge as he struggled to get up to speed with the new technology.

"Before I felt comfortable with it, it was about nine months or so. By the end of that, I could cruise around and I knew what I was capable of, and how to do it. But it was tough for a while," he recalls. "I definitely wanted to throw the computer out the window and pick up a pencil–'cause I knew exactly what I wanted, but I didn't know how to *do* it!" Luckily, he had Lasseter sitting beside him, explaining how the computers and the tools worked.

About a year later, they began creating *Toy Story*, the first 3D computer-animated feature film–which opened in 1995 and took the world by storm. "I'd had the great experience of just basically shadowing him all through *Toy Story*," Docter says of working with his mentor. "I mean, I definitely had my own things to take care of–I was working on story and supervising the animators on that one. But I got to sit in on model reviews, and recording sessions, and go to the scoring sessions . . . so I really got to see how this all works."

When *Toy Story* finally came out, they saw how long CG (computer generated) films take to develop and produce–about four-and-a-half years each. As Pete Docter points out, "We realized that if we want to be a real studio, we're gonna have to do films more frequently. Andrew Stanton had already started, and then John jumped on with him doing development for *A Bug's Life* (1998). And so, John then said, 'Pete, why don't you go ahead and think about what'll happen after *A Bug's Life*.'"

Docter got right on it. In a brainstorming session with Jeff Pidgeon and Harley Jessup, Docter lobbed an idea that ended up as the seed for *Monsters, Inc.* It was about a guy in his thirties, disgruntled with work, and not thrilled about his love life: "So, one night, he gets a package from his mom, and inside are these books that he had as a kid. He opens one and a bunch of drawings fall out, and they're drawings that he had done of monsters. He doesn't think anything of it, and puts them on the shelf and goes to bed. . . . That night, the monsters show up in his room–he thinks he must be going crazy, he's freaked out. Next morning he wakes up and thinks, 'Oh, it was just a bad dream,' but no: They're eating his cereal out of his fridge . . . and they follow him to work–only *he* can see them–so it completely destroys his job, his love life, everybody thinks he's crazy. Well, it turns out that the monsters are fears that he never dealt with as a kid. As he gets to know and respect these monsters, they help him overcome those fears. And at the end, once he overcomes them, the monsters disappear, to go on and presumably help other kids . . . so it's a bit of a bittersweet ending."

A few elements of that original idea stuck–the monsters stayed, obviously, as did the notion of a bittersweet ending. By February 1997, after much brainstorming and tinkering, they pitched a movie to Disney that was essentially and structurally *Monsters, Inc.*

The story that ended up on the screen is set in a bustling industrial town called Monstropolis, home to Monsters, Inc., the largest scare factory in the world. Their top scarer is a huge, furry, horned, blue and purple

Mike Wazowski and James P. Sullivan making a big entrance onto Monsters, Inc.'s Scare Floor. Note Sully's two worshipful geeks standing on the left. © Disney Enterprises, Inc./ Pixar Animation Studios.

monster named James P. Sullivan (voiced by John Goodman)–Sully to his friends–who's assisted by his roommate and best pal, a wiry, green, one-eyed creature by the name of Mike Wazowski (voiced by Billy Crystal). Their job: to sneak into kids' bedrooms at night (through their closet doors) and get them to scream, which in turn powers Monstropolis' energy supply. One day, all hell breaks loose when a sweet little girl name Boo accidentally finds her way through her closet into the Monsters, Inc., factory–where the monsters believe that children are toxic–and it falls on Sully to somehow get Boo back home before anyone finds out.

"The heart of the film, to me, was about Sullivan," Docter observes. "He goes from being a completely job-obsessed guy, like a lot of us are, to having his life turned upside down in becoming a parent. Y'know, he actually becomes a father to this kid . . . and that rearranges the way he sees everything."

But the director and his fellow creators wrestled with the details for years. Sully's character ranged from being run-of-the-mill scary to not scary at all. And Boo's demeanor was even more tricky to determine: "We knew we wanted this cute, innocent girl that Sully has to fall in love with, but we thought it would be really cloying to portray her as such. So we were just thinking that she'd be more like Tatum O'Neal's character in [Peter Bogdanovich's classic 1973 film] *Paper Moon*, where she's really tough and scrappy and bosses him around–and he's a little bit out of his element. He doesn't know how to control this kid, who has her own opinions about stuff. So that was the dynamic."

In that version, Boo was around six years old. She was feisty and opinionated . . . and, says Docter, bilingual: "You know how, in science fiction films, you go to outer space and everybody speaks English, right? We thought, let's try something where the monsters speak monster language, and the kid speaks human language–English or whatever. It would start out where the monsters start talking to the kid, saying, 'DO . . . YOU . . . UNDERSTAND . . .' and then you'd cut to her point of view, and they're going, '*Bglrghrlrlblgrgh!!!*' And there'd be this lack of communication . . . but slowly, she'd learn a couple words, and so on."

Docter and his cohorts decided to conduct a little test in their efforts to find Boo's voice–rather than trying to teach a youngster a made-up language, they brought in "a *real* little kid who's sort of on the cusp of language, and we just used that gibberish sound. Maybe that would *sound* like a different language," he muses. "Well, it didn't. It sounded like a kid on the cusp of language! But that was really appealing . . . and people said, 'Oh, we have to keep this voice.' She was the daughter of one of the story guys. So we used her voice. And that influenced the character quite a bit. She got younger."

Meanwhile, they had to convince Peter Schneider at Disney that there was real potential in Sully's relationship with Boo. "He was more interested in a relationship between Sullivan and a friend of his . . . more of a buddy film," recalls Docter. The director didn't yet have the confidence to emphatically state, *Yes, dammit, this will work, I know it:* "So we then kinda shifted gears and said, 'Well, alright, let's try doing something like that.'" That's how the character Mike ended up in the picture.

Docter realized that he would have to prove himself as a director by proving the viability of the story. "In the back of my head, I'd always believed in this relationship between Sully and Boo, and felt that it would be a great emotional hook for the audience. For whatever reason, though, it wasn't landing for people. That and the fact that–'Hey, this is not John Lasseter directing this one–this is some other guy. Are we going to get the same quality that we have on these other films?' So we went for quite a long time without a green light."

The turning point, he believes, was when story artist Nate Stanton boarded a sequence where Boo has to go to the bathroom, and she and Sully end up playing hide-and-seek in the locker room. When the execs saw those scenes on story reels, they began to sense the appeal of the relationship between monster and child. "So we ended up with sort of a great combination of a buddy film . . . and that relationship," notes Docter. "It added a lot."

The director points to some wonderfully funny supporting characters as well, including a pair of squeaky-voiced nerds who worship Sully, now the top scarer at the company: "They were actually involved [in an early draft], when he was a loser. He was relegated then to working in the Scream Refinery–he used to be a scarer, but he can't do that anymore . . . and he's back with these pencil-necked geeks, who are, y'know, bossing him around–*'Hey, Sullivan, get back to work!'*–and they're just scrawny kids. It was a way of showing how miserable his life was. We just loved them as characters."

Monsters, Inc. boasts some great-looking character design. According to Docter, a few were easier to lock in than others. "Mike was pretty nailed down from the beginning. Of course, like we do with everything else, we tried a lot of variations. . . . There was an early one that was basically a big round body, with one eye and two legs. No arms. He just had these two appendages that he would walk on, and also be able to hold things and gesture with. And it seemed like we were really just tying our hands with all these restrictions . . . so we ended up going back to the four limbs."

Sully's design, however, proved to be a more onerous task. "It was largely because the story changed so much," notes Docter. "If you don't know whether he's a janitor, or a has-been, or what, then it's really hard to design that." Once Sullivan's character came into sharper focus, of course, his appearance followed suit. But the physical contrast–Sully big and intimidating, Mike a pint-sized, lovable schnook–was there early on.

One of the ingredients that makes *Monsters, Inc.* so much fun to watch is the chemistry between those two–thanks in large part to actors Goodman and Crystal. "The amazing thing for me about John Goodman was how instinctive he is," Docter raves. "He would show up, he'd barely read the scripts, and right out of the gate he's getting the lines right. You could tell he understood right away what was needed. . . . And Billy Crystal was an amazing guy to work with . . . he's not only a great actor–he's like working with a team of writers! We all encouraged the actors–and this is something that I learned from John Lasseter–to ad lib, and make it their own. Even if the structure of a sentence doesn't change much . . . it's just the way they say it. What you're looking for is that real natural [delivery], like they just thought of it."

Following Billy Crystal's suggestion, Docter pushed to record the two actors' voices in joint sessions, despite the normal routine of recording voices separately. "Some folks were very skeptical . . . but it really, really worked," he muses. Thanks to the actors' quick wit, recording the two together provided the kind of spontaneous interaction they could've never

Mike and Sully (leaning on scream storage canisters) in front of little Boo's flowered bedroom closet door. © Disney Enterprises, Inc./Pixar Animation Studios.

gotten otherwise. "An example of that is a scene in the locker room, which we'd written to some degree, where Mike says, 'Oooh, can I borrow your odorant?' And Sully says, 'Yeh . . . I got Stinky Garbage, or Old Dumpster.' They just went back and forth, trying to out-gross each other in a way that we could still use in the film," the director smiles, "and, of course, they crossed the line several times, but . . ."

Docter is quick to acknowledge his co-directors, David Silverman (of *Simpsons* fame) and Lee Unkrich, who both made very specific contributions to the development of *Monsters, Inc.* "David ended up helping pretty much exclusively in story . . . he was largely responsible for the relationship between Mike and Sully. He brought a lot to that. Between him and Bob Peterson, who was our head of story, those two had a great handle on this sort of buddy relationship, and the energy between those two guys. We were conscious at the beginning that we could easily fall into *Sully the straight man, and Mike the comic relief* . . . but I think David worked really hard to make Sully have as many funny lines as Mike. That they could rib each other back and forth, play practical jokes on each other . . . I think that creates a little more believability in terms of why they're still friends, and have been for so long."

Lee Unkrich jumped in after the development had begun. With a background in live action, he turned out to be the perfect master of the project's editorial phase. "After the story is close to being figured out, you give him the sequence on boards, and he cuts it and makes it work," Docter explains. "It's amazing how you can have the exact same boards, the exact same scratch track–you cut it one way, it falls on its face. You cut it another way, it looks great. On *Monsters, Inc.*, we asked him to come and help out, because, there again, the reels are the sales tool. If they're not cut well, you start to lose faith in the show. So he came in to help advise, and then stayed on and helped us throughout the production in layout. He has a great skill in the visual cinematic language of film: the staging, compositions, and then taking those back to the editing room and helping Jim and Ken, our editors, put it together in a way that was as strong as it could be."

At first the filmmakers tried dividing responsibilities between the co-directors, but, says Docter, "It really feels like there needs to be one person who's calling the shots, one person's vision. From the very beginning to the very end, I was the one . . . who saw every aspect of production. And it was the most difficult thing I've ever done in my life. It was a challenge on every level. The thing that I think affected me the most was, you could not turn it off. You can't go home; it follows you everywhere–it turned out there were 450 people that worked on the show, and everyone was waiting for the director to have that clarity, that vision of what to do, and how all their work fit into it."

Having John Lasseter around didn't hurt, of course, if the first-time director needed advice. "He would always have some words of wisdom," Docter says. "Or even when I would think, 'This is really great, I wanna show this to John,' he would be able to push it further, make it even better. That's the way he is; he's an amazing, creative guy." Pete Docter also valued Lasseter's objective take. "You know how it goes. When you're working on something for five years, you get very close to it. And I knew I could trust John's opinion . . . he would come in and look at things with a fresh eye. I think that's just invaluable."

As many other directors have discovered before him, Pete Docter learned the merit of viewing the film, or even portions of it, with an audience. "Whether that's two animators here, or people down at Disney . . . you can see something again and again and again, and as soon as you *show* it to someone else, you see it through their eyes and you go, 'D'oh, that's not clear at all!' Or, it's really dumb, or whatever."

Monsters, Inc., was easily the most sophisticated film Pixar had ever created . . . until their *next* production. Since everyone keeps raising the bar technically with each new computer-animated feature, one might wonder how much further they can all go. "I think technical innovations will continue to come along, and, hopefully, continue to surprise people," Docter says. "What every director wants to do is put your money on the screen, so you can see it. Like Sully's fur, or clothing on Boo–things that you wouldn't be able to do unless you had this particular technology. Hopefully, at some point, those become less research & development projects and more *out of the box*–type solutions, so we don't need to continue to spend so much time and energy developing totally new systems. Then again, that's kind of the fun of it, too. I think, if you told the technical directors here, 'Our next film's gonna be about spheres on a white void,' they would hate it 'cause there's no challenge in it. Even when I'll tell them, 'Okay, look, all I want is a blue box. It doesn't have to open, or anything.' Well, they can't help themselves–they have to put the hinge on the back, 'cause it just looks a little *better* with the hinge!"

Still, Docter insists, it's never about the technology for him. "Mainly, our job is to tell great stories," he concludes. "In the five years that I worked on *Monsters*, I think probably three-and-a-half was *just* story–and then you continue to work on story as you're doing everything else. The technology follows the storytelling."

Sub-Zero Hero at the Helm

Directing Blue Sky's Surprise Hit *Ice Age*

"Animation is the least spontaneous performance art known to man," declares Chris Wedge, director of *Bunny*, which won the Academy Award for Best Animated Short in 1999.

Wedge's very next project happened to be his first feature film–Twentieth Century Fox's CG animated hit, *Ice Age*. "We work through these layers of convoluted technology to get a performance on the screen that we can't work on in real time . . . it's more visualization than anything. Y'know, animators really have to call up their powers of concentration to get that performance up there. It's something they have to visualize, and hold, and apply. It just requires *a lot* of time . . . and that's the miracle of animation–that the performance, once it plays on the screen, can feel spontaneous, but the technique behind it is everything but.

"Most animators are just very shy actors," he believes. Wedge ought to know a thing or two about animators–he's devoted himself to the craft for years now, slowly working his way up the ranks to feature director. "I was a self-taught stop-motion animator. I started when I was twelve, and I did it all the way up through film school at SUNY-Purchase, and just stayed with animation there. I would spend three years at a time on elaborate stop-motion movies."

Despite his obvious love of stop-motion techniques, Wedge never pursued it professionally. "It just interested me," he explains, "and that's what I did from the age of twelve to about twenty-two. That's about *all* I did. Then I started in with my career in computer animation–the first job I ever had was at Magi. And then, that was that." He joined the company in 1980, working and learning there for four years. You might say Chris Wedge happened to be in the right place at the right time: Magi was one of several computer imaging studios hired by Disney to create visual effects for *Tron* (1982), the very first motion picture to feature true CG–and Wedge cut his computer animation teeth working on it.

Tron may not have been a very good movie, but no one had ever seen visuals like that on the screen before. The experience convinced Wedge that "the people who were going to be really good at computer animation, the people who were gonna help pioneer it, were the people that *understood* computers and programming. Those guys that were writing the software were coming up with cool ways to make different textures or effects . . . and I wanted to learn that."

So Wedge went off to graduate school in 1984 at Ohio State University. It was there that he met Chuck Csuri, who'd created a laboratory where artists and computer scientists were developing software together and making short films. "I made a couple of shorts, then I taught there for a year and a half . . . and then–well, I was gonna have to commit my wife if we didn't move out of Columbus, Ohio. So we moved back to New York and started Blue Sky with some former colleagues from Magi."

Throughout the ensuing years, Blue Sky Studios created some stunning CG effects and animation for movies and TV, including the singing and dancing cockroaches of *Joe's Apartment* (1996), aliens for *Star Trek: Insurrection* (1998) and *Alien Resurrection* (1997), and the famous "talking fish" for the 1999 season of HBO's *The Sopranos*, but they had never produced a full-length, narrative feature film. By the time Wedge won his Oscar for *Bunny*, he and his partners felt they were ready. "Frankly, I had never made a bit of animation where the characters talked until *Ice Age*– aside from the roaches in *Joe's Apartment*, but you never really saw their mouths move," Wedge says today.

Once Fox and Blue Sky agreed to proceed with the film, they spent a great deal of time hammering out the story, doing visual development while working simultaneously on the script. "At the beginning of the project, the studio felt, understandably, that if they let us just storyboard our way through the movie on our own, they were going to lose some control . . . and they weren't gonna know where we were headed. We came up with a way to work together, so that we tried to put as much as we could into a script page before we started boarding it. That way, they knew what we were doing."

They got their go-ahead from Fox in October of 1999. "We'd started thinking about it in February or March . . . we had a couple of presentations, one in May, and one in October, and that's when we got the green light. They'd had the concept kicking around for about a year before I got on it." Part of the challenge, Wedge felt, was that *Ice Age* wasn't generated within Blue Sky. "We were interpreting somebody else's script," he points out. "I don't know if it's fair to say, but I much prefer a kind of 'explore and experiment' way of working, over 'plan the whole film out and execute it' without any changes . . . which doesn't leave much room for discovery. What I think makes *Ice Age* so much fun is that we let ourselves use what we were discovering."

One of their discoveries came about as Wedge searched for an interesting way to open the film. It led the director and his team to create the Scrat–a small, frantic, prehistoric squirrel who tries desperately to bury his

As the human baby walks toward him, Diego the saber-toothed tiger wrestles with his conscience while Manny and Sid look on.

acorn throughout the story, only to be thwarted again and again. Scrat never actually appeared in any of the original script drafts: "The movie is called *Ice Age*, but in the script you didn't see any ice until you're halfway through. I just thought it would be fun to make the Ice Age itself a character . . . and we decided to represent it with a glacier. There's a migration at the beginning of the movie, so we decided that the glacier is *chasing* the animals down out of the hills. And as we went in to simplify this idea, we thought maybe just one character is being chased, and it should be the smallest one we can find so we can have fun with the scale. And then, we had a very short meeting one afternoon–we just went nuts on this one idea, and sent [story artist] Bill Frake off for the weekend. Bill is a very prolific illustrator, and he came back with a lot of the core ideas for the Scrat . . . including his interpretation of its kinda manic poses. It was just great raw material, and we started from that."

The opening sequence was so entertaining, they decided to use it as a coming attraction teaser in theaters almost a year before *Ice Age* was even released. "I just thought that the Scrat sequence could stand on its own as kind of a short," Wedge relates. The marketing people at Fox thought so, too, and wanted to make sure audiences were not only primed for *Ice Age*, but that they'd understand its appeal. "There was quite a bit of debate about whether or not we should put one of our favorite sequences right out there, as a teaser. But that's what we did, and it didn't hurt at all."

Mainly due to budgetary constraints, the director says that the characters took precedence over the environments. He felt that the locales would be more effective if they were imbued with a flatter, more storybook quality–a look which was served perfectly by Blue Sky's *Ray Tracing* software. The technique is something the studio had been developing for more than fifteen years, making it "robust and efficient enough to use in production. That's the biggest trick."

Wedge says that, in order to understand the difference between their system and, say, Pixar's, it helps to picture yourself as an artist using the software. "It might be fair to say that using our system, you think more like a photographer, and using their system, you think more like a painter. A lot of the lighting and dimension comes for free with our technique. So you can put a light source on an object in the camera, and then turn on all the bells and whistles, and feel fairly confident that you're going to get an image that looks photo-realistic. The challenge for us is to *stylize* things so that everything pulls together."

The art direction and design of *Ice Age* was a group effort, Wedge relates. "Designer Peter de Sève came in early on, around April 1999, and I just felt as though he was going to be able to find every character. So he was it. We gave him carte blanche. I really hate watching movies that look like they were designed by a hundred people . . . where every character looks like it came from a different movie. We used two designers on *Ice Age*–one, Peter de Sève, to do the characters, and then Peter Clark, to do

One of the many beautiful Ice Age *landscapes rendered by Blue Sky's computer animators.*

the environments. Clark has a great, efficient style, that I just thought helped kind of suggest the rugged environments they'd be in without explaining. We worked to balance de Sève's style with Clark's style–and a lot of it comes together when you're lighting it. So the technical directors here contribute a great deal to the final look that we're able to achieve."

Ice Age's co-director, Carlos Saldanha, allowed Chris Wedge to stay more focused on the development of the film's story. "Carlos spent more time with the animators than I did," Wedge explains. "He kind of led the animators; that was his primary responsibility. We gave him his title when we were about halfway through the movie. I just felt he deserved it. Carlos has an innate animation talent, and he's a great people person–he understands how people feel. A great communicator, too."

Since so many creative people collaborate on a project as enormous as *Ice Age*, it's fair to ask how much of the director's personal stamp he feels is on the finished film. "I'd hope a great deal," Wedge says. "I directed it . . . and people were either naïve or deluded enough to listen, but I tend to not let go until I think it's right. You tell people what you wanna do, and then they come back with things. Sometimes they come up with something better, and sometimes they come up with a performance that enhances your idea so much that it makes it *realer*. That's the fun, even up till the last minute."

In fact, Chris Wedge and his crew worked tirelessly to mold and shape *Ice Age* almost until the very end. That meant cutting lines that weren't working, whole scenes that had already been animated, even characters who'd been recorded–like Sylvia, Sid the Sloth's love interest. In the original version, Sylvia chases him around for the whole movie, finally to reveal that she's bearing his child(!) . . . which, naturally, made Sid a rather sleazy, unlikable character. "The actress did an amazing job," sighs Wedge, "with some of my favorite stuff, too." Still, she had to go.

As for the greatest lessons learned, Wedge asserts that the director must roll with the punches, actively influencing the process as the story evolves. "You don't have the master plan in your head when you start. . . . You make a movie over the course of however many years it takes, but, at each moment in those years, each moment that you're on the movie, your performance is contributing to it. And every little thing you do, every minute, every day, ultimately, it all adds up to one gigantic pile of hay. And that's the movie!"

CHAPTER 7 THAT EXOTIC, RARE BIRD—THE ANIMATOR

Using Pencils and Pixels to Give Their Creations Life

"We used to sleep on our desks and continue the next morning. . . . I used to feel that I'd drop dead on my drawing board many times because the tension was so great. But after I'd flip the stuff, I was proud. And when I saw it on the screen, I was prouder."

—Joe Oriolo, pioneering animator of *Popeye* and *Felix the Cat*

Every production needs its actors. Without them, there'd be nothing for an audience to do but sit and gape at the scenery. Animators, the true performers of the medium, are a rare breed–they put the *anima* in animation. Until just a few years ago, an animator's chief tools were a pencil and paper, an animation desk, and his or her imagination. While the latter is still a major requirement, many of today's finest animators do their work entirely on computers–a development that once seemed almost unthinkable. There are young animators now who've never worked on anything *but* a computer. Others have made the transition from traditional to digital, while still others prefer to feel a Mars Staedtler 3B pencil between their fingers.

Whatever mode one chooses, it's a craft that requires patience, since the actual process of animating is, by its nature, slow and methodical. In the heyday of the classic Bugs Bunny and Daffy Duck cartoons, a top animator at Warner Bros. could usually turn out about fifteen seconds of animation per week. A supervising animator on a feature film needs a few years to complete work on his or her character.

As in any other profession, the toon world has its share of all-stars–men and women who are regarded as the best in the business. Some of them have gone on to direct and produce their own projects; others have chosen to stay focused on the hands-on craft . . . while a few will alternate between the two, drawn back to animating again and again through sheer love of the process. In this chapter, we'll take a closer look at a few of these artists, and see how their contributions enhanced some of our favorite toons.

Deja's View

Animating Disney's Modern Heroes and Villains

Andreas Deja was only ten as he sat in a dark movie theater in his hometown of Dinslaken, Germany, watching Walt Disney's 1967 feature, *The Jungle Book*, unspool on screen–yet it was the defining moment of his life. The boy's discovery turned into an obsession. He went back to see the film again and again, and began dreaming of one day working for the studio. A few years later, he finally wrote to Disney, asking how he could become an animator.

"They replied with a form letter, which I still have. It's like my little treasure from way back," he recounts. "And it was very smart in its response. It said, 'If you are serious about getting into a profession like animation, don't send us any copies of Mickey Mouse and Donald Duck, 'cause we can teach you those later here. You have to become an artist in your own right, and go to art school. Learn about anatomy, and go to the zoo, and watch the animals and watch life around you. Observe life around you, and sketch that.'"

It all made sense to him. And though his parents had a different future in mind for their son–"Their dream was that I'd become either a physician or a priest. I had to drag myself through Latin for *nine years* . . . it went into one ear and out the other!"–Deja pursued the letter's advice with single-minded determination. He took trains to a nearby town for life drawing classes at night, continued drawing through a year and a half of army service, and enrolled in art school full time in Essen.

In 1980, following a long-distance correspondence and several meetings with one of Disney's legendary "Nine Old Men," animator Eric Larson (who'd seen Deja's work and told him he had what it takes), Andreas Deja finally saw his dream realized. He moved to California and began working at the studio. Following a short training period, he was given his first assignment at Disney Feature Animation: "They were impressed with my drawing ability, and they said, 'You know, we don't have designs for *The Black Cauldron*, we're just doing storyboarding right now. . . . What we'd like you to do is be in one room with Tim Burton, and you two design characters. Tim has this sort of bizarre, zany style, and yours is very solid. Maybe we can mix it up or something.'"

So, for about a year, Deja worked in a small room at Disney with Tim Burton. "I guess they wanted us to mate and have offspring of some kind," Burton has pondered. "He would sit on one side of the room and I would sit on the other. It was like a friendly version of *The Odd Couple*."[1]

What they did was brainstorm. "We filled up storyboards with designs, and story situations, whatever we could come up with," Deja adds. "He would take some of my drawings and add his touch to them, and vice versa. Unfortunately, the management at the time decided that a marriage of the conventional Disney style and Tim Burton's wasn't possible, and we should do it completely conventionally. It lost some spark . . . and Tim got so frustrated that he left." Burton was never heard from again–aside from directing *Pee-wee's Big Adventure* (1985), *Beetlejuice* (1988), *Batman* (1989), *Edward Scissorhands* (1990), and *Ed Wood* (1994), and creating *The Nightmare Before Christmas* (1993), and a few other works of similar obscurity.

Meanwhile, Deja turned to some *Black Cauldron* designs done by legendary animator Milt Kahl as one of his last assignments for the studio . . . which points to a major perk of being on staff at Disney: the opportunity to study the work of one's heroes up close. Andreas Deja spent a huge amount of time in the archives poring over everything that Kahl had ever animated, analyzing it, and taking it apart drawing by drawing–which has its advantages and drawbacks. On the plus side, he notes, "you really learn a lot, and find out how this particular animator approached a scene, what his methods were. What is *not* so good is that you have to realize you'll never draw like this person–you shouldn't even try." That took Deja some time to realize before he began to try different things. Nevertheless, Kahl remains his hero: "I don't think there was anybody in the last century who drew better than Milt."

Equally significant in Deja's development was his discovery that it's mostly about *acting* and actually less about drawing–that what really matters is how insightful an animator is in terms of a character, how he or she can develop it. Interestingly, Andreas Deja has never taken an acting class, nor did he even set foot on stage in, say, a class play when he was a boy. "We didn't have that," he says of his schooling. "I think my work has its roots in observation, observing people, and movies, and just everything, mostly."

After his year of development on *The Black Cauldron*, he suddenly found himself out of that pot and into the fire–as a full animator on the film. "It was fun," he remembers with some hesitation. "The only thing is, there was a lot of resistance to the treatment of the story by some of the senior artists. They wanted a much *cartoonier* treatment . . . I don't know, I just did as I was told. I mean, let's face it, I came fresh off the boat. It was my first job!" The young animator worked on the feature for about three years, the longest he's ever worked on a single film. *The Black Cauldron* (1985) tanked at the box office–perhaps the Disney Studios' biggest animated embarrassment–but none of that diminished Andreas Deja's excitement at seeing his name roll up the screen on his first credit crawl.

He moved on to a little work on *The Great Mouse Detective*, then *Oliver & Company* . . . and then *Who Framed Roger Rabbit* came along. The animation was to be produced at director Richard Williams' London studio, but Deja really didn't want to move back to Europe. It took some friendly persuasion to get him to go. "They finally convinced me. [Associate producer] Don Hahn and Richard Williams took me out for margaritas at a local Mexican restaurant, and talked me into it," he chuckles.

Deja was first assigned the task of bringing Disney's famous *Fantasia* characters to life in the movie's various cameos. "Eventually, I did Roger Rabbit himself, quite a bit of footage of him . . . and the Gorilla Bouncer, those few scenes . . . and lots of crowd scenes at the beginning, when Bob Hoskins comes out of Maroon Cartoons' studios. I did all of those."

He admits being intimidated by the technique of marrying his animation to live footage, especially given director Bob Zemeckis' constantly moving camera. "I was scared like crazy . . . I had no experience in it. But my first scene was the Ostrich going upstairs, opening the door while Hoskins comes out. The Ostrich gives him a little look and a little attitude, throwing her head back–and it turned out okay! They all liked it . . . so I was very excited, and I had passed this test as far as I was concerned."

His confidence grew with every scene, aided by Dick Williams' guidance as mentor and friend, and by his brilliance as a director. "The man was on fire," Deja raves. "I just loved it. It was a great working relationship."

When *Who Framed Roger Rabbit* finally wrapped, Andreas Deja's star continued to rise at Disney. He quickly developed a reputation as one of the two best animators at the studio–Glen Keane being the other–and segued from one project to the next. He served as supervising animator of King Triton in *The Little Mermaid* and Mickey Mouse in the shorts *Prince and the Pauper* (1990) and *Runaway Brain* (1995), as well as tackling a diverse series of memorable villains in some of Disney's biggest hits of the nineties: Gaston in *Beauty and the Beast*, Jafar in *Aladdin*, and the duplicitous and deadly Scar in *The Lion King*.

Animator Andreas Deja relaxing in his home studio.

It's probably no coincidence that Deja was so adept at bringing animated nasties to life. The character who'd influenced him most profoundly in *The Jungle Book* was Milt Kahl's tiger, Shere Khan, whose aloof villainy was a direct forebear of *The Lion King*'s Scar. "I enjoyed working on *Lion King* a lot," he says. "I liked Scar because of the type of character that he was. . . . He just had fun being evil. He enjoyed himself . . . he had a way with words–I thought the dialogue was very well written–and, of course, on top of it all you had Jeremy Irons. How can that fail?"

Deja started on the project early on, back when the film was called *King of the Jungle*. "Things were still pretty flexible," he states. "What happened internally at the studio was, for the first time, our group–the one that had pretty much done every animated movie–was split into two. One group was offered work on *The Lion King*, and the other option was *Pocahontas*. Because of my love for animals, and this whole *Jungle Book* enthusiasm that I had as a kid, I wanted to try that even though *Pocahontas* looked more solid. It was going to be about Indian legends, and their beliefs about spirits in the water and trees . . . and there was some beautiful pre-production artwork that we didn't really have on *The Lion King* yet. I remember [fellow animator] Ruben Aquino and myself being left in the dust because everyone else stormed to *Pocahontas!*"

Disney animation honcho Peter Schneider confided his concern about this development to Andreas Deja. "What are we going to do?" he wailed. "This is going to require the most experienced animators. These are *animals*; there's going to be some realism in it . . . and we don't have the crew."

"We'll just have to give new people a chance to rise to the occasion," the animator told Schneider at the time. "He seemed pretty hopeful," as

Deja recalls, "but I was scared and frustrated. And that's basically what happened: There were some people who came through the ranks, who were given a chance to take on a character."

Deja first set himself to the task of designing Scar, King Mufasa's treacherous brother, by studying Jeremy Irons' films to see if there were some characteristics of the actor he could use. He quickly hit pay dirt. The animator noticed that in many roles, Irons' hair was slicked back . . . which he applied to Scar's black mane, a look that immediately distinguished him from the other lions. Next, he elongated Scar's face, mirroring the distance between Irons' nose and upper lip.

Throughout the design process, Deja was very conscious to avoid any physical resemblance between Scar and Shere Khan. "You could take some of those features of Shere Khan and just slap a wig on him and say he's a lion now–you've got a new character. I did not want that," Deja emphasizes. "Shere Khan has a very horizontal face. Scar's is more vertical . . . and I wanted to use the black that real lions have around their mouths. These black lips. I think the other animators [used that] to a certain degree, but I really went a little further with it."

Deja was also aware, when designing Scar's body, that the character should have a markedly gaunt appearance. "He says, in the film, that he ended up at the 'shallow end of the gene pool' when it came to strength, so he would have to be somebody who couldn't take on his brother physically. He would lose, 'cause he was scrawnier. And so his head is usually lower than Mufasa's, who was more majestic, and his walk is a bit more sneaky . . . things like that."

Irons' vocal performance was also of enormous help to the animator. He felt that that was the springboard for everything. "There wasn't a bad line that Jeremy Irons read. . . . It's like half the work was really done. Even *drawing-wise*, it seemed to be half-done." Deja studied Irons' film, *Reversal of Fortune* (1990), which the actor had won an Oscar portraying real-life accused murderer Claus Von Bulow. "He was so icy and intelligent, and so underplayed . . . that was a good inspiration. [Scar] is hammy at the same time, just really enjoying his sense of humor and point of view on things . . . and yet, he's a ruthless killer."

When *The Lion King* ran into some trouble and the story began changing, Deja found himself having to redo scenes that he'd already completed. "There were changes as they were going along," he notes. "You know, you would animate a twenty-foot scene, and [then hear], 'Well, we just went over the reels and the dialogue has changed. You can keep half of the scene but the second half has to be re-animated."

Deja's very first piece of footage for the film depicted Scar appearing over the horizon and calling out, "*Mufasa! Quick! Stampede in the gorge–Simba's down there!*" The directors liked the animator's handling of the scene very much . . . with one small caveat. "They said, 'You know, our camera angle is going to be higher now, a little bit higher. So can you animate the whole scene from a different angle?' This would be *nothing* now for a computer animator!" Deja laughs. "You push a button and you have your different angle. But with traditional animation, you have to re-animate the whole thing. So I animated it from a different angle–the same poses. This was at the beginning, so you say, 'Well, this happens' . . . but it's all part of it. And there are enough scenes to balance it, enough scenes that do go through the first time . . . you know, so you just take these things as they come."

Andreas Deja's very first scene in The Lion King, *in which Scar had to be re-animated to accommodate a slightly different camera angle. © Disney Enterprises, Inc.*

As you've read in several earlier chapters, *The Lion King*'s production was riddled with problems, making the yet-to-be completed picture the subject of much industry gossip. Andreas Deja heard all the talk. "The word on the street, or at least in the halls of the studio, was that this was just trying to be 'Bambi in Africa' . . . But once we were past the halfway point, I think people started to realize this was really *about* something, and the theme of the film was coming through. And people got really excited." Deja always had high hopes for the project, even when many were skeptical of its chances for success. "We had been on a roll, starting with *Roger Rabbit*, *Mermaid*, *Aladdin* . . . things had been going very well, but then, nobody expected this to go *that* much through the roof!"

Following *The Lion King*, John Musker and Ron Clements approached Deja to animate the villain Hades (voiced by actor James Woods) for their new production of *Hercules* (1997).

"I said I was really flattered, and it was going to be a great role–but I felt I'd be repeating myself." He explained that he needed a break from all the villains he'd been working on. Instead, Deja asked if he could tackle a tougher assignment: Hercules himself. "I know he's not gonna be as much fun," he told the directors, "but I think it's an important character." Clements and Musker understood where he was coming from, and quickly said *yes*. (Animator Nik Ranieri ended up on Hades, who all but stole the show.)

Animators are actors, in essence, and its stars are eagerly sought out by directors in much the same fashion. Similarly, they must perform with one another in scenes just as two thespians would on the stage or screen. Since these performances are drawn or rendered, however, just how does that work–how do two (or more) different animators' characters interact so seamlessly on screen?

"You need to be in tune with the other animator," Deja explains. "So you meet and you talk things over. The first question is always: Which animator starts? That's fairly easy, unless it changes throughout the scene. I would always say that the aggressive character starts, and the reacting character tends to be second. But sometimes, that changes . . . and occasionally, you have to work back and forth."

As an example, he cites an encounter in *Aladdin* between his character, Jafar, and Princess Jasmine, who was animated by Mark Henn. In this particular sequence, a distraught Jasmine runs into Jafar's headquarters, where he coolly informs her that Aladdin is to be beheaded. The script called for some moments where he would touch her, feigning concern, and put his hands on her shoulders. Henn began the scene first. Jasmine sinks down into a chair at the news; she can't believe that Aladdin is to be beheaded . . . then she does a little *take*–like a shiver–and exclaims, "*How dare you!?*"

"What I did then, just before Mark had animated that sort of jerky move on her, I had [Jafar's] hands sort of touch her shoulders–like a spider, the fingers would come down very slowly, to make it creepier. And it worked really well because Mark was very careful in terms of placing her head and eyes where Jafar would be," Deja explains with relish. "To this day, that's one of my favorite sequences that I've done with another animator. I really think the acting is so good in it."

Of all the Disney films he has worked on, the one he claims as his personal favorite is the irreverent hit comedy *Lilo & Stitch* (2002), in which he animated the little Hawaiian girl, Lilo. "It was such precious material that we were given by Chris Sanders and Dean DeBlois, the directors–it had real roots in real life. So tender, and genuine."

When asked for his take on the state of animation in general these days, he grows pensive. "People's perceptions of what animators do are always surprising to me," he reveals. "They still look at it as something . . . I don't want to say *superficial*–because obviously, when it's done well, people do go to see it–but because they only see the end product, people think it's all fun and games. They have no idea of the degree of frustration . . . the concentration. It's not an easy medium. You can get frustrated because you might not be able to draw the way you want to draw . . . or you just have trouble finding the best acting pattern. But this is all a sign that you're really involved. And you're problem-solving each day."

Clearly, Andreas Deja passionately embraces his craft–problems and all.

"It's the best medium in the whole world," he feels. "As a means of expression, I don't think there's anything like it. Because it's about drawing, which I love . . . it's about acting, which I love . . . it's about putting on a performance. You can become any character–it has nothing to do with your looks. You know, actors always are so limited by the way they look . . . But we can be an animal, we can be a chicken, a dinosaur, a little girl, anything. It's very freeing. That's what I love about it!"

Ya Gotta Have Courage

Dilworth's Cowardly Dog Leaps into Action

John R. Dilworth, a self-described "animation filmmaker," just lives to animate. "It brings me the most sensual experience," he purrs. "Animating really is *sexy* for me, to make something move like that. It's a lot like sex or drugs, where there's not much else going on. It roots me in the moment. . . . I don't think about death, or the outside world."

Although he's experienced considerable success in his career as a producer and director–his short film, *The Chicken from Outer Space*, was nominated for an Academy Award in 1993, and then turned into a hugely popular Cartoon Network series, *Courage the Cowardly Dog* (1999)–he still finds himself compelled to pick up a pencil and animate again and again. The reason, for him, is a simple one: "Because that's our *art*." When he's not doing it, he says, "I miss the drawing . . . and making objects and forms move. I miss the expression."

Details from Courage the Cowardly Dog*'s model pack, drawn and notated by John Dilworth, showing how to animate Courage walking, running, and in various states of alarm.*

Back in the mid-eighties, when he toiled as an art director for a small ad agency in New York City, a job he admittedly wasn't thrilled over ("it was the stuff that makes you wanna leap from a window"), Dilworth began creating his first cartoon short. "I was doing a film I thought would make me a great independent filmmaker, like the Europeans, called *The Limited Bird* (1989). It was a long piece, about seventeen minutes . . . my idea was to try to use as few drawings as possible to capture the most intense emotion," he recounts with a bemused grin. "I don't know if I was successful or not. I worked on that for over three years. Every night, I'd come back from the studio and draw, draw, draw. . . . It got into a few festivals, and that was it. I moved on."

Since then, he never stopped making short animated films, teaching himself as he went along . . . playing with color, experimenting with mixed media . . . but never quite feeling satisfied with himself or his work. "I'm a chronic disaffected person," he believes. "I don't think there's a film of mine I'm completely happy with. It's like when the Pope boiled an egg for the bishop, and the Pope asked the bishop, 'So, how's the egg?' And the bishop looked up at him and said, 'Well, it was good in *parts*.' You're not gonna be totally satisfied, but you're not gonna say everything you've done sucks, either," he chuckles.

Dilworth gets misty as he recalls his very first piece of animation. "I think that's like your first lover, ever," he sighs. "Those moments you don't forget. I was in school, and I did a little picture, thirty seconds long, about a trapeze artist. It was called *The Swinger*. This guy was overconfident . . . and as he proceeds he loses his confidence; he just falls apart in mid-swing. Seeing that move, I can't even tell you the *electricity*–it was truly like Zeus had come down and given me a bolt of enthusiasm!"

Fast-forward to the early nineties, by which time John Dilworth had already created numerous short films and TV commercials, been hired to direct series pilots for MTV and Nickelodeon, animated and drew boards for other people's shows, and had generally earned a solid reputation as a filmmaker, when an idea hit him for another cartoon–a 1950s-ish science fiction short, in black and white, to be called *The Chicken from Outer Space*.

He wanted it to be suspenseful and humorous, yet devoid of all the standard fifties sci-fi metaphors about McCarthyism, communism, and technocracy. Influenced by the popular TV series *The X-Files*, and fueled by his love of Rod Serling's *Twilight Zone* and *Night Gallery*–"Those are the shows I used to love when I was a boy"–Dilworth approached the Sci-Fi Channel with the idea. When that saucer didn't fly, he persevered–and ended up procuring the necessary funding from Hanna-Barbera. He spent about nine months working out the story, fleshing out the characters, running ideas and gags past his friends for feedback. As it happened, we were having dinner together one evening at the time, and he was regaling me all about his new toon–which was to feature a pink dog so cowardly he was afraid of his own shadow. "What's his name?" I asked casually. Dilworth thought for an instant, before making it up on the spot. "*Courage!!!*" he blurted out–and that was it. The canine was christened over sushi.

With an able crew assisting him, Dilworth wound up doing about half the animation himself in the eight-minute cartoon. "I also did all the key poses . . . and I did the layouts," he adds. Once they had the story locked in, the short itself took just five months to complete. When it was finished, it aired to overwhelmingly positive response on Cartoon Network's *World*

Premiere Toons, prompting the filmmaker to try to win an Oscar for Best Animated Short–so he submitted *Chicken from Outer Space* to the Academy of Motion Picture Arts and Sciences.

He didn't take home the trophy–but he had a hell of a ride along the way. "Were the Oscars a tremendous experience? They sure were. . . . What animator hasn't dreamed of going to the Oscars and losing? I thought, 'My God, this is my perfect opportunity to not go up there,'" Dilworth cracks.

As the nominees' names were being read off, one by one, all he could think was, "'*Oh God, let it end . . . let it end . . . let it end . . .*' All sound dropped out. I just heard my heart beating so loud I thought I was going to have a heart attack. I was looking *down* . . . y'know, you're just listening and listening . . . and I snuck a look over at Nick Park, who was sitting on my right–and *he* was looking down, too. And then they said, 'The winner is . . . *The Wrong Trousers*, by Nick Park,' So he got to take home the golden naked boy. But it was fun. As soon as that was over, I can't tell you the amount of perspiration that had escaped my body! I literally had to change my clothes. And then, I was *so voracious!* We went and ate, and I think I ate three tables' worth of food. Because of all the stress that was building up."

Following *Chicken from Outer Space*'s nomination, the entry rules were changed by the Academy. "There's a law now on the books: no pilots, no films made for television are eligible," Dilworth says. "But when I made *Chicken*, I always felt it was an independent film. It was never really a pilot. The truth is, I was exhausted from financing the films I had done already."

After *Chicken from Outer Space* was nominated, Hanna-Barbera (which owned the short as well as its characters) approached John Dilworth about turning it into a series, which he resisted. They wanted him to move to L.A. and work out of their facility there–but the filmmaker had grown accustomed to a degree of independence. He had always run his own studio, Stretch Films, and wanted to keep doing so–so he grew very patient. Of course, it didn't hurt that he'd gotten wind that Hanna-Barbera would eventually be absorbed into Cartoon Network. So he waited . . . and he waited . . . for about two years.

In the meantime, Stretch Films kept busy producing *Ace & Avery*, a charming series of thirteen animated shorts for Cartoon Network, and Sesame Workshop's pre-school series, *Big Bag* (1996). He also did commercials, made another well-received short film called *Noodles and Nedd* (1997), and generally bided his time. "I was still working with Cartoon Network, incidentally, the way it worked out," he quickly notes. "So, then it happened. And when it was official, I rang up Linda Simensky, we met in New York, and I pitched her *Courage* again. And, y'know, she dug it. The best thing about it was that they didn't forget it, and they still wanted to work with me."

"There had been talk of a series, but John wasn't that interested," Simensky recalls. "He didn't wanna work for Hanna-Barbera. He wanted to do it out of New York. And he was very smart, because I don't think any of us knew how this was gonna pan out . . . so he waited until he could do it directly with Cartoon Network, out of his own studio."

The short film officially morphed into *Courage the Cowardly Dog*, a weekly half-hour series chronicling the life of an incredibly timid dog who's regularly forced to defend his owners–Muriel and Eustace, an old couple living on a farm outside the small town of Nowhere–from paranormal and criminal elements that threaten their simple existence. Dilworth and crew were given a green light by the network, and what followed were five intense years (and four seasons) of practically nonstop production.

The animator took his new assignment seriously. "I don't want to sound pretentious, but the fact is, I'm very conscious about having a series on television, and the responsibility that enables one. I mean, I didn't want

Poses from a Dilworth model sheet of Muriel, Courage's sweet, kindly Scottish owner whom he does his best to protect.

the stories to just be funny. . . . It's a good opportunity to lay some themes down. Even though it's a hell of a lot of work, TV production, it's a real opportunity to voice your concerns.

Dilworth is quick to clarify his intentions–he's not throwing jargon down the throats of TV watchers. "I'm not a moralizer, although I'm a humanist. But [the stories] get diluted, just through the process of going through so many bodies, and having to do them so quickly. You don't have the control, the individual control that you'd like to have on a theme. And so, maybe eighty-five of the cartoons have a real theme, and the others were just fluff that was made up to fill," he admits, though quickly adding, "Funny cartoons often have insights into human behavior, anyway. Not as the driving force, but as by-product."

Courage the Cowardly Dog sports a richer look than the short film it was based on. While Dilworth's character designs remained consistent, the backgrounds were now filled with texture and dimension, much of it enabled by the new digital technology–and skilled artists who became more and more proficient at wielding it. "The background artist on the short was Margaret Frey, but the look is what *I* desire. I mean, when you see those cartoons, I'm interested in real time," he elaborates. "I want you to feel a moment of time. It's not just blue skies–and the clouds aren't all just fluffy like sheep. Light has so much to do with how colors react. My whole thing is, I want to give you that *dimension*. I mean, okay, we didn't really capture it in the original short . . . but when I look at it, it's still not so bad."

They worked closely on the background textures–focusing on surfaces like wood and sand. And when he had a certain type of lighting or time of day in mind, Dilworth would bring in photographs to demonstrate what he was after. "It took about a season before we really started to make it *happen*. I'm interested in composition, how it all works together, what props and characters are on what background. I just wanna see it all. Because to me, that whole composition, that *is* the art. Y'know? And the frame just happens to your television, no matter what size it is."

Since Dilworth seems deeply concerned with the art of his television creation, it's only fair to ask if, in retrospect, does he feel that *Courage* managed to bridge commercial success with artistic success? He nods his head. "Uh-huh. Of course, the animation could be so much better. Working overseas is a difficult process . . . it's nearly impossible to get the sort of acting required that really gets a gag over, or really captures an emotion. We've done 104 cartoons. The thing is, I went into this knowing that if I could get at least 70 percent of what I would do myself, I'd be happy. It's TV, it's mass-produced."

Dilworth, a talented animator, found the process maddening at times. "It's *so* frustrating. But I had to learn to become an adult. And I stopped having these tirades, y'know, when we called retakes with my producer. Because there's really nothing more she could do. We sent them the letters, the faxes, the models . . . we'd go there every year. I wouldn't physically reanimate a scene, but I would give them keys, and show them how it could be done. And, of course, the first time I went out there, before we started the show, I spent a great deal of time going over how each character moved, what I wanted to see, the laws, how they should go about the layouts and composition . . . but, most important, the biggest aid was the short. 'Cause we animated that here at Stretch. It was their visual bible, and they studied that."

Every single cartoon got shot as an animatic before it moved on. "'Cause I like to see the sense of timing, I like to see how gags are being put over. . . . I like to look at the composition." Once the animatic was approved, the designs would have to be worked out. Dilworth gave a lot of autonomy to his design personnel, as well: "We'd meet, and I'd give them an idea of what I was looking for–we would do that with backgrounds, props, and characters. I would give rough designs for the lead characters, and everything else I'd just give a little description. Or, if they were stuck on something, I would sort of sketch it out for them there, and then they would just go off and do everything on their own."

Naturally, all the designs were created to look very much like the work of John Dilworth, as if he had personally touched it all. "They did a good job. It's that 70 percent again–if they could give me seventy of how I'd do it myself, then I was okay . . . but I'd give 'em all the parameters." Did they have trouble getting it the first year? "Yeah, of course," he says, adding that he had to occasionally sit down and redraw things. "I spent a lot of time with the designs . . . but it arced down as the seasons progressed."

The years of intense production haven't been easy, he concedes. "It's been very difficult. Because of my emotional involvement in all aspects, and in the artists' lives . . . and in nearly every element of the cartoon. It's very obsessive. I wouldn't recommend this for a person who obsesses a lot about what they do. 'Cause it just makes things worse. I think they should, like, work in the woods . . . or transplant trees . . . and be in nature."

He also stresses that it hasn't been all just *him*–Dilworth appreciates his crew more than he can express in mere words. "Every artist here does tremendous work . . . and their contributions cannot be praised enough. I mean, every soul here. I *am* involved, but I'm collaborating with the artists that are helping to do this thing. . . . But I have to say that, without a strong leader who can answer a question or make a decision right there, nothing goes forward. I mean, *that's* what I do. I just have a strong vision for this thing. If I were doing it for somebody else's show, I probably wouldn't be as strong because I'd be second-guessing what the other person wants."

Cartoon Network couldn't be happier with the show. "It all came together pretty nicely," Linda Simensky confides. "I mean, there were things about the first season . . . like, Courage talked too much. It didn't seem right for him to do all that talking. The network basically went to John and said, 'We don't like it, how do you feel, would you change it?' And then he tried it, and it worked. A lot of stuff with that show just came together . . . and it's such an odd show. It's another one where I really felt some of the early scripts weren't quite right . . . but after a season, they nailed it. We knew it would get better, and it did."

Meanwhile, Dilworth has never stopped animating his short, personal films. As production on *Courage*'s final season began winding down, he created a simple, funny short called *The Mousochist* (2002), depicting a mouse that's tempted by a huge wedge of cheese lodged in a lethal-looking mousetrap. The creature tries to ignore the cheese, but cannot . . . he tickles it repeatedly with his tongue, lusting for it while clearly aware of the potential consequences should he give in and take a bite. In the end, he can't help himself: the rodent chomps down on the cheese and the trap snaps his head off . . . but the disembodied head is thrilled, anyway, now that it got what it craved.

Dilworth confesses that all of his shorts have something to do with his own life. "*The Mousochist* is absolutely what I went through on *Courage*, being a jurist at Annecy, my relationships . . . things that I thought I wanted, that I *must* have . . . and now that I've got 'em, I have to *live with them*, y'know? You see the mouse, but he's got no fuckin' body . . . but he's got the cheese and he's happy."

Sheer Genie-us

Eric Goldberg Conjures Up *Aladdin*'s Kinetic Comic Centerpiece

When Disney's *Aladdin* was let out of the bottle in 1992, a new animation star exploded onto the scene in a blinding blue flash, garnering more publicity and acclaim in the public eye than any animator had in years. Magazine covers, newspaper articles, TV and radio interviews–the works. It played like a glossy, overnight Hollywood success story . . . except for the fact, of course, that it wasn't exactly overnight.

Eric Goldberg was an animation prodigy, drawing flipbooks when he was just six and animating his own award-winning toon, "For Sale," by the time he was eighteen. He cut his college education short–basically, there was nothing more they could teach him at Pratt Institute–to go work for director Richard Williams as an assistant animator on the meticulously crafted but uneven musical feature, *Raggedy Ann and Andy* (1977). Still, his real education began there, as the young artist got to work alongside and learn from such legendary animators as Ken Harris, Art Babbitt, Tissa David, and Williams himself.

From there, Goldberg moved to London, where he continued working for Williams' studio as a director and animator on projects like the charming TV special, *Ziggy's Gift* (1982), and the forever-in-production feature film, *The Thief and the Cobbler* (started in 1968, finally released in 1995), before starting his own production company, Pizzazz Pictures, and making more commercials between 1983 and 1990 than he claims he can ever count.

Throughout his time abroad, he wondered when he'd eventually return to the United States. Although it was always the New Jersey–born artist's dream to direct and animate for Walt Disney Feature Animation, it was his bad luck to have come of age just when Disney was going through its extended down period. His dream was put on long-term hold–but that wait was soon to end.

Goldberg's wife, Susan–a former CalArts student who would later emerge as the first credited female art director on a Disney feature, *Fantasia/2000* (you can read all about it in chapter 5)–had introduced him to director John Musker years earlier. They'd managed to stay in touch, keeping up "a kind of mutual admiration relationship over the years," Eric Goldberg says. So, when Musker and co-director Ron Clements extended an invitation to come back home and work on a new picture called *Aladdin*, the animator felt it was finally the right time and project.

"That was a big inducement, to know that John and Ron were going to be doing something," Goldberg explains. "I didn't know at the time *what* I was going to be doing. No character was discussed . . . but I thought, 'Okay, if it's John and Ron, it's probably going to be good.'"

With that, the Goldbergs packed up and moved to Los Angeles. "When I arrived at the studio, they gave me a script and said, 'We want you to read this, and, y'know, see what you think.' So I read the script, and, of course, the Genie–written in their hand as if they had Robin Williams already signed on the dotted line–leapt off the page. One of John and Ron's major talents is that they can actually write in the voices of the characters that they intend to cast. And while they're completely open to the riffs and suggestions of various people, they start with something very, very specific in mind. And I thought, 'Well, I hope they give me the Genie.' So I go in, and they say, 'Well, uh, we'd kind of like you to do the Genie.' And I went, 'Yeah. Okay, that sounds good.' I played it cool," he laughs, "but, y'know, I was thrilled!"

The impish couple, Susan and Eric Goldberg, in their basement animation studio at home.

First off, the character's design had to be locked in. The visual development crew at Disney had already been struggling with it for quite a while. "We had the worst time trying to get a design of the Genie," vis dev artist Sue Nichols recalls, "because Jeffrey Katzenberg wanted something that looked pretty much like a guy in a genie outfit, and we kept trying to do these multi-arms–or, y'know, hands but no arms . . . or something magical, a fun cartoon version. He just didn't want any of it."

When Eric Goldberg sat down to figure out the Genie, he wasn't quite sure what direction to take him in, either. He drew caricatures of Robin Williams, horned-and-clawed genies, variations on Fats Waller (the character's original musical inspiration)–a wide range. "I remember Peter Schneider walking into my room the first week, and, of course, what I'm drawing is very, very cartoony and off-the-wall, and he said [very clipped], 'Well. That's very nice. Might be a little too *way out* for Disney, but very nice.' And he walked on," Goldberg chuckles. "He had no idea what he was getting at the time."

As he continued to experiment, Goldberg found that the Fats Waller idea and the Robin Williams persona didn't mesh. He began to simplify the design, finally hitting pay dirt the day he drew a caricature of Williams as a Genie–in a swooping, boldly linear style reminiscent of famed *New York*

Times theatrical caricaturist Al Hirschfeld. "I have to give [production designer] Richard Vander Wende a lot of credit here," the animator notes. "He was very inspirational on where we went with the character design, because his concept paintings for *Aladdin*–they were what I would call 'Hollywood Arabian'–were very S-curvy, very caricatured . . . really, really taking into account the curvy calligraphic shapes. So, naturally, I thought, 'What kind of characters fit in a curvy environment? *Curvy* characters.' Bingo: Hirschfeld."

At that time, design trends in animation had been leaning decidedly the other way. *Angular* had been the style of the day. Most of the commercial studios, like Goldberg's Pizzazz, had been doing work in an angular, rather post-UPA mold. "I was starting to get tired of angular," he says, "and I just thought, 'God, I miss curves. I miss curves in animation!' They're so *natural* in animation."

Goldberg seized the opportunity to depart from the angular norm. "Here was a movie that was made for curves. And a character made for curves. The first test I animated, the character had a turban and he had a vest, yet the more we stripped off of him, the better he became. Richard Vander Wende, in particular, was very responsive. He realized the more we took off, the more movement we were getting. And John and Ron liked it, too."

By then, Musker and Clements were very eager to get Robin Williams on board as the Genie's voice. The actor had just finished performing a wacky bat for Twentieth Century Fox's ecologically minded animated feature *Ferngully . . . The Last Rainforest* (1992), and the directors weren't sure he'd want to tackle a cartoon role again so soon. More importantly, they needed to sell Jeffrey Katzenberg on the idea, and then, in turn, sell the concept to Williams. "So they suggested that I pull a couple of pieces from a comedy album, and animate the Genie to them," Goldberg says. "I did three tests. Probably the most successful one at the time was, we took a riff where Robin was talking about schizophrenia, and he was saying: '*Tonight, I'd like to talk to you about the very serious subject of schizophrenia.*' '*No, he doesn't!*' '*Shut up, let him talk!*'" On that last line, Goldberg grew the Genie an extra head, "to argue with himself."

The animator, at that early stage, was already experimenting with the lightning-quick transitions from one character to another that would become the Genie's hallmark in the finished film. As Goldberg explains, Clements and Musker had originally written the Genie as *character types*: "He would transform into an evangelist. He would transform into a game show host. He would transform into various people–but they hadn't written it so that he transformed into known personalities. That came when Robin got to the mike the first time."

Another reason for the Genie animation tests was to see if the character, which Goldberg was conceiving in more of a graphic two-dimensional style, could exist successfully in a three-dimensional Disney universe. "It wasn't until Eric came on and did his tests, and Jeffrey could see it moving to Robin Williams' dialogue, that he said 'Yeah, yeah! That's it, that's great!'" Sue Nichols notes. "'Cause it's so hard to develop something that's pure imagination, and has never been done or seen before."

By the time Goldberg animated the third 'schizophrenia' test, design on the Genie was done. Not only did those tests lock in the character–they managed to sell both the studio and Williams in one fell swoop. "There were many times I realized, on *Aladdin*, 'Okay, I'm actually in the movie business now, after years and years in commercials,'" Goldberg muses. "The first time I realized it was when Jeffrey Katzenberg brought Robin in to look at the animation. I pitched some boards, and showed the test." Williams thought they were hilarious. "That was an honor in itself–to make Robin Williams laugh! That was *great*."

The next question was, how were the *other* characters going to get designed? Goldberg attributes their success to John Musker and Ron Clements, Richard Vander Wende, and Glen Keane (Aladdin's lead animator). Keane wielded his considerable clout at the studio, gathering Musker, Clements, and Vander Wende in a room with the supervising animators where, together, they designed the cast. "Historically, I think it was the first time the studio had ever done it in this current generation of Disney studio animation," Goldberg says. "That's why the cast looks so unified. We all got together and just kept *Hirschfeld-izing* our designs. And we defined the *Aladdin* universe: If the Genie is the wackiest end of that universe, then Aladdin and Jasmine are the most conservative end, and you design everything else in between. But you still design Aladdin and Jasmine so that they have that same Hirschfeldian curve to them. It's just that they're drawn less caricatured, less broadly than the other characters."

Surprisingly, for all the artists' channeling of Hirschfeld's style, he was never a consultant on the film; nor did he have anything to do with it. In fact, he never even saw a single frame of *Aladdin* until its pre-premiere screening at the Museum of Modern Art. "He was a very gracious man," offers Goldberg. "Earlier, I'd called him up out of the blue–we were in New York to do a publicity launch–and I said, 'Please, would you come to one of these things? You've been a huge influence on this movie, and we would love for you to see what we're doing.' And at the time, he said, 'Well, y'know, I would love to, but I've got these deadlines. . . . I gotta do, like, eight drawings for the *New York Times.*' And I'm thinking, 'You're ninety-two!!! When does it *stop*?!'" Goldberg roars with laughter.

When Goldberg arrived at Disney, he was told that the studio's computer animation system, CAPS, couldn't yet do certain things. Back then, only one film–*Rescuers Down Under*–had fully utilized the new process, which could scan the pencil animation, digitally ink and paint the images, and incorporate computer-generated effects. One stylistic flourish that had not been accomplished yet was a thick-and-thin line–which the animator was envisioning for his character. "A thick-and-thin line carries color better," he explains. "With a pronounced thick-and-thin, it would look like an old ink line."

So he and his key cleanup assistant, Lori Noda, began experimenting with CAPS to prove to the naysayers that it could work. Not only did they succeed, but it looked so good that everyone else soon followed suit. "There are people that chafed against it," Goldberg recalls, "because it takes longer to build up that kind of line . . . it's more work. But the result was on the screen, and nobody could deny it."

Eric Goldberg's tangible contributions to *Aladdin* were far greater than most people realized at the time; his design and animation sense had a profound influence on many other aspects of the movie. Since he was on the film for a year before his fellow animators hopped aboard, his test animation on other characters brought him in contact with Tina Price, one of Disney's computer mavens. They collaborated on the Magic Carpet and Abu's animation well before either design had even been finalized. "Basically, the carpet was all hand-drawn, hand-animated, and hand-cleaned up," Goldberg explains. "But because it's a rectangle, what they could do was basically have the intricate carpet pattern on a computer rectangle–so they could manipulate that rectangle to match the outer outline of the *carpet's* rectangle. When Randy Cartwright came on to animate the carpet, they texture-mapped the design to match the forms of Randy's animation. But we did the first test . . . he sneaks around a corner, he takes, and then, because he's frightened, he rolls himself up. My actual animation did not make it into the film, but the concept of it did."

Goldberg also did a few tests on Iago, who'd originally been written as a British character. (Gilbert Gottfried came in later; he was one of Katzenberg's suggestions.) "The joke at the time," recalls Goldberg, "was supposed to be that Iago was an *'Awwk! Awwk! Awwk!'* parrot when everyone was looking at him, and then *disdainful* when everybody turned away. I think a lot of that British disdain became part of Jafar to a certain extent, when we got Gilbert on board."

As for his main assignment on *Aladdin*, the big blue Genie turned out to be the ideal marriage of animator and voice actor, perfectly suited to Eric Goldberg's and Robin Williams' respective talents. Soon after Williams signed on, they flew up to Skywalker Sound in San Francisco to record him. Musker and Clements were sure to include the animator in the recording sessions, so he could study the comedian's mannerisms.

Goldberg realized, as he watched Robin Williams perform, that he wanted the Genie to be physically broader than Williams is in real life, especially given how unrestrained the vocals were. "He recorded what was written, and then he would riff," Goldberg recalls. "And, of course, we *wanted* the riffs. But what we didn't expect was that he would bring out his entire arsenal of celebrity impersonations, as well!"

Eric Goldberg made a terrible mistake at that first session. When offered the opportunity to move closer so he could better observe the actor as he spoke, he allowed himself to be seated inside the recording booth. That meant he had to remain absolutely silent. Not even a peep–or the microphone would pick it up and ruin Williams' explosively funny takes. It was sheer agony: "Robin goes for about half an hour before he takes a

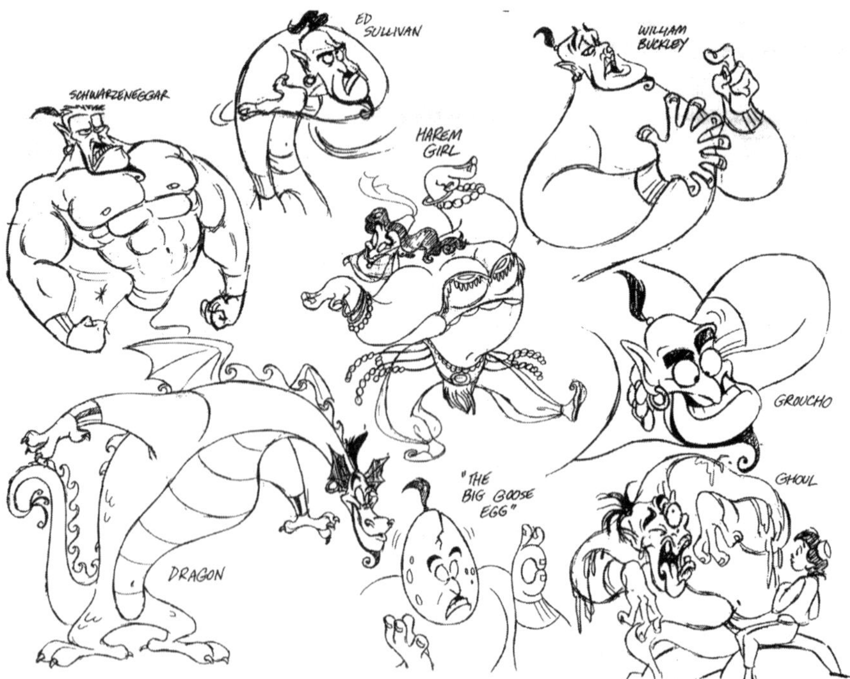

Detail of a vivid Eric Goldberg model sheet depicting the Genie in just a few of his colorful personas. © Disney Enterprises, Inc.

break," Goldberg grins, "and I'm sitting there in the stage with him, creased up, *killing myself* and trying not to laugh. Finally, he takes a break and I fall out of the chair and say, 'Okay, I'm going behind the glass now!' . . . It was a lesson in *torture*."

When the creative team returned to the studio in L.A., they realized that they absolutely *had* to use the unexpected material. Working with editor H. Lee Peterson, Goldberg, given free reign by Musker and Clements, cobbled together the first couple of takes of what the Genie actually said. "We worked out story sketches, and cut together the funniest Robin stuff we could. Then, John and Ron and I would sit there and–aside from laughing ourselves stupid–we would all pick the takes that we thought were the funniest. I remember we were all sitting together, cracking up about the Robert De Niro *Taxi Driver* stuff, thinking we'll *never* get this in the movie . . . well, we went ahead and stuck it in the movie–and it's still in the movie! And come full circle, when *Aladdin* had its Museum of Modern Art pre-premiere, and they had lots of New York luminaries there, who's in the audience? [*Taxi Driver* director] Martin Scorsese. And, of course, he busts a gut at it, so it was great!"

The animator and performer didn't have many conversations during the recording sessions, and rightfully so–after all, Ron Clements and John Musker were directing the film. "But he knew, and I knew, that we were on this unspoken wavelength," Goldberg says. When Williams tossed off one of his trademark riffs–such as when Aladdin promises the Genie that he'll use his third wish to set him free, and the Genie responds, "Uh, huh. Yeah. Right. *Booo-wooop*!"–Goldberg knew immediately that it was supposed to be Pinocchio's nose growing: "I said, 'Hey. We *own* Pinocchio!' So I boarded it that way." At first, Ron Clements didn't know what the '*Booo-wooop*!' was, but Goldberg implored him to retain it. And it turned out to be one of the biggest laughs in the film. "In fact, at previews, it was such a big laugh that we had to add footage to the scene, till the laughter died down."

Robin Williams' wild riffing offered the animators an enormous smorgasbord of choice. For every single line of dialogue, he would sometimes do it as fifteen characters–affording the filmmakers the luxury of going back to the studio and saying, "Let's see . . . he did Groucho, W.C. Fields, Peter Lorre, Ed Sullivan . . . okay, the Ed Sullivan goes right *there!*" They could then plunk in a Groucho line somewhere where it felt most appropriate, and so on. With the unexpected infusion of so much unbridled insanity from Williams and Goldberg, people found they had to adjust everything else accordingly. In the original draft, the tale had revolved around Aladdin and his widowed mother. No longer: Mom was chucked from the story on

Jeffrey Katzenberg's command. And, with the action-adventure motif out of the picture, Goldberg found that the film could be infused with even more gags and laughs.

Jafar's parrot sidekick, Iago, was one of the main beneficiaries of the new tone. Gilbert Gottfried, along with Iago's supervising animator, Will Finn, were able to play up Iago's edgy comedy to the hilt, notes Goldberg. "That character allowed a lot of physical humor into the film that might not have been there. Gilbert's thought, as he was watching it unfold, was, 'When in doubt, hurt the bird!'"

Comedy was always Eric Goldberg's métier. So it pleased him to no end that *Aladdin* was getting funnier by the day. "There was a type of humor that was getting into this movie that I had never, ever seen in a Disney film before," he says. "To a certain extent, we were trying to see on *Aladdin* how far we could push it without it breaking. One of my favorite things that Gilbert did as a riff, which wound up in the movie–and it typifies the kind of humor that *Aladdin* could have–is when Iago is panicked, and he's saying to Jafar, '*We've gotta get outta here! I've gotta start packing! We've gotta travel light–I'll bring the guns, the weapons, the knives, and how 'bout this picture? I dunno. I think I'm making a weird face in it.*' That was improv–and you *never* heard Disney characters saying that kind of stuff before! It's just off the wall, y'know, kind of, well, where did they pull *that* from?!"

Aladdin became wild and irreverent, bursting at the seams with pop culture references, Williams' impersonations of famous personalities, sight gags, clever songs, and sharp scripting. "It just felt like such a breath of fresh air," Goldberg says in retrospect. "And yet, it has the values of a traditional Disney movie: It has a moral, it has personalities that you invest in, it has scope, it has all the things that the great Disney movies have. But it just had that *extra* thing."

Eric Goldberg's next assignment at the studio was as different from *Aladdin* as could possibly be: He and Mike Gabriel co-directed the serious animated musical drama, *Pocahontas* (1995), an entertaining and beautifully crafted retelling of the young Native American princess' story. The experience of helming his first movie, especially one so different in tone from the rest of his oeuvre, left Goldberg proud but completely exhausted.

Since then, he's found a comfortable balance, dividing his time between his first love of animating–*Hercules* (1997), the character Philoctetes, voiced by Danny DeVito–and directing movies, the "Rhapsody in Blue" and "Carnival of the Animals" sequences in Disney's *Fantasia/2000*, and Warner Bros.' *Looney Tunes: Back in Action* (2003), co-directed with Joe Dante.

CHAPTER 8
BIG-SHOT TOON PRODUCER
The Nuts and Bolts (and Falling Anvils) of Producing Animation

"[The Beatles] loved it. They started to hang around the studio, especially Ringo. He was taken by it. He commented one day that his nose wasn't quite long enough, and would the animators do something about that? We said 'sure,' and we didn't do anything about it. But . . . in subsequent scenes, I said, 'You notice your nose?' He said, 'Thank you, Al.'"

—Al Brodax, producer of *Yellow Submarine* (1968)

The title of producer may be the most casually bandied-about credit in show business. And it's no different in animation. There never seems to be a shortage of them on a project, and the variety is bountiful: You have executive producers, line producers, associate producers, co-producers, creative producers, writer-producers, animation producers, show runners (they're producers, too), and then, just plain old producers. Most people have no idea what the distinction is between one or another, and if you asked some of the producers themselves–as I did while writing this book–even they have trouble defining the differences sometimes.

It takes years to put together an animated feature film, and many months to construct even a single episode of a cartoon TV series. In features, the producers have to focus on one large story. In television, they quickly find themselves juggling many episodes and overlapping deadlines all at once. Producing in either medium is a formidable task, which can't be accomplished by one person working alone. Someone has to put together a team, assemble the right talent in all areas, and then oversee the many different aspects of production–from the very cute and cuddly beginning to the sometimes bittersweet end, with deadlines and impending air/release dates looming all along the way. Not only do producers have to formulate and remain mindful of their budgets, but they need to find the delicate balance between a project's creative goals and its financial limitations ... which can be a neat juggling act.

Since there's so much to get done, it makes sense to divvy up responsibilities among several capable leaders–and that's where the vast array of producers comes into play. With that in mind, let's take a look at a few different *types* of toon producers.

THE MOTHER OF ALL SIMPSONS

Margot Pipkin, Animation Producer

If you were to ask most people who *The Simpsons'* mom is, they'd answer "Marge" without hesitation. But they'd only be partially right–the show actually had two. Its first was Margot Pipkin, animation producer of *The Simpsons* from when they were short cartoons on *The Tracey Ullman Show* right on through the end of the first full season as a half-hour series. Her title reflected the fact that James L. Brooks, Matt Groening, and Sam Simon, the show's executive producers, were essentially creating a sitcom, albeit an animated one. Furthermore, as Pipkin explains, "in prime time, all the producers are usually writers. This was the first time a prime-time writing crew had combined with an animation crew. On *The Flintstones*, it was all animation people."

The job of animation producer means, literally, just that: Margot was the one physically running the production of the animation at the studio, which was Klasky Csupo for the series' first few seasons. To this day, Pipkin is still spoken of by the show's early creative staff with reverence and true affection. Getting the fledgling show up on its feet was a formidable task, to say the least–no one had done a prime-time toon in many years, and certainly not one with the lofty ambitions or complexity of *The Simpsons*.

"My God, she had her hands full from the moment she walked in," Ken Bruce, early *Simpsons* animator and layout artist, says today. He recalls how Pipkin was able to hold things together: "Margot's a really good people person. She's an amazing problem solver, and, at the end of the day, even though it's about getting the job done and cracking whips, she still has human characteristics: empathy and heart. Beyond producing–and I say this without any condescension, because it's part of what makes her so amazing–she was also a good mother figure for the stupid, childish, day-to-day infighting that happens between immature artists."

Pipkin began her job as producer of the short *Simpsons* cartoons at Gabor Csupo's urging. Already on staff at Klasky Csupo, she was working on animated TV commercials for them when he came to her one day with his new project. "I'm actually proud of the fact that I saw, in Margot, her production skills," he beams. "She didn't even wanna do it in the beginning–she thought it was too much responsibility . . . but she was so organized, and so dedicated, and so hard working, that I said, 'Margot, you would make a great producer.' And she said, 'Oh, no, no, no . . . that's not me.' And I said, 'Yeah, that's *exactly* you!'"

She finally gave in and accepted the promotion. First thing, she brought in Bill Kopp, Wes Archer, and David Silverman. "Those were the three guys who did everything–layout, animate, in-between–and Gyorgyi Peluce did the ink and paint." As you no doubt read earlier (if you haven't, shame on you–it's all in chapter 2), this small crew was able to churn out a mountain of work in practically no time at all–and on an absurdly low budget.

When the Fox network decided to spin *The Simpsons* into a half-hour series, it fell on Pipkin's shoulders to transform the small operation into an efficient production machine on a much larger scale. "Back then, Klasky

Director David Silverman and animation producer Margot Pipkin, proudly displaying their Emmy Awards from The Simpsons' *first win in 1990.*

Csupo was this tiny little outfit . . . essentially a husband-and-wife team that did commercials. Then, they did these little *Simpsons* interstitials . . . and then, the network decided to do the spin-off and wanted us to take it to series."

There was just one problem: the studio wasn't equipped for such a massive undertaking. Fortunately, just at that time, Filmation–a powerhouse producer of animation during the creatively moribund early eighties–had closed down. "So we bought their cameras, we bought their desks, everything," says Pipkin. "We just went over there and took everything we could, and they were selling them at wonderful bargain-basement prices 'cause they were closing down and nobody else wanted them. And that's how we started up."

Once production began, Pipkin realized that there'd have to be some changes made to accommodate the demands of the series. Drawing from her background in TV commercials, the producer decided to create animatics for each episode–filming each storyboard in sequence, and presenting it with dialogue to the executives. This method worked well with producers Jim Brooks and Sam Simon, Pipkin explains, because of their background in live-action comedy: "In live action, you write a script, you go watch the actors perform it, you rewrite right there on the stage. They needed the ability to rewrite." Looking at an animatic before anyone proceeded to the next phase meant that the writers could see how a show was playing, and make the necessary adjustments. "You've got to be able to do that in prime-time animation," Pipkin adds. "You've got to be able to make the jokes better."

She also reintroduced the practice of drawing all scene layouts here in the United States, then sending them overseas for the animators to use as a clear guide. This was how Hanna-Barbera had done *The Flintstones* back in the sixties, but gradually, over the years, more and more animation work got sent to foreign studios. It finally reached the point where practically all layout was being done abroad–with often spotty results. "When you send it over to Korea, which is where we were sending it, you have non-English speakers," Pipkin explains. "They don't have the sense of the comedy timing–and, in comedy, timing is everything. How you deliver the line . . . what is the look . . . and that was something that I'd hoped to control here. The layouts were to help the Korean animators know what the expressions were to be, much more so than you could give them with just the storyboard."

As Pipkin is quick to add, *The Simpsons* is very American comedy. "You're slamming Homer as a father . . . that's not something Koreans were going to understand." And yet, as she points out, the show has grown in popularity all around the world—"it's interesting that now that humor has become global."

Margot Pipkin stayed with the series through its first full season, and would have remained with it longer if she hadn't gotten pregnant. "I thought, 'I can't be pregnant and work twenty-hour days.' So I quit, and went home and had my baby." Producing the show had thoroughly exhausted her, so she actually welcomed some time off. "But I did feel bad that I couldn't go and participate more in the glory, because I'd worked so hard to birth that animation baby," she says. "And then, I had to leave it to somebody else, which was very hard. We really felt that we were breaking ground. . . . I loved the crew, and I enjoyed working with all those incredibly bright writers and executive producers. It was a very exhausting, positive experience."

Gabor Csupo and the rest of the crew were all sorry to see her go. "Very much so," he says. "But then, later, she came back for a few years." When Margot eventually returned to the workforce, she picked up where she left off, producing animated series like *Duckman* (USA, 1994) and *God, the Devil, and Bob* (NBC, 2000).

Talking Babies Are Born

Producing Nickelodeon's *Rugrats*

Then, we have another curiously worded title: "creative producer." Working alongside Margot Pipkin on *The Simpsons* was a young guy by the name of Paul Germain. As he recalls it, when they all received word that the short cartoons would be turned into a half-hour series, "people who had been paying no attention to it suddenly are saying, 'Oh, this is the gravy train!' and, all of a sudden, all the big shots are jumping on." Germain had been absolutely instrumental in putting together the creative team for all the *Simpsons* shorts that aired on *Tracey Ullman*, as well as having overseen their actual production.

But when the show took off on its own, he suddenly found himself on the periphery. "I was being relegated from the guy who's putting the whole thing together to being sort of a servant-like line producer," he says today, "which is not what I wanted to do. So I decided to leave. I'd actually gotten very disillusioned, to where I was going to become a teacher."

Germain gave his two weeks' notice and was about to depart . . . but, at the last moment, Gabor Csupo came to him and offered a better position, in development. Germain wasn't too keen on the idea at first: "I said,

'Oh, I've been doing development for years, for Jim Brooks . . . I was reading seven feature scripts a week and I hated it. I don't wanna do that any more.'" Still, Gabor talked him into trying out the job for the summer, before Germain's teaching job was to start in September.

Quietly and simply, that set the stage for the creation of one of the most popular animated TV shows in the history of the medium.

When he began working directly for Klasky Csupo, Germain found himself "doing what Gabor *thought* was development." In other words, Csupo expected Germain not simply to find projects, but to create them himself and convince the network they were worth taking on. "Now, I had never created anything on my own. . . . Suddenly, I was put in the position to come up with ideas. And I thought, 'Okay, I'll come up with ideas!' So I wrote all these little notions of what we might do for an animated show. . . . Y'know, a city of insects . . . a space alien show . . . all kinds of stuff."

Meanwhile, the networks began calling Klasky Csupo–*The Simpsons* was really taking off now–wanting to know if they had anything else up their sleeve. One of these folks was Vanessa Coffey from Nickelodeon. Back then, the cable network had no animated shows yet, and was looking to create a block of original programming. What they *weren't* looking for was the same old stuff that everyone had been seeing on the tube for years. "I had about three days to prepare," Germain remembers. "I had all these ideas I'd put together, all these pitch boards and stuff . . . [designer] Everett Peck had done artwork for some of these. And the night before the pitch, Arlene Klasky called me and she said, 'I want to do a show about babies.'"

What happened next has been the source of considerable debate, depending upon whom you talk to. Gabor Csupo recalls that "the original idea for *Rugrats* was a very quick one that came from Arlene, who was sitting home with our boys. She told us this one-liner idea: 'Let's do a show with babies, you know, from their point of view–and they can only talk between themselves, not to their parents." Paul Germain contends that, when he asked Klasky to elaborate on her baby idea, she responded, "You know, little babies. They walk around, they're really cute," whereupon he said okay, hung up the phone, and didn't quite know what to do with the idea until he awoke in the middle of the night with an epiphany. As Germain tells it, "When I was a child, my youngest brother would just sit around and drool. He couldn't talk, he wasn't walking, and he would just sit in his playpen. And when you're a kid, you think, 'God, babies are so stupid. They don't do anything–they just kind of sit there like idiots.' And I remembered thinking to myself, 'I wonder if, when I leave the room, and I'm not looking, suddenly he gets up and he walks around and he does

stuff?'" However the actual genesis occurred, clearly, all three parties played a huge role in the show's creation, and all three are now listed as creators in *Rugrats'* opening credits.

Two facts that are absolutely not in dispute: Paul Germain was creative producer of the series for its entire original run of sixty-five episodes, receiving the unusual title due to his roles as a writer, co-creator, and producer. And, at the pitch session to Vanessa Coffey, the show that Nickelodeon snatched up on the spot was *Rugrats*. "I read my other ideas, but Vanessa gave me a lukewarm reception," says Germain. "And then I got to the very last idea: 'A bunch of little babies, they seem like dumb little babies . . . but the minute the adults leave the room, it turns out the babies can talk and they're cognizant.' That was my entire pitch."

"We had no artwork on *Rugrats*," Csupo adds. "We didn't even know what to call it. We just called it 'the baby show'. . . . Actually, I think it was Paul's idea to call it [*Rugrats*]." Coffey requested a treatment and character designs, which Germain, Csupo, and Klasky got cracking on immediately.

"When we knew we were gonna do this baby show, we started to draw like crazy," Gabor Csupo recounts. "Hundreds of baby characters . . . and the funnier they were, the more we liked it. We didn't wanna draw cutesy cute, sweet babies–we wanted to kind of have a roughness to it, and a strange design sensibility. So we drew a bunch of these, and then we started to pick the best, whatever made us laugh more . . . and that's how we assembled the cast."

"I put together a four-page treatment," Germain relates. "Gabor designed the mother, the father–that's Stu and Didi, Tommy, the house, and Grandpa. Arlene designed Phil and Lil. The concepts were mine . . . the character descriptions, who they were. I named the main character. Originally, we called the kid Ollie, and I changed his name to Tom, 'cause

I didn't like Ollie. . . . I wrote up what the characters were going to be, how the show was going to work, at least for the pilot. . . . I wrote all that up without looking at any artwork. I just said it's gonna be about this little baby who talks when nobody's looking, and gets into mischief, and unlocks his crib with a screwdriver and gets out . . . the two parents [are] oblivious–they're yuppies, always worried about their yuppie things; they think they're being good parents but they're oblivious. Which is, incidentally, kind of a Nickelodeon theme: generally, your parents are stupid, they don't know what they're doing; *you're* the one who knows."

Detail from a model sheet of Rugrats' *Phil and Lil, showing rotations from an overhead angle–making the babies look even shorter.*

Vanessa Coffey and the network were actively involved in the development of *Rugrats*. "I *wanted* some designs that didn't look normal," she says today. When they came back with Csupo and Klasky's characters, Coffey says, "I loved them. The only change I had was Chuckie's legs were too long. I had them shorten Chuckie's legs so that he seemed more vulnerable. Initially, he was taller."

The Klasky Csupo crew then spent months assembling a six-minute *Rugrats* pilot. Quite a few artists and animators from *The Simpsons* helped design and bring it to life, including David Silverman, Wes Archer, Ken Bruce, Teale Wang, and Gyorgyi Peluce. Germain explains, "In the pilot, which has never been broadcast, we had Tommy, Phil, and Lil. Chuckie and Angelica did not exist yet. We had Stu and Didi, and Grandpa, and the dog. And then, there were some peripheral characters who didn't come back, who you just saw in the background but didn't have any lines." The pilot was almost silent, with just a small amount of dialogue. Its director and lead animator was Peter Chung, who went on to create *Æon Flux* for MTV a year or so later. "He's brilliant . . . he animated it and refined the characters. Chung could do perspective changes and things like that, which are now done in computer . . . but he was doing 'em in cel. Gabor brought him in to direct the pilot, and I kind of sat over him, driving him nuts, because I wanted the story to be a certain way."

As for the story, Germain struggled to come up with an idea that would set the right tone for the series. The answer came from *Simpsons* producer Margot Pipkin and her husband, Ben Herndon. "I thought it was a perfect idea," Germain says. "Ben and Margot remembered that their nieces and nephews were always attracted, when they were little, to the toilet. It seemed like it was alive and it was talking . . . they'd hear it burbling and they'd say, 'That toilet's burping, it wants to talk to me,' and they were always wanting to explore the toilet. I thought, 'God, that's perfect!' We knew the pilot was going to be tested . . . and that level of just vaguely, vaguely *naughty* was going to be exactly the right tone for the show. So Ben Herndon and I wrote the pilot together ['Tommy Pickles and the Great White Thing']. Ben didn't stay with the show . . . but he wrote an episode or two when we went to series."

When the pilot was finished, they took it to Nickelodeon. Vanessa Coffey began showing it to focus groups–and it tested through the roof. The following summer, Klasky Csupo was given the green light to go ahead with production, and Paul Germain hired *Rugrats'* first story editor, Craig Bartlett. They needed twenty-six episodes, each eleven minutes long. Bartlett and Germain wrote the first few together, bringing in Germain's film-school pals, Steve Viksen and Joe Ansolabehere, for work on others. Additional writers included Mike Ferris (who'd written the features *The Game* and *The Net*, among others), Peter Gaffney, and Jon Greenberg. "They were just brilliant writers," Germain raves.

In fact, Joe Ansolabehere and Steve Viksen were so good that, when Bartlett left the show–he went on to create *Hey Arnold*, also for Nickelodeon–Germain offered them positions as story editors for the second season. (Joe took up the offer; Steve didn't.) "In the first season, Joe wrote some of the best episodes," Germain recalls. "I'd say the breakthrough episodes that really determined how this series was going to work, what the stories were gonna be like, that was Joe and Steve."

Paul Germain was a very active, hands-on producer–"a total pain-in-the-ass micromanager," is how he puts it. "I was the show runner. I oversaw all the scripts, I directed all the voices, I cut the voice tracks, I oversaw storyboards, I would cut the animatics. At first, we did them on videotape, and then, pretty quickly, we went over to computers. We edited them together, then they'd be timed . . . and then they'd be sent overseas. They'd come back and I'd edit the hell out of them, until I got 'em as close to being what I wanted as I could. And then I posted them." During the final edit sessions, Germain worked with composer Mark Mothersbaugh and his protégé Dennis Hannigan: "I would tell them exactly what I wanted with the music . . . and then go over the effects and we'd mix 'em right there in the studio. Gabor and I put together a mixing stage so we could actually mix the shows there. So we did everything in-house, which was great."

On August 11, 1991, *Rugrats* was launched, sandwiched right in between *Doug* and *Ren & Stimpy*. *TV Guide* described the show as, "An animated view from down underfoot is provided by Tommy Pickles and several other diaper-clad tots, who journey into the grown-up world." Originally planned as a Saturday morning block by the network, Nickelodeon president Gerry Laybourne decided to air them a day later for a very specific reason: "Counterprogramming," Coffey says. "'Cause nobody had cartoons on Sunday morning. It was the biggest launch in Nickelodeon's history, and the biggest financial commitment that they had ever made."

It took a while to catch on, but *Rugrats* steadily grew in popularity, both with audiences and the show's staff. "The crew loved what they were

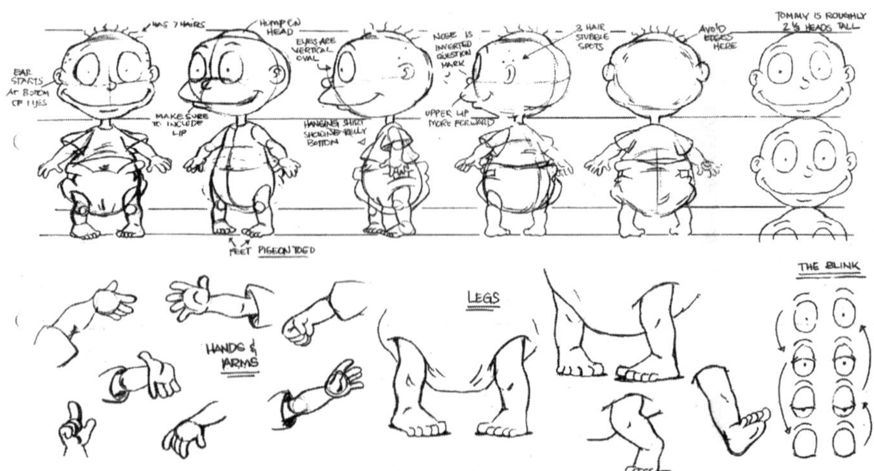

An expressive model sheet of Tommy, with lots of detail on how to correctly draw his limbs.

doing," Germain says. And the writers' different styles really came through in each of the episodes: "If you watch *Rugrats*, there's this incredible feeling of variety. You watch different shows, and they take you in different directions. I mean, they have a consistency to them . . . but they also have the individual sensibilities of all these writers."

Germain is proud that he was able to co-create a cartoon series featuring babies, without it ever feeling too soft. "I wanted it to be kinda hard-edged," he explains. "I said, 'Look, babies are cute as it is. Let's fight the cuteness and try to work *away* from it. Which, I think, is why the show works. That was a real concrete decision on the part of the writing staff, and on the part of Nickelodeon, who loved it. They never called us and said, 'This is too harsh, don't do this or that.'"

The producer saw the series through its first classic run of sixty-five episodes before leaving Klasky Csupo. "I oversaw all sixty-five half hours, at least through the writing . . . the last few, I'd gotten into a dispute with Gabor and Arlene and I finally left the show. But, by the time I left, I had recorded the sixty-fifth episode. So I consider myself there for all sixty-five."

The network decided in 1994 to start airing *Rugrats* repeats in prime time, which sent its ratings soaring. "It was always kind of semi-successful, kind of a low-key success," Gabor Csupo acknowledges. "But it didn't break out big-time immediately. It was just, all the kids kind of liked it . . . and we always thought that parents kind of like it when they sit with their kids . . . but when they put it on *every day*, syndicated on their own network, that's when kids really got into it. That was just, like, a really great surprise."

The series resumed production a few years later–without the participation of Paul Germain. In 1998, the first theatrical feature based on the popular series, *The Rugrats Movie*, was released, followed up with *Rugrats in Paris: The Movie* (2000). Both were phenomenally successful. As for Germain, he moved on with former *Rugrats* scribe Joe Ansolabehere to create another popular series, *Recess*, for the Disney Channel in 1997.

WHO P-P-P-PRODUCED ROGER RABBIT?

Don Hahn is widely considered one of the top producers in the animation world. A quick glance at his knockout résumé reveals *Beauty and the Beast* (1991), *The Lion King* (1994), *The Hunchback of Notre Dame* (1996), and *The Emperor's New Groove* (2000) as some of the Disney feature films he guided to completion. Along the way, the man has earned the respect and undying devotion of practically everyone who's ever worked for him.

The Lion King's story head, Brenda Chapman, says of Hahn, "He has this wonderful way of . . . always being in there, and just sort of coming up with ideas with you, but you never feel like he's thinking, 'I'm the producer, so I get the final say around here.' He's *very* collaborative, he's very soft-spoken, but, boy, he gets the job done. He is, bar none, one of the best producers in the business. He's amazing."

Don Hahn worked his way up the ladder at Disney in the most unassuming manner, starting there with a summer job in 1976 when he was just twenty years old. "I always loved Disney. . . . I was still going to college at Cal State Northridge, and the studio at that time was a very interesting place. It was a little bit of a country club atmosphere, a very family-run studio," he remembers. "The guys who had worked with Walt were all still there. Frank Thomas and Ollie Johnston were animating on *The Rescuers* (1977), and Milt Kahl was there . . . John Lounsbery, and Eric Larson, and Don Griffith, and Ken Anderson–all those guys still came to work in the morning. And my first job was to deliver scenes to them, because I worked in the animation research library, or 'the morgue,' as it was called back then. Someone would call up and say, 'Ken Anderson wants a package of story sketches from *One Hundred and One Dalmatians*,' so I would go up to Ken's room and get to say 'hi' to Ken Anderson. Or I would go up to Milt's room and say 'hi' to Milt."

During the ensuing years, Hahn moved through a variety of assignments at the studio, learning as he went along. "I just kind of bummed around between cleanup, rough in-betweening, and production management–those three things. You would think I had some big nefarious plan, but I was just a little kid from Bellflower, and I was honestly quite happy just to have a job at the studio. And we were working really hard–I worked on *Pete's Dragon* (1977). We had ninety-hour weeks a lot of times trying to get that movie done."

The cutthroat competitiveness one might ascribe to a typical movie producer did not apply to Hahn. Ambition, maybe. Genuine enthusiasm, definitely: "I always thought, y'know, if I keep my head down and try to do a good job, I'll be able to excel and go on to do other things. I worked on a couple of movies as a cleanup artist, and I have some animation scenes in films like *Mickey's Christmas Carol* (1983) . . . but I realized pretty early on that I wasn't [a natural animator like] Glen Keane or Andreas Deja, and that my real love was working with people. I loved working with people. I loved the variety of producing. Of course, it wasn't till a full ten years later that I got a first chance of producing something, and that was *Roger Rabbit*."

Big-Shot Toon Producer

Don Hahn ended up as associate producer of *Who Framed Roger Rabbit* (1988), and helped to kick off animation's modern renaissance–almost by happenstance. It began when Steven Spielberg expressed interest in producing the film, which had been knocking around for a few years at Disney with no real momentum. What's more, Bob Zemeckis, fresh off his huge hit, *Back to the Future* (1985), wanted to direct. "It really took off when Zemeckis got interested in it. And the studio wanted to work with Spielberg, so I think those two elements brought it together. It couldn't have gotten done without Steven because he and [co-producers] Frank Marshall and Kathleen Kennedy helped pull together all the Warner Bros. characters, and the Tom and Jerrys, and all the other characters that played cameo roles in the film."

The brand-new head of animation at Disney, Peter Schneider, had taken the call from Amblin Entertainment and was heading over there for a meeting. "Peter was just off the Olympic Arts Festival Committee, and didn't know much about animation, and he said, 'Okay, who here knows about live-action/animation combination movies?'"

Hahn, who'd worked on *Pete's Dragon* years earlier, chimed in, "Well, y'know, *I* do." So Schneider took Hahn with him. "And about–gosh, three weeks later," muses Hahn, "I was on a plane to London to meet with [animation director] Richard Williams and Bob Zemeckis and start setting up shop in Richard's studio to do the early tests on *Roger Rabbit*!"

There were many producers credited for the film: Spielberg and Kathleen Kennedy executive produced, while Robert Watts and Frank Marshall were the overall live-action producers. Then, there were two associate producers of *Roger Rabbit*. As Don Hahn explains it, "Steve Starkey, who went on to do *Forrest Gump* and *Contact*, was the associate producer along with me. Steve was kind of riding herd on the West Coast, and I was riding herd in London. So I produced the animation, basically. And even though we went to the set, I was all about Richard Williams getting the animation done. So it was truly a first break for me to be able to do that. To say I produced the animation on *Roger Rabbit* was a great thing, and, in the end, got me the *Beauty and the Beast* movie."

Although Hahn had never produced a feature film before, he says he felt fairly confident that he could handle the assignment. "I had a lot of experience in animation, and I had, at that point, ten years of knowing where the bodies were buried. . . . I knew where the artists were, I knew the process . . . and I knew enough to be able to contribute a big missing piece of the puzzle on that film. What I *didn't* know, 'cause I was just a young'un, was how to deal with the larger issues of making a movie of that scale."

Brenda Chapman and Sue Nichols (left and right) flank producer Don Hahn at the wrap party for Disney's Beauty and the Beast.

What made it particularly daunting was the way the production was spread out all over the place. Most of the live-action scenes of *Who Framed Roger Rabbit* were being shot in London, with some exteriors shot in L.A. The optical effects marrying the live footage with the animation were being handled by Industrial Light & Magic in San Francisco. And Disney (also in L.A.) was dealing with an outside company–Richard Williams in London–for the animation. "Basically, we set up from scratch," Hahn recounts. "I showed up with a suitcase in my hand, and we grabbed Dick Williams' animators and went to a warehouse in Camden Town, and built up a studio from scratch. We built desks, and a production room, and all that–and that was *overwhelming*."

Next, Hahn needed to come up with a crew: "The old axiom about producing is, *you hire the best people you can, and then do exactly what they tell you*. Or the other one is: *Make yourself the dumbest guy on the set*. Which is basically saying the same thing . . . you just surround yourself with great people." Hahn knew he could fly a few animators in from Los Angeles, but then there were the other *hundred* or so he'd need in addition. How, he wondered, would he find such a large crew?

They decided to literally advertise the positions–in newspapers, as well as in animation and art journals. "You have to remember," notes Hahn, "at the time it wasn't like it has been over the last fifteen years, where it's just been a boom in animation. Back then, there wasn't a lot going on." They ran ads on both continents–in Europe, Canada, and New York. The turnout included a small handful of talents–including Tom Sito–who passed the word on to their willing and able peers. "By kind of playing a game of 'telephone,'" says Hahn, "we were able to piece the crew together."

The total London staff reached about two hundred at the height of production: "A real gypsy crew of animators. A lot of them came from Canada, some from France, Spain, Germany, Italy, a lot of English, obviously . . . it was a real United Nations animation group. And a lot of those people–like the Nik Ranieris or the James Baxters–are people who are still in the industry, and turned out to be these real senior leaders . . . Andreas Deja was over there, and Simon Wells, who later turned into a live-action director."

The animation studio was being pulled together even as Bob Zemeckis was directing the live action, starring Bob Hoskins as gumshoe Eddie Valiant and Christopher Lloyd as his nemesis, the evil Judge Doom. So Don Hahn had to at once keep his eye on both sides of the London production.

A few of the animators would occasionally venture onto the set, as well. Andreas Deja still cracks up recalling an incident he witnessed during shooting one day: Valiant, Roger Rabbit, and Judge Doom were part of the scene. So, naturally, the actors were talking to thin air. Charlie Fleischer (Roger's voice) was present–he wouldn't be in the shot, of course; he was just there for rehearsing, and to feed them lines–wearing floppy rabbit ears, and a silly, slapdash costume . . . sort of halfway made up to look like the rabbit, merely for fun. "I remember there were some construction people who helped with the set," Deja says. "They were outside, and I overheard a brief conversation. One said, 'Yeah, this is gonna be the new Spielberg/Disney film . . . something about a rabbit, Roger Rabbit.' And he said, 'You know what? It's gonna be awful! I just saw the rabbit down there; it's *terrible*!' They thought it was the real thing!"

One of Don Hahn's daily routines was to pick up Dick Williams each morning, have coffee, and drive out to the set at Elstree Studios. Zemeckis and Williams worked closely together, conferring over details, planning shots. "It was definitely collaborative," Hahn says. "I think Bob knew that he needed a visionary guy from the animation point, and when he found Dick he was really happy. He knew that Dick knew all the old Tex Avery and Bob Clampett cartoons like the back of his hand, but he also knew that he would have some great ideas about how to design the characters and how to stage them . . . the collaboration was really good. They got along great."

The co-directors would go through the live action together, after it had been edited, with Williams rendering quick drawings for each and every shot, essentially creating a storyboard. Hahn recounts Williams' effort: "They would look at the movie, which was almost an 'Invisible Man' movie, and he would sit down and say, 'Okay, Roger [will be] in this drawer here, so this is what it should look like.' And he would do a little sketch. For every shot, every one of the 850 shots in the movie, we have a Richard Williams sketch of what that should look like. And where Roger was, and where Jessica was. And how tall they were in the frame, and what that looked like. And *that* was the bible."

When Williams had to assign a scene to an animator, he would just go to a shelf, pull out a sketch from when he'd sat with Bob Zemeckis, and explain it in full detail, using the drawing as their guide. Hahn explains that the system wasn't all that different from other animation/live-action features, like *Mary Poppins* or *Pete's Dragon* . . . with one major exception: Zemeckis' camera moved all over the place. Which meant that, for the first time in a film of this nature, the animators couldn't simply draw against a stationary background; they had to account for the moving image and keep the characters in corresponding motion. "The mechanical process of making photostats from film, and then drawing on top of them, and then shooting it and re-compositing it, was all the same," Hahn notes. It was just more difficult and more expensive.

This, of course, meant *lots* of extra work for the animators: "Loved the movie, hated the job," says Brenda Chapman, who worked on *Who Framed Roger Rabbit* as a cleanup artist. "I had to clean up the Weasels chasing Benny the Cab. I was trying to hook up their feet to the oil spots in the live action, just so that they wouldn't float around. Because the camera was never still, you had to find something to anchor them to–so you'd look for oil spots on the road, or anything, in the photostats. It was driving me crazy."

Breaking this taboo against the moving camera turned out to be a brilliant decision–making *Who Framed Roger Rabbit* an unprecedented masterpiece combining live action and toon action. "Actually, it was Richard Williams who said, 'No, you gotta throw all those ideas out and just make your movie, and we'll follow you up.' And so Zemeckis did that, and I think that's what made the movie so special," Hahn says. "For years, people were afraid of moving the camera . . . and of the interaction of toons and live-action props or characters. And what *Roger Rabbit* did was kind of toss all that on its ear, and say, 'Well, no, what makes it good is that Roger walks in, and knocks over a chair or a lamp, and it's *very* interactive–and the camera always moves.' *That's* what makes you believe that those characters exist in that setting."

As for the story, Hahn says it changed a lot along the way. Although screenwriters Jeffrey Price and Peter Seaman made major adjustments from the source material, Gary K. Wolf's original novel, *Who Censored Roger Rabbit?* (see chapter 1), the main characters, and the story's dark undertones were retained. "It's a film noir detective movie, so it had to have some of that *mysterioso* kind of quality to it," the producer feels. "But I think, story-wise, it was pretty fearless, set against Los Angeles and the red cars and all that, in a really interesting way." While Price and Seaman revised the script, story artists Joe Ranft and Hans Bocher worked on the boards–an effective, collaborative team effort, notes Hahn.

In fact, the production only suffered one major meltdown that he can recall. In the fall of 1987, Jeffrey Katzenberg noticed things weren't coming together on time. He called "a summit," recounts Hahn. "I flew with Robert Watts and Dick from London, and all the West Coast people flew out to New York, and we met in the Disney offices with everybody: Bob, and Frank Marshall, everybody," for a roundtable gathering to discuss the problems with production. (The story and other details weren't under fire, since Spielberg was at the creative helm of the project.) "So, on a business level, Jeffrey was just saying, 'All of our butts are on the line here. I've never had my neck stuck out so far in my life, and the movie has to get done.' That meeting was the big turning point. From then on, it was actually much, much better. Because Jeffrey would come over more frequently, make one-day trips over to London. . . . Bob Zemeckis would come over more frequently. We had daily phone calls where I called up Bob and told him how things were going on a daily basis."

The fact is, they were all still feeling their way through the process, as none of them at that roundtable, with the exception of Dick Williams (*Raggedy Ann and Andy* in 1977), had made an animated feature before. "They were working on *Little Mermaid*, and *Oliver & Company*, all those movies, but they were only in the dream phase," Hahn asserts. "This was kind of the first of that whole line of movies."

Then came the test screenings before live audiences, which turned out to be a debacle. "At the early screenings you think, 'Oh, God, is anybody gonna go see this?' A lot of it wasn't in color, so people couldn't read the pencil tests. Now you have a fairly literate audience that, over fifteen years, understands how animation is made. Then, it was in black and white, and some of the animation wasn't done. And the animation that *was* done hadn't been painted yet. People just said, 'What the hell is this? A rabbit gets framed for murder?'"

Hahn was present at one of the test screenings where people actually walked out in the middle. Quietly, he says, the producers flipped out. "It was disastrous. But the other thing, though, is you know you have to finish the movie and you have to believe in the material. For the *worst* screening, I wasn't there. I was in London finishing the movie . . . and it was back here [in L.A.]. Everybody just huddled afterwards and said, 'Y'know, if anyone asks us how this screening went, we're all gonna say it went spectacularly well, and we're never gonna let word leave this room.' So we all put our heads down and just finished the movie–and it worked out okay."

When all was said and done, *Who Framed Roger Rabbit* was one of the most fulfilling experiences of Hahn's career. "A lot of us cut our teeth on that film in a number of ways. And it was great–y'know, the fact that we got *through* it," he laughs. "It was a very difficult movie, on a very short schedule, yet if you talk to people that worked on it, most all of them will say it was one of the high points in their lives, just because it was one of those great times when you all got thrown together with what turned out to be some really brilliant guys. Certainly Zemeckis was, certainly Richard Williams was, and it's what made the movie great."

Who Framed Roger Rabbit was the first blockbuster Disney toon in years, even if, technically, it was also half live action. As Don Hahn observes, it marked a turning point in how audiences perceived animation: suddenly, it wasn't just for kids anymore: "If you remember before that, it was, 'Well, *maybe* I'll take my kids by the theater to see *Fox and the Hound* or *Rescuers*, and maybe I'll go with them, but I won't enjoy it that much.' Because *Roger Rabbit* put a kind of funny, irreverent spin on the whole world of toons and animation, it was a huge box office hit for its day. . . . People went on dates, and adults went and took their kids, and it was kind of the first thing where people went, 'Y'know, I *love* animation!' And then we were lucky enough to follow that up with the *Mermaid*s and the *Beauty*s and other films after that."

While Hahn was packing up the London studio, he got a call from Katzenberg and Peter Schneider. "We wanna do *Beauty and the Beast*, and we want you to produce it," they told him. Of course, he took the assignment. *Beauty and the Beast* went on to become the first animated motion picture to garner an Oscar nomination for Best Picture–a feat Hahn followed by producing *The Lion King*, which became Disney's biggest hit, ever.

Not bad for a little kid from Bellflower.

CHAPTER 9
WHO SAID THAT?!
The Art of Giving Voice to Cartoon Characters

"While recording Sylvester cartoons, my scripts would get so covered with saliva I'd repeatedly have to wipe them clean."

—Mel Blanc, voice of Sylvester the Cat (1988)

There are actors who've given the most brilliant performances of their careers, all for the privilege of hearing the words emerge from the mouth of a rooster. Or a Chihuahua, or a flying squirrel. When performers do voice work for cartoons, they get to portray a wide range of roles–people, ghosts, ogres, genies, stupid cats, wily coyotes, jabbering donkeys, homicidal monkeys, and even talking teapots and candlesticks. They never have to memorize their lines, and, if they're having a bad hair day, well, who cares?

However, ask most of them if it's an easy job, and they'll tell you that doing voice-overs is hard work–sometimes harder than performing live in front of an audience or camera. As *Shrek* co-director Andrew Adamson points out, "I think it's very challenging for an actor–particularly a comedian–to not have other actors to play off, or an audience to play off." Of Mike Myers, who voiced Shrek, he says, "He'd done a lot of stand-up before, and to suddenly be in a room where he would just see us through the glass, y'know, maybe we'd be laughing but he wouldn't *hear* that . . . it's very challenging."

Of course, it wasn't always like that. Back when radio was still in its heyday, and even afterwards, many cartoons were still recorded with more than one actor in the booth. They could develop chemistry, play off one another. These days, it's much more common for each individual performer to record his or her lines separately, after which everything will be cut together as seamlessly as possible.

But getting a great performance out of an animated character is still a hugely collaborative endeavor. In the recording studio, a voice director does what he or she can to help the actor "see" the scene. "You show many visuals, you describe the scene as much as possible," Adamson goes on. "You don't have that wonderful thing that happens in live action, where they walk onto a set in a period costume and it helps them get into character. You don't have that, so you have to help them find other ways."

Later on, of course, the animator can take his cue from the voice artist's recording to create a subtle physical portrayal. Some studios like to videotape their performers during recording sessions, allowing the animator to reference and incorporate facial expressions or particular body language, if they feel it's helpful. On a TV series, the animation is usually more stylized and limited in movement, so the vocal performance has to do a lot more of the work. Jay Ward Productions' witty, pun-filled *Rocky and His Friends* (1959) is a great example of a toon that hardly moved at all–reportedly, about four drawings per second, instead of the usual twelve–but is as beloved as anything that ever hit the tube. *Simpsons* creator Matt Groening once put it succinctly: "I'm a huge fan of Rocky and Bullwinkle. What was great about that show was not the animation, which was terrible. It had great writing, great music, and great voices. And, I think, if you have that combination, the animation can be clunky."[1]

While the media spotlight is often focused on star turns by famous movie and TV names, the lion's share of toon voice work is still performed by skilled, professional voice-over actors; people like Christine Cavanaugh (*Rugrats*), Tom Kenny (*SpongeBob SquarePants*), Nancy Cartwright (*The Simpsons*), Will Ryan (*The Little Mermaid*), Jim Cummings (*The Lion King*), Tara Strong (*Powerpuff Girls*), Marty Grabstein (*Courage the Cowardly Dog*), and others. One performer–despite her modest physical stature–stands head and shoulders above the pack . . .

JUNE'S FORAY TO FAME

The Queen of All Voice Artists

A huge part of the aforementioned *Rocky and Bullwinkle*'s success was June Foray, the undisputed doyenne of animation voice-over work. Today, she's a living–and still working–legend, who gave voice not only to Rocky the Flying Squirrel and the ultraglam Russian spy, Natasha Fatale, but to practically every female character (and some of the males) in that series, as well.

June Foray has performed hundreds of voices over the years, starting off doing feline effects as the evil Lucifer the Cat in Walt Disney's

Cinderella (1950) and moving on to memorable roles like sweet old Granny in the classic Tweety and Sylvester cartoons for Warner Bros., Bugs Bunny's gleeful nemesis, Witch Hazel–the scraggly old crone who'd leave a mass of swirling hairpins in her wake every time she dashed off screen, wide-eyed young Cindy Lou Who in Chuck Jones' acclaimed Dr. Seuss TV special, *How the Grinch Stole Christmas* (1966), curvaceous Ursula on Jay Ward's *George of the Jungle* (1967), perennial damsel-in-distress Nell Fenwick in Ward's *Dudley Do-Right* (1969), the School Teacher in the classic *Frosty the Snowman* TV special (1969), plucky Grandmother Fa in Disney's *Mulan* (1998), and even a reprise as Rocky in the feature-length *The Adventures of Rocky and Bullwinkle* (2000).

Ask her which character is her favorite out of all the voices she's performed, and she'll coyly offer, "I love all the characters I did, and I still do." But surely, she must favor *one* over another? "I know that the public says Rocky. I love Rocky and Bullwinkle. . . . I'm obviously partial to them," she confesses, "because it was so brilliant and wonderfully done. But there's a little bit of me in all the characters I've done, whether they're evil, or [good]." The fact is, June Foray can barely go anywhere these days without someone beseeching her to say a line or two as Rocky–usually his famous line, "That trick *never* works!" from one of the show's amusing bumpers.

Two of Foray's most famous voices: nogoodnick Pottsylvanian spy, Natasha Fatale, and our flying hero, Rocket J. Squirrel.

The adventures of the plucky squirrel and the genial moose aired on ABC for about two years, before being picked up by NBC in 1961 to run in prime time. "It was *Rocky and His Friends* when we first started, but then NBC didn't want that–so that's when they changed it to *The Bullwinkle Show*," she explains, noting dryly that "it was the same show."

Unlike so many feature films and TV series today, where each individual voice-over is recorded separately and then cut together to form a scene, *Rocky and His*

Friends was performed as an ensemble, with the four principals often doing several different voices within the same recording session. The fact that Bill Scott (Bullwinkle), Paul Frees (Boris Badenov), Daws Butler (assorted characters), and June Foray were all such versatile veterans of live radio had a lot to do with their chemistry. These were actors who were used to picking up a script, reading through it once, and then going out on stage to perform a show in front of a live audience.

The result was a loose, freewheeling voice track, where everyone played off one another–and, sometimes, off themselves. Foray recalls one recording session in particular where she played three characters in the same scene: a princess, a fairy godmother, and a loudmouthed old woman. By the time the session was over, she laughs, "I would walk out talking to myself." And how did she keep from getting mixed up when performing so many parts in the same scene? Different colored pencils to highlight each character's lines–Rocky's in blue, Natasha's in red, and so on.

Working on *Rocky and Bullwinkle* was "like a party," Foray says, "with a lot of jokes and a lot of fun." And, perhaps surprisingly, with hardly any improvisation. "There was no ad libbing at all," she states. "Those scripts were so beautifully written, how could you ad lib? The only time, maybe, I'd ad lib was to say 'Hokey Smoke' every so often, just to be different."

It was always a joy for her, she claims, never a chore. As she told *Animato! Magazine* in a 1994 interview: "The writing, the stories, the satire, the conception, the acting, the direction . . . it was very intelligent, very sophisticated. We offended sports stars, congressmen . . . but all the time, it was gentle, friendly satire. Nothing cruel. I look at my time there and I can say, with a fair amount of certainty, that this was the zenith, this was the high-water mark of my career. The Warners cartoons were great, too, but the techniques they used for recording voices didn't allow for the interplay between the actors. The rapid delivery was just incredible. It couldn't have been done line by line." As Foray points out, because the scripts "were recorded very quickly, when they came to you for your line, you had to be ready"–and they usually had to get it in one take. Daws Butler once remarked, "Working in that company was like getting to play for the Yankees at the top of their game. And June was Mickey Mantle, only cuter."

The merry ringleaders of this talented bunch were creator/producer Jay Ward and Bill Scott, who not only did Bullwinkle's famous voice (as well as Fearless Leader, Mr. Big, and many others on the show), but was also the head writer and co-producer at the same time. He presided over a dazzling group of scribes–George Atkins, Allan Burns, Jim Critchfield,

The big three who brought Rocky and Bullwinkle *to life: good friends Jay Ward, June Foray, and Bill Scott.*

Chris Hayward, Chris Jenkyns, Jim MacGeorge (also a prolific voice artist), John Marshall, Paul Mazursky, Jack Mendelsohn, Larry Tucker, and Lloyd Turner–many of whom went on to create or write such classic sitcoms as *Mary Tyler Moore, Rhoda, Taxi, Barney Miller, Get Smart,* and *Maude.* With a talent pool that dense, the writing on the show was head and shoulders above most cartoon scripting, often bursting with wicked punnery and tongue-in-cheek irony.

"Those scripts were so sophisticated and hilarious," June gushes. And even though they lampooned the Cold War and other targets of their day, most of the episodes still hold up well. What she misses most about the whole *Rocky and Bullwinkle* experience: "The love for each other. We loved Bill, and Jay . . . always laughing heartily . . . never any altercations of any kind. It was fun just going to the set . . . and going to their homes. We were dear friends–together for so many years. After we did *The Bullwinkle Show*, we did all the Cap'n Crunch commercials, and all the other commercials."

Looking over the rest of her oeuvre, June Foray's funniest characterization might well be Witch Hazel, who appeared in a handful of Warner Bros. cartoons, including "Bewitched Bunny," "Broom-Stick Bunny," "A Witch's Tangled Hare," and "A-Haunting We Will Go." A mad, cackling hag who embraces her own ugliness, Witch Hazel revels in backhanded compliments ("Tell me now, who undoes your hair? It's absolutely hideous!"). As Foray explains, "I made her *funny*–I didn't make her mean." And that insane cackle . . . Foray's witch cackle is so distinctive, to this day, many voice casting agents report that they rarely hear a female demo tape that doesn't include some approximation of a June Foray witch voice. Amazingly, she'd played *another* cartoon crone–also named Witch Hazel–in Disney's Donald Duck short, "Trick or Treat" (1952), before Chuck

Jones brought her over to Warner Bros. to voice his own witch. "Disney couldn't copyright [the name], 'cause there's an alcohol rub called Witch Hazel," she notes.

Foray has been performing for over half a century now. Most actors can only dream of that kind of career longevity. When she began working, and throughout much of her early career, voice artists rarely, if ever, received screen credit for their contributions. That practice continued for years–until one man finally broke the trend: "Walter Lantz," she relates, in his *Woody Woodpecker* cartoons. "He gave all the actors screen credit, whereas nobody else ever did. I mean, you don't know who [voiced] *Sleeping Beauty* . . . unless you're in the business. Then, you know Pinto Colvig did Goofy, and so on." Nevertheless, she insists that she didn't let the practice bother her too much at the time, for one simple reason: "I was *working*."

A 1991 model sheet of Warner Bros.' classic crone, Witch Hazel, indelibly voiced by June Foray. TM and © Warner Bros.

Clearly, she loves what she does. And, as far as she's concerned, there are distinct advantages to voice work. "The great thing about doing voice-overs is that you don't spend too much time. And, when you get it right," she muses, "they don't make you do it again!" She admits that she usually knows what she wants to do, anyway, and doesn't rely too heavily on a director's guidance. Has she ever been at odds with a director over line delivery, or how a character should sound? "Many times. But I'll say something . . . and, if they still *insist*, I'll do it [their way]," she smiles, "because they're paying me. But I'm easy to get along with, and I don't like to be contentious."

As one of the many animation directors who've experienced the pleasure of working with her, I can confirm that June Foray's technique is flawless. For each line in the script, she'll perform three consecutive readings with just a short pause in between. Each is slightly different, yet perfect in its own right. It makes selecting your favorite take a bit harder sometimes, but we should all have such problems.

SOMETHING WICKED THIS WAY SLIMES

The Malevolent Tones of Ursula

Animated Disney features have a long-standing tradition of depicting classic scoundrels, but none have been so unsettling as their female villains. Perhaps it stems from our expectations of nurturing, comfort, and honesty from our mothers. When those expectations are betrayed, they horrify us all the more: The vain, evil Queen in *Snow White and the Seven Dwarfs*, *Cinderella*'s malicious stepmother, Lady Tremaine, the icily wicked fairy Maleficent in *Sleeping Beauty*–all women who chilled us to our marrow. *One Hundred and One Dalmatians'* flamboyant Cruella De Vil was both frightening and hilarious. And, in 1989, *The Little Mermaid* presented us with Ursula the sea witch, brought to life by animator Ruben Aquino as a delectably dark addition to Disney's pantheon of villainy.

Pat Carroll, veteran stage and screen actress, was completely oblivious to the studio's difficulties in attempting to cast Ursula. The film's creators had gone through dozens and dozens of auditions for the vengeful sea witch, searching for just the right performer who could put across the deep-voiced, world weary, deadpan villainess they had in mind–but never quite snaring their catch (see chapter 2 for more). Carroll had simply received a phone call from her agent one day, asking if she'd be open to the idea of auditioning.

When he told her it was for a new animated Disney feature, she jumped at the opportunity–it was one of her lifelong goals. "After I read the script, I thought, 'Oh, this is going to be so wonderful . . . and then, I heard the music and thought, 'Oh my God, that's like a Broadway score!' So I went out to the studio, and looked around the room at all of us ladies . . . there were ladies I recognized from film, there were ladies I recognized from television . . . it was a highly sought-after job. And in New York, they were doing the same thing. So I knew I was one of many. . . . This was not, 'Oh, we must get Pat Carroll.'"

As she recalls it, both her spoken and singing auditions went well. And that was the last she heard from anyone on the subject . . . until a full year later, when her agent called to congratulate her for getting the Disney film. "I said, '*What* Disney film?' Come on, it was a year later! I'd done a lot of things in the meantime. Can you believe that–I didn't even know what the hell he was talking about! Y'know, you finish your audition, you go away, you do other stuff. It's like fishing: You bait the pole, you stick it in, you never know if you'll get a bite or not. Any other way, and you'd end up in a crazy house! And that's all you can do."

Veteran stage and screen actress Pat Carroll, voice of evil Ursula, the sea witch, in The Little Mermaid.

After some time spent walking around in a daze, Carroll joined the other cast members at an L.A. recording studio–one she knew well from all her commercial work. The entire cast, including the New York crowd, was gathered at the space. "I looked around at this group of people and I was gaga," Carroll remembers. "We were surrounded by photographers because it was the first time in the history of the Disney studios that they ever had a read-through with the entire cast! And I know that Howard Ashman and Alan Menken were the ones who were responsible for that, because they were theater men."

The principal players, which included Carroll as Ursula, Jodi Benson as Ariel, Samuel E. Wright as Sebastian, Buddy Hackett as Scuttle, Kenneth Mars as King Triton, and René Auberjonois as the Chef, did the table reading with all the songs . . . but the extraordinary session's audio went undocumented due to a problem with one of the recording devices. "It was done, but there's no record of it," sighs Carroll. "I was so disappointed . . . because I thought, 'Maybe they'll give us copies of this, a historic first in the history of the Disney studios.'"

Some time later, she began recording her part–music first, with "Poor Unfortunate Souls," Ursula's big production number. Session after session involved an additional set of instruments–and a more exacting set of demands. "The first day, it was just Alan accompanying me at the piano. The next session, I went back, there was rhythm. The next session I went back, maybe horns or strings. . . . I think we did over a dozen. And those men were absolutely military in their adherence to what they wanted. Many times, I'd go home with my vocal chords blown. Because you have to do it over and over and over again . . . and I would occasionally have to say, 'Gentlemen, may I take a five-minute break to breathe, and get some water, and just rest.' They'd say, 'Absolutely.' But they were relentless in their pursuit of excellence, and I *adore* working with people like that."

Carroll is quick to point out that many of the embellishments that make Ursula's number so chillingly provocative came from Howard Ashman. Ursula's catchy "innit" in place of "isn't it," for example, was pure Ashman. "I asked, 'Howard, may I use that?' He said, 'Of course, I wished you would!'" These "attitudinal things," as Carroll calls them, often came from the lyricist's own reading of the lines. "I said, 'Y'know, before we do this, would you do the number the way *you* see it and *you* do it?' He did–and I said, 'I got you, Howard. I know exactly what you want.' He *gave* me that performance! Come on, I'm honest enough to say that. I got the whole attitude from him . . . and his shoulders would twitch in a certain way, and his eyes would go a certain way. . . . I got more about that character from Howard singing that song than from anything else."

When she first read the script, Carroll had a distinct image in her mind of how she envisioned the sea witch. "I wanted her to be an ex-Shakespearean actress who now sold cars. It's the attitude . . . the voice was very Shakespearean: *Hello, my dear! Oh, no, dahling.* . . . Very theatrical–but the pitch was a used car salesman. Very, very patently obvious. No subtlety there. She was being unctuous, and oily, and ever so wily . . . but you saw right through her. I'm surprised the kid didn't!" Ariel couldn't–the movie would've ended right there.

Altogether, it took close to two years to record all of Ursula's lines. Because an animated film evolves as production goes on and on, there were many rewrites and adjustments made along the way. Pat Carroll says she gave her commitment to *The Little Mermaid* precedence over all other jobs during that period. "It was a lifelong ambition of mine to do a Disney film," she states. "So I was theirs, hook, line and sinker."

At times, the demands of the performance completely drained her, both physically and mentally. She vividly remembers coming home one night after another long session, completely exhausted. "And I was griping, as actors are wont to do instead of being grateful they're working," she recalls. "My youngest daughter, Tara–who's now an actress and director–said, 'Mom, may I remind you, you're in something that fifty years from now may be shown, and all the work you've done in the theater will have gone by the boards and disappeared. What you're working on now will be seen by our children, and our grandchildren, and our *great*-grandchildren.' I looked at her and I thought, the kid is right. And I said, 'Tara, are you telling me that my grandchildren will only know me as a *squid*?' We both began screaming with laughter, because she knew what I was saying was right."

Sure enough, younger *Little Mermaid* fans still think of Carroll as Ursula the evil sea witch, not as a voice artist with her own name. "Ursula is Ursula. It has nothing to do with *me*. So I always sign pictures–and I'm still getting requests from the little people–'*Dear Sweetlips: I hug you with my tentacles. Oceans of love, Ursula.*' And then, underneath, in parentheses, I put, 'Pat Carroll,' very small. They don't know who this Pat Carroll is, but they do know who Ursula is!"

When the film was finally completed, the actress got to slip into a private screening in New York, to see and hear the entirety of her performance for the first time. As the evil sea witch appeared onscreen, Carroll recalls slinking down into her chair. "Ursula scared the hell out of me. I thought, 'Oh my God, who *is* that?! It's huge and it's wonderful . . . and oh my God, it's scary.' And then, afterwards, I thought, 'I'm going to frighten the hell out of kids. I'm going to be the next Margaret Hamilton!' You know, she was a kindergarten teacher and she adored children. She was *so* scary in *The Wizard of Oz* (1939) . . . and Margaret hated that till the day she died because she adored kids and they were all scared to death of her! Isn't that something?"

Pat Carroll has performed many voices for cartoons aside from *The Little Mermaid*, most notably for several Hanna-Barbera series. "I love it, because it's lovely, clean work. You can show up in your gardening clothes, if you wish, and all that's demanded is from your neck to your jaw. Your voice box, and an operative mind, sometimes."

The energy required, she says, is equal to that of stage work. In fact, it can demand even more energy, since it's up to the voice artist to visualize the toon's surroundings. Plus, all of the character's persona must come through solely in the voice, not in any body language that's going unrecorded. That's what makes a good voice artist successful. "The better your voice is trained," she notes, "the more you can do in that field. You have to have range. It's also very bravura acting, this voice-over stuff. It's very big. So, if you tend to be subtle, it's not the field for you . . . the demands are very loud, and vocal, and in primary colors. But I *love* it, because you can go wilder than you go in front of a camera . . . or wilder than on a stage."

There are also certain very lucky performers, as she points out, who are gifted with markedly different-sounding voices . . . which can be perfect for cartoons. "A certain kind of quirk in their voice is also usable, though they might be limited because of that–but I say, 'Bravo!' Look at that darling man who was in films for so many years, Sterling Holloway. His was a voice that you always recognized [Winnie the Pooh, Kaa in *The Jungle Book*, Mr. Stork in *Dumbo*, etc.]. A very unusual voice, and was it not perfect for those particular characters? That voice was so right for children . . . for the gentleness of it, and the eccentricity of it. It was exactly perfect for what they did with it. Arnold Stang is also instantly recognizable–what a perfect voice he has, because it cuts glass! You know, it's brilliant. And Arnold has used his voice and his persona for years to be a headliner."

As for her work in *The Little Mermaid*, Carroll calls it "the one thing in my life that I'm probably most proud of. I don't even care if, after I'm gone, the only thing I'm associated with is Ursula. That's okay by me, because that's a pretty wonderful character and a pretty marvelous film to be remembered for. And I bless it."

WAY OUT WEST

A Versatile Voice Artist Named Billy

If anyone can be said to have inherited the mantle once worn by voice-over genius Mel Blanc, it would be Billy West. As with Blanc, whether you realize it or not, West's voice is permanently etched into your brain. Ever watch Nickelodeon's *The Ren & Stimpy Show*? Billy West was the voice of Stimpy for the show's entire run, as well as Ren from Season Two on. Catch any of Matt Groening's *Futurama* (Fox, 1999)? West voiced three of the series' main characters: Dr. Zoidberg, Professor Farnsworth, and the twenty-five-year-old pizza delivery boy (and star of the show), Fry. On Nickelodeon's popular series, *Doug* (1991), West was Doug.

West has also performed a staggering array of character voices on shows like *Batman, Catdog, Dilbert, Hey Arnold, Johnny Bravo, King of the Hill, The Oblongs, Pepper Ann, Pinky and the Brain, Sabrina, Scooby-Doo, Toonsylvania, Time Squad, Timon and Pumbaa*, movies like *Joe's Apartment, Rugrats in Paris*, and *Space Jam* (voicing Bugs Bunny and Elmer Fudd), celebrity impersonations and comedy bits on radio's *Howard Stern Show*, scads of TV commercials, and the list just goes on. It all started kicking in for him at a very early age–perhaps at six or seven–and yet, Billy West doesn't believe that this was a profession he actually chose for himself. "At the risk of sounding cliché, I think something like that chooses you," he says. "It's not like you choose it. What would possess you to run around and make noises, glued to the radio, and start singing all the songs that came out of the radio? What makes a kid do that? My world was a sonic world. . . . I wasn't so into the visuals, as I was *hearing* things."

The versatile comedian and voice actor, Billy West.

West was drawn to the sounds of Warner Bros. and Hanna-Barbera cartoons before he could read. And, when he was finally old enough to read the "Voices" credits, he became instantly intrigued by the appearance of one or two names–actors who seemingly supplied all those different voices. "But I never took it seriously," he says, "because people treat you like you're annoying them when you're trying to develop something like that. It's like, if a kid chooses to be a drummer, where does he go to practice without driving everybody shithouse?!"

In school, his natural ability for mimicry led him to indulge in the kind of pranks you'd expect from a kid like that. "We had a shop teacher named Mr. Stuart, and everybody hated him. If you asked him a question, instead of going 'Yup,' he'd go, '*Yawmp . . . Yawmp, yawmp, yawmp, uh-huh, yawmp*.' I used to write it on a piece of paper, and look at it–he said 'Yawmp,' like a Dr. Seuss character . . . I would do those kinda teachers,"

West says. "And the hags. We had a finance teacher. . . . One time, I was sitting there in a quiet, quiet study class, and I was making little noises. She would look up, and then, she'd go back to her books. And then, she'd look up again, and go back to her books. And then, she popped up and went, '*Who's making that noooise? It sounds like something from a swaaaamp! A filthy little creature!*' She was so dramatic–she sounded like [character actor] Joe Flynn."

West was born in Detroit, Michigan, but moved with his family to Boston in 1963. His early dream was to be a musician, not a voice actor, so he performed with his band whenever he could. "But what had been happening onstage throughout all those years, whenever we had a busted amplifier, or somebody broke a string, you had to kill time. So, in those clubs, I wouldn't stand around looking at the floor–I would just start talking to people. I'd start foolin' around with voices and stuff . . . 'cause I was hell-bent on keeping them there. Keeping them entertained. I was afraid they'd just walk away."

West finally gave up music and tried his hand at stand-up comedy. "But nobody told me you hadda have an act. I just said the things I felt like saying, and did the things I felt like doing . . . so I imagine it came off as really abstract. Sometimes it would work . . . and other nights, it would go to hell in a twisted metal fireball." Billy West realized that stand-up comedy wasn't the life for him, either.

His turning point occurred when a buddy helped him snare a job producing WBCN's morning radio show. "It was like a playpen," he recalls fondly. "You could just do anything you wanted back in those days. Radio then was not all so tight and restricted by corporate confines." So, he began writing bits for himself and performing them on air, in many different voices.

West became popular at the station, and says that got him to do some real thinking: He'd heard a few national radio spots, wondered how some of their voice actors had ever gotten hired, and figured he'd take a shot at work on that level, himself.

He and his wife, Violet, moved to New York City and took up residence in a tiny walk-up apartment "in the ass-end of Chinatown." They made the best of it. "I had a feeling that I was headed for something," West remembers. "I just didn't know what it was."

In 1988, he voiced his first cartoon, a revival of *Beany and Cecil* directed by John Kricfalusi. Unfortunately, it only lasted a few episodes before ABC unplugged it. So, West got in touch with an agent in L.A., who set him up on an audition for Barney Rubble in some cereal commercials. "I thought I did pretty well," the actor recalls. "Next thing you know, this agent calls me up and she goes, 'Are you sitting down?' And I go, 'Yeah?' She says 'You got it.' I go, 'What?' She goes, 'You got the part! The Barney Rubble part in these cereal commercials!!!' And I went, 'Oh my God!' I was all excited . . ."

And he never heard from her again. "She never called me back! When I finally called her, she said, 'Well, they decided to go in another direction'—a nice way of saying they just kicked you into a six-foot hole, and now the dirt is over your face. That was my first taste of Hollywood baloney . . . and it didn't taste good. I began to see that there are some people who have no problem with just kinda gliding through everything with no remorse."

So music was out. Stand-up comedy was out. And voice work was starting to look like yet another dead end.

Thankfully, John Kricfalusi and his people hadn't forgotten Billy West's work from *Beany and Cecil*. They called him up to tell him some stuff was on the way. "I thought it was great that they remembered me," beams West. But when the package arrived, its contents baffled him: "It said, 'These are the characters.' Well, honest to God—I didn't know what the hell they were! What're they—mosquitoes? Or microbes? Or maybe they're from, like, outer space? I had no idea that it was a cat and a dog."

The next thing the performer knew, he was starring in a bona fide cartoon cult sensation: *The Ren & Stimpy Show* on Nickelodeon. "The beauty of it was that it's almost Picasso-esque," West muses. "One week, Ren would have little dots on his head, like freckles. And then, another time, he didn't have 'em. These inconsistencies drive some people crazy . . . but I happen to *adore* it when it happens. And I love amalgams of voices—fusions."

For Stimpy's voice, West says he "supercollided" Larry Fine of *The Three Stooges* with something else. Kricfalusi had felt that West's first stab at the voice—which was more Larry Fine than anything else—sounded too much like "a depressed old Jewish guy." The actor told the director that he knew how to handle that. "I pumped it up," he explains, "to where it was childlike—not retarded—just very childlike, but still with a Philly type of accent."

As for Ren Hoek, West had at first been asked to do his voice, as well. It, too, was a supercollision: "Peter Lorre . . . fused with Kirk Douglas' *EMPHATIC DELIVERY*—and he's a Chihuahua, so there's a little south-of-the-border mixed in there . . . it comes and goes . . . and then it starts to sound a little Danish—'cause look at the name, Ren Hoek . . . mixed with the screaming of Burl Ives." When the show kicked into production, however, John K. decided to do Ren's voice himself. Later on in the series' run (once Kricfalusi was gone), West picked up where the creator had left off. "My original demo for Nickelodeon of both characters is probably still around somewhere," West speculates. "We recorded it in a closet at MTV Networks in New York, because we were about to go in and talk to people."

Early on, while he was still living in New York and doing comic bits for Howard Stern's radio program, he didn't have an inkling that *Ren & Stimpy* was taking off into the stratosphere. "The thing started becoming a cult show, and I didn't even know it. I had no idea that people were going *crazy* over it out there. Until, suddenly, I started getting calls from all over the place, from people I knew. And then, suddenly, people like Alan Arkin wanted to know who I was. It was, like, his favorite show! Something clicked . . . and then I knew: I was takin' the *elevator*."

Things really did begin to happen for West from that point on. As he observes, "Madison Avenue watches anything that's popular. And then, suddenly, I'm popular–and they see this cultural cult buzz going on. They even stole the font that *Ren & Stimpy* was written in–that weird, kinda crazy font–it wound up on every cereal box in the United States, it wound up on toy commercials. It meant, 'This means *cool*.' So I was starting to get hired for kids' toy commercials . . . and suddenly, instead of these somber faces that invite you in to audition once they've gone through two hundred guys, it was like, 'When do you wanna come in?' They were starting to accommodate me. I couldn't believe it, honestly."

When West finally moved west, he was warmly received by his peers in Los Angeles. They had heard him on the radio, seen him on TV. Their praise brought him long-awaited redemption, hard-won validation. "I was once told that I would not be a good voice-over person, because I had flaws," he notes. "This was a teacher-type, a pedant, where everything had to have a rule or a formula. And to me, I don't know any of the rules . . . I don't know any of the formulas. I never took voice lessons. I just said, 'This is what I wanna do, and here's how I'm gonna do it, I don't care what anybody says.'"

Perhaps because it took him awhile to reach his goals, all this hasn't bloated the actor's ego. Ask him how he prepares for a role, and he'll tell you he doesn't dwell on it. "It's just a part of my life. My whole life isn't about that stuff, so I think it has a proper perspective, even though I've been tremendously lucky. But I don't think much about it."

West does insist, however, that voice acting is not just a matter of voice. Rather, it's a skill that's refined by an active, intuitive, spontaneous mind. "That's how anybody who creates voices can dial up anything at once–they remember the musicality of the character in their head, their cadence . . .

and the accent, the voice falls right into place. I like spontaneity. . . . I like things to be askew. It causes something, like an energy, that's different . . . You know, if you've barely got it, and you just start messing with it on the spot . . . you'd be surprised what you come up with when you really have to be resourceful."

This doesn't mean that a voice actor has free reign to revamp the script. And by no means does he have the last word. "You *do* have to please a director," cautions West, "and you do have to make the casting person happy. . . . I've never lost respect for that. I love direction, especially if a director is real fussy about what they want. I'll even take line readings–I'm not that important. I pretty much read the words that they tell me. The *important* thing is to be easy to work with. Y'know, just because you can sound like Basil Rathbone doesn't mean you can split the atom!"

West attributes much of his own success today to a practical attitude that he adopted years earlier, back when he was still sneaking out of the radio station to go to auditions. "I believed in the craft, and began to take it seriously," he says. "And I began to notice that, hey, sometimes you don't get the edgy, cutting, cult project. Sometimes, you've gotta do narration, and sometimes, you've gotta do a commercial for a product you don't even buy. But this was equally as important as anything else . . . and you come prepared. It's like being a carpenter–y'know, if you build a doghouse, make sure you bring the right tools and everything you're going to need. And that's how I felt."

Chillin' with Sid

John Leguizamo's Lovable *Ice Age* Sloth

He may have starred in something called *Ice Age*, but John Leguizamo's career has been on fire lately. Winning awards and drawing raves for his sold-out satirical one-man shows *Mambo Mouth*, *Spic-O-Rama*, and *Sexaholix*, making a splash in movies like *Moulin Rouge* (2001), *Summer of Sam* (1999), *Romeo & Juliet* (1996), and *Carlito's Way* (1993), and creating, producing, writing and starring in his own comedy TV series, *House of Buggin'* (Fox, 1995), Leguizamo's talents seem boundless. But his biggest box office hit to date has been Twentieth Century Fox and Blue Sky's CG, animated feature *Ice Age*, (2002), in which the actor voiced a lovable, lisping little sloth named Sid.

Not so surprisingly, considering his penchant for wild, edgy humor, John Leguizamo turns out to have been a major cartoon freak since childhood. "I love animation, man," he gushes, noting how addicted he was to toons on

Film and stage actor John Leguizamo, voice of Ice Age*'s Sid the Sloth.*

TV. "All the Warner Bros. stuff. I watched them over, and over, and over. Bugs Bunny was my favorite–I loved all the super hero stuff, too–but to me, the comedy of Bugs Bunny was just unreal. There was nothing like it, ever. It was hilarious."

Divulging a bit of hero worship, Leguizamo is quick to credit the voice of that Warner Bros. sensation: "And Mel Blanc was the god of all animated things–I mean, he did *every voice* on those cartoons. Each one was unique and really came to life . . . so when I did *Ice Age*, I wanted to really make that character come to life, make the voice fit the physicality of it."

Ice Age was not Leguizamo's first time voicing an animated character. He was a riot as a CG-animated rat in Eddie Murphy's hip remake of *Doctor Dolittle* (1998), but went quietly into the dark of outer space as an alien named Gune in Fox's visually impressive bomb, *Titan A.E* (2000). "The idea was great. Sci-fi . . . doing Animé, American style. But somehow, it didn't quite gel," he understates kindly. Luckily, *Titan A.E.* didn't sour the studio on producing more animated features, or *Ice Age* might never have happened.

Fox producer Lori Forte approached Leguizamo to voice Sid very early on in the film's development. His presence at the studio predated even the hiring of the director, and his input in developing the screenplay was instrumental to the final shaping of the plot.

"I had a *lot* of input. Y'know, I'd talk about the characters and the character arc," he recalls. "I gave lots of notes. 'Cause [the story] was very dramatic at first. It was really dark, and I *liked* that aspect. I said, 'All you've gotta do is make it really funny.' My character was very comedic, but the other guys weren't at all." Sid was originally meant to be the comic relief in the story, but, as things evolved, "he became a lot warmer. He'd had a lot of girlfriends and stuff, so that got taken out 'cause the innuendo didn't work. It was just a 'B' story that wasn't necessary."

Once director Chris Wedge and his New York crew were on the project, Leguizamo put a lot of effort into finding Sid's voice–from the other side of the globe. "I was in Australia doing *Moulin Rouge* and I couldn't get back to the U.S. for ever, and [Wedge] kept wanting me to give him a voice. . . . I had to test some voices, but I was like, 'I don't know, man, I don't know what to do.' So I made a mini-disk of, like, *thirty voices* . . . I tried giving him all kinds of stuff. Like Yertle the Turtle-type voices–[very slow] *Uh, yup, yup, yup . . . like, real slooow type voices there, ya know?*–Southern voices, English voices, French . . . you name it, I gave him everything. And he wasn't sure–none of it really worked for him."

At that point, Wedge was leaning toward having Leguizamo use his own speech mannerisms, but the performer wasn't thrilled with that idea. "I was like, nah . . . I thought it would be kinda flat," he opines. "I wanted the sloth to have a unique personality, 'cause he was so goofy-looking. They'd given me a [maquette] of Sid . . . he had these big eyeballs, and all that. I knew the voice couldn't be myself–he was this little creature who was very self-involved . . . and kind of a loser . . . I wanted him to have enough endearing qualities so that you'd like him." Things finally began to click when Leguizamo watched some documentary footage of sloths from the Discovery Channel, noting that the creatures store food inside their cheek pockets. "That's when I started coming up with the lisp," he recalls.

Leguizamo figured that the sloth's two huge front teeth would also cause something of an impediment, all the more reason for the *lishping*. Even then, Chris Wedge wasn't convinced . . . but the actor's performance grew on him. "I really liked it more than perhaps Chris did, at first. And then he dug it. And then they tested it–it tested really high." The lisp stayed.

Ice Age's central relationship is between Leguizamo's lovable little Sid and a gruff, lumbering woolly mammoth named Manny (comedian Ray Romano) who's pretty much a loner and wants nothing to do with him at first. The sloth befriends Manny out of necessity–he needs protection from two giant angry rhinos that he's provoked.

Leguizamo found he could identify with Sid, and used his own past, growing up in Queens, New York, to help motivate his performance. "Totally. That whole thing of trying to survive, and using other people to protect you," he laughs. "I thought of my early years, when I was thirteen and I wanted to hang out with the cool guys . . . and how I used to have to work my way into their clan. Y'know, charm them and be funny, and goof, and try to hope that they'll accept me." And, just like Sid, the actor claims he felt helpless at times. "Oh, yeah. I was skinnier, smaller. . . . I wasn't as

Sid hightails it as two angry prehistoric rhinos come after him in Ice Age.

tough as the other guys–especially the guys that I wanted to hang out with. They were all really, really tough."

John Leguizamo was the first performer to record lines for the film, alone in the booth. "I totally motivated myself at first, and I recorded my whole part–and then Ray Romano recorded with *my* guide track–and I was like, '*Aha!* He got his little *jabs* in there for me!' Then the next time I recorded I did it with Ray's track, and, eventually, [the voice of saber-toothed tiger Diego] Denis Leary's. I got to record last, which was fun 'cause I got the final word most of the time."

The recording went on for about two years, which meant that the busy actor often had to lay down his lines long distance while working on other projects. "It wasn't easy, man. I had to do it in Boston while I was shooting a movie . . . and in Australia while I was shooting a movie." Wedge's direction and Leguizamo's recordings were done via satellite, and they made the most of their circumstances. "Chris was fun–he has a really goofy sensibility, he's very easygoing, he's got great ideas, and he lets you play. And, together, you two can chisel out what you want to create."

Leguizamo's previous animation experience came in very handy, he says. "I knew, whatever you want the voice to be on screen, you have to *be* that in the studio. Like, if [my character's] out of breath, I'll run till I'm out of breath . . . or if I'm supposed to be fighting, I'll throw my body around. I mean, you've got to really be emotionally, psychologically at that level for your voice to be as full. And I value that, so I try to do it as best I can." Interestingly, for someone who thrives on performing before live audiences,

Leguizamo doesn't mind the solitude of the recording booth. "It's cool, 'cause then, I get to try so many different things. I'm my own best audience, and I laugh at my own jokes, so I have no problem!"

The very first time he stepped into a booth to record a voice-over, however, it wasn't as easy for him. "That was tough. When I did *Titan A.E.*, or the other ones–it was a little weirder because I didn't know what to do. . . . I was like, 'Wow . . . how do I respond to voices that aren't there?' I only had a script," he recalls. "And then I got it. 'Oh, wait a minute . . . this is kinda cool, because I can say whatever I want as *often* as I want, until I get that line perfect. So it was kind of a real Zen thing, y'know . . . like at a driving range, you just hit that ball until you can hit it as far as you can. Until I'm satisfied with enough variety of choices that I think they can do something with it."

Still, he considers voice acting more challenging than performing in front of an audience or camera. "It's much harder. You've gotta visualize stuff that's not there . . . you've gotta project your personality into a character–make it come to life just with your voice. But I *use* my body–I'm totally as physical as I can be when I'm recording, so that my voice is as full when it stands alone in the picture. It'll make that picture come to life; it'll pop. You can tell if it's full of life or not, you can tell if it's flat and mundane. And I'm a perfectionist."

When Leguizamo finally saw the finished version of *Ice Age*, he was ecstatic with the results. He'd been too busy to attend any of the private screenings, so he got his first look at the premiere: "It was great! I *loved* it. I saw it three times–I never see any of my movies that often."

Since the film was such a smashing success–its budget came in well under that of most other animated features, and it grossed an astronomical sum–expect an *Ice Age* sequel at your local multiplex fairly soon. And John Leguizamo will be very much a part of that.

"It'll be very different than last time," he believes. "Last time, we took a serious script and made it funny. This time, there'll be a comic premise already included in the storyline." And an inventive comic actor behind the microphone.

MISSED IT BY *THAT* MUCH
The Part Almost Went To . . .

When voice actor and cartoon character are perfectly matched, it becomes impossible to imagine someone else in the role. Could anyone other than Mel Blanc have voiced Bugs Bunny or Daffy Duck? Would the public have embraced Homer Simpson without Dan Castellaneta's lovably buffoonish characterization? Could any actor besides Robin Williams have given voice to the Genie in *Aladdin*? It's hard to picture it, so indelibly etched are these performances. Ironically, when Williams opted not to play the Genie in Disney's 1994 made-for-video sequel, *The Return of Jafar*, it was Castellaneta who was chosen to provide a Robin Williams-esque performance, instead . . . with decidedly mixed results. Williams himself returned to reprise the Genie in the somewhat better second video sequel, *Aladdin and the King of Thieves* (1996).

Choices have to be made, of course, and it's often fascinating to learn who *didn't* get the job. Before Williams was finally convinced to sign on as *Aladdin*'s Genie, the creators had discussed the possibility of several other comic actors to voice the character, including Steve Martin, Dana Carvey, and Martin Short. And although animator Eric Goldberg even went so far as to do a rudimentary sketch of a Steve Martin-esque Genie, no one but Robin Williams was ever seriously considered.

Shortly before *Monsters, Inc.* opened in November 2001, *Entertainment Weekly* reported that Billy Crystal had actually been offered the role of Buzz Lightyear for the original *Toy Story* back in the early nineties. "There's a whole test of Billy Crystal as Buzz Lightyear," Disney's Thomas Schumacher confirmed. But because a very close friend of the comedian had been in a tiff with the studio at the time over publicity issues, Crystal's manager presumably advised him against voicing Buzz. "The biggest mistake I ever made in my life," Crystal admitted, according to *EW*. "I voted [*Toy Story*] for Best Picture that year. Only thing I ever turned down that I felt [bad] about." The role went instead to Tim Allen, who provided just the right mix of warmth and clueless pomposity. As for Billy Crystal, he wasn't about to make the same mistake twice. The actor eagerly accepted the role of short, green, one-eyed Mike in *Monsters, Inc.*–a part that the filmmakers basically wrote with him in mind.

As you read earlier, *Shrek*'s title character was originally voiced by *Saturday Night Live* funnyman Chris Farley, until he tragically died in the middle of production (see chapter 2). Immediately following his passing, several different actors who might deliver a similar performance were discussed–"But we realized that we would be making a mistake to try and duplicate a Farley-like persona," says Kelly Asbury, one of *Shrek*'s original directors. "Once that was decided, Mike Myers was the first and best choice." And you know the rest.

Would it surprise you to learn that, before Jim Carrey became *Jim Carrey*, he actually auditioned for Prince Eric in *The Little Mermaid*, and didn't get the role? It happened. "We sort of knew who he was," director Ron Clements says. "It was after *The Duck Factory* [a short-lived sitcom set in an animation studio], and he came in with his baseball cap on, to look younger."

Who *didn't* play Roger Rabbit? Few realize that Roger's famous voice in *Who Framed Roger Rabbit*, performed so distinctively by Charlie Fleischer, was originally vocalized in early tests by none other than Paul Reubens–yet to gain wide acclaim as "Pee-wee Herman." Michael Giaimo–then a Disney story artist who'd worked for almost two years on early development of the film–recalls how terrific Reubens was in the role. "Our early take on Roger Rabbit was a little more internal," he remembers. "He was a clown, but he wasn't quite so manic. There was a little more heart to him. We did some test animation, and got Paul Reubens to do the voice for Roger. Actually, not many knew him at the time–he had just finished a run at the Roxy on Sunset Strip of 'Pee-wee' as a live show [there was no TV series in sight yet]–but Paul actually is a very good actor, and has quite a range. We used that in the test footage. He did two different voices: one where he's being silly, and one where he's talking to Eddie Valiant, where Roger feels put upon for being a cartoon character and he tells Eddie, 'You just don't know how it is, and I wish you could be in my skin to see how it feels.' He's very down and very dejected, and it was really quite a touching performance."

Ultimately, director Robert Zemeckis decided to go another way with the rabbit's character–much broader and zanier. "If you've ever met Zemeckis, well, he sort of *is* what Roger Rabbit became. He's kind of a big, funny, clown-like guy!" Giaimo chuckles.

Sometimes, even when you've got the part, you haven't got it. A performer can record all of his or her lines, only to discover that the character has been completely cut from a film, which is exactly what happened to actress Kristen Johnston (of *3rd Rock from the Sun* fame) in the movie *Ice Age*. She'd given voice to Sid the Sloth's love interest, Sylvia, in several scenes–and, by all accounts, was wonderful. But because the filmmakers decided that Sid needed to be portrayed more sympathetically and as less of a skirt chaser, Sylvia had to go. "She was great. She added so much life to that character," laments John Leguizamo, who got to perform lines in the recording booth with just one fellow actor–Johnston.

Obviously, these (and many other) projects, where certain performers ultimately prevailed over others, would have turned out significantly different from the gems we know them to be today.

CHAPTER 10
MAKIN' TOONS CROON
Those Musical Marvels Who Compose the Merry Melodies

"I love to singa! About the moon-a and the Jun-a and the spring-a!"
—Owl Jolson, "I Love To Singa," *Merrie Melodies*, July 18, 1936

Around the same time that motion pictures started talking, cartoons began to sing. Walt Disney's third Mickey Mouse short, *Steamboat Willie*, premiered on November 18, 1928, and audiences were delighted by the sounds of the famous critter's melodic whistling and toe tapping. Ever since that day, music has been an integral component of animation.

A little-known musician by the name of Carl W. Stalling–who'd begun his career playing organ accompaniment for silent films in Kansas City–moved to Hollywood to work for his friend, Walt Disney, for whom he basically invented the process of scoring music for cartoons. Stalling (who was also one of Disney's original investors) egged the producer on to create a new series of shorts in which animation would be matched to music (instead of the other way around, which was more common then), and with *The Skeleton Dance* (1929)–composed and arranged by Stalling–Walt Disney's *Silly Symphonies* were born.

In the early 1930s, Warner Bros. introduced their *Looney Tunes* and *Merrie Melodies* cartoons with music scored mostly by Frank Marsales, Bernard Brown, or Norman Spencer. By 1936, Carl Stalling found himself at the studio–where he went on to compose and arrange practically every theatrical short for over twenty years. In the process, he revolutionized the way we perceive cartoons. You can hear the track to any of Stalling's Warner Bros. shorts and instantly recognize his work, with its lush orchestrations, clever sampling of popular songs of the day, and hair-trigger shifts in pacing, from manic and furious to slow and gentle, then back again to frantic. Whatever mood was called for, Stalling enhanced it with his musical genius.

Among his contemporaries, Scott Bradley also enjoyed a nearly twenty-year run as sole composer of MGM's animation, including many dozens of *Tom and Jerry*, *Droopy*, and *Barney Bear* shorts. In the decades following the retirement of unique talents like Stalling and Bradley, the quality of cartoon scoring declined dramatically. Once the theatrical short went the way of the dinosaur, television picked up the ball and became the prime source of toon production, for the most part, with one overriding credo: Get 'em done fast and cheap. To save the expense of composing, arranging, orchestrating, and recording new compositions for every cartoon, the same stock cues were used and reused over and over again.

From the early sixties through the eighties, most TV shows' opening theme songs were their musical saving grace, some standing out more than others. Is there anyone alive who *doesn't* know Hoyt Curtin, Joe Barbera, and Bill Hanna's original 1960 theme for *The Flintstones*? Among the rest of the pack, that same team's theme for *The Jetsons* (1962), Stan Worth and Sheldon Altman's ditty for *George of the Jungle* (1967), and Bob Harris' kicky *Spider-Man* song (1967) are a few of the most memorable, along with the *Pink Panther* series (1969), which appropriated Henry Mancini's suave, jazzy licks from the live-action films' music.

Once the early 1990s rolled in, there was an awakening–and hallelujah! Original musical compositions were being scored to picture again in cartoons.

Alf Clausen has been doing marvelous work for *The Simpsons* since joining the show during its first season, composing, arranging, and conducting a thirty-five-piece orchestra to create an average of thirty to forty music cues for each episode. The show's sharp-edged satire has even allowed the composer to musically parody various pop culture institutions. In an episode called "Two Dozen and One Greyhounds," Clausen and writer Mike Scully cross-pollinate *One Hundred and One Dalmatians'* Cruella De Vil with *Beauty and the Beast*'s Lumiere as Mr. Burns warbles "See My Vest" to his lackey Smithers, vilely (and hilariously) conveying his desire to craft a perfect outfit made up of dog, cat, gopher, gorilla, and other animal skins. Clausen's efforts haven't gone unnoticed–along the way he's managed to amass a pile of Emmy awards and nominations.

Ren & Stimpy, with its distinctively retro riffs culled from the stock library vaults of Associated Production Music, was one of the first daytime toons to dispense with the awful synthesized junk that had been in use for years. Composer/arranger Shirley Walker's brilliantly subtle and dark underscoring of *Batman: The Animated Series* brought out all the drama and tension the filmmakers were hoping to convey. James L. Venable's standout musical direction of *Powerpuff Girls* and *Samurai Jack* continue to complement the wit and dazzling graphics on display. Jody Gray's playful compositions for *Courage the Cowardly Dog* only heighten the pink pooch's comic terror as he tries to protect the farm from a gallery of bizarre creatures and otherworldly fiends.

I wish I could insert a musical chip into this book for you to hear some of the great scoring being done for toons these days, but you'll just have to flip on the TV and listen for yourselves.

Turning to the realm of motion pictures, by the time the first full-length animated feature was produced, music was already driving cartoons every bit as much as their storyline or sight gags. So it made perfect sense that *Snow White and the Seven Dwarfs* (1937) would be a musical, using songs (by Frank Churchill, Larry Morey, Paul J. Smith, and Leigh Harline) to help move its story–songs so memorable that several endure as classics to this day: "Heigh-Ho," "Some Day My Prince Will Come," and "Whistle While You Work."

Throughout its peak years, Disney features turned out one hit after another, songs that lodged in our heads and never went away: Leigh Harline and Ned Washington's "When You Wish Upon a Star" (*Pinocchio*, 1940); Allie Wrubel and Ray Gilbert's "Zip-A-Dee-Doo-Dah" (*Song of the South*, 1946); Mack David, Al Hoffman, and Jerry Livingston's "Bibbidi Bobbidi Boo" (*Cinderella*, 1950); Sonny Burke and Peggy Lee's "Bella Notte" (*Lady and the Tramp*, 1955); Sammy Fain and Jack Lawrence's "Once Upon a Dream" (*Sleeping Beauty*, 1959); Richard M. Sherman and Robert B. Sherman's "Supercalifragilisticexpialidocious," "A Spoonful of Sugar," "Chim Chim Cheree," and "Feed the Birds" (*Mary Poppins*, 1963), just to name a few. It's fair to say that no Hollywood film studio has consistently contributed to our musical pop culture for as long as Disney.

Around the late sixties, the studio slid into a fallow period that lasted several decades, producing films without any particularly memorable songs. At the same time Disney was falling out of step, musical tastes were changing. Even *The Jungle Book* (1967), a rollicking cartoon feature (created during the heart of the British rock 'n' roll invasion), harkened back to the musical era of its middle-aged creators: mostly Dixieland jazz and swing. And, when British vultures Buzzie, Flaps, Ziggy, and Dizzy–an obvious nod to The Beatles–finally open their beaks to sing "We're Your Friends," it's not even rock 'n' roll that comes out, but pure barbershop quartet.

Speaking of the real Fab Four, they allowed producer Al Brodax to adapt their personas and music to a smashingly popular big-screen animated feature, *Yellow Submarine*, in 1968. Loosely spun off from the success of the animated TV series, *The Beatles* (1965), the film boasted wild psychedelic colors, stylized graphics mixed with some very cartoony designs, the irreverent, pun-laden wit that John, Paul, George, and Ringo were known for, and some terrific Beatles songs, including "Eleanor Rigby," "All You Need Is Love," and the title tune, "Yellow Submarine."

As for Disney's output over the next few decades, regardless of how fondly one thinks of the films, most people would be hard-pressed to recall a single song from *The Aristocats*, *Robin Hood*, *The Rescuers*, *The Fox and the Hound*, *The Great Mouse Detective*, or *Oliver & Company* (which featured tunes by a plethora of pop songwriters and performers, including Billy Joel and Bette Midler). The late eighties, however, saw the arrival at the studio of two key figures who'd change all that . . .

The Songs Always Come First

Alan Menken and Partners Raise the Musical Bar

When you talk about great songwriting teams of the twentieth century, you have to include Alan Menken and Howard Ashman. Although their collaboration was tragically cut short by Ashman's death from AIDS in 1991, with *Little Shop of Horrors* on stage and screen, followed by *The Little Mermaid*, *Beauty and the Beast*, and *Aladdin*, they had four staggering successes. Not only did they leave a legacy of unforgettable songs–a trend that composer Menken has continued to this day, working with various other collaborators–they revived and redefined a genre that was considered all but dead until they came along: the animated musical.

Unlike a lot of people who grew up head over heels for musicals, Menken wasn't drawn to them until much later in his development. "When I was a kid, I was in love with classical music," he confides. "I dreamed about becoming a composer, not necessarily a songwriter. At the same time, my family loved theater songs, so I grew up with them around me. I wasn't particularly into or interested in musical theater beyond what anyone else would be, but they were a fabric of my life . . . and, because of my sensitivity to music, that became a part of my being."

By 1964, Menken was hitting adolescence just as The Beatles hit U.S. shores and took the music world by storm. It had a profound effect on the young composer. "Even though I found pop music exciting before that, to a degree, The Beatles and the synergy between pop music and songwriting, and our lives, you know, became very palpable to me. So I wanted to *be* The Beatles . . . then, I wanted to be the Rolling Stones. I was always playing piano, and then, I took up the guitar. I started writing songs."

As he grew older, he decided that that was what he wanted to be: a songwriter.

More to appease his parents than for any other reason–they were worried that he'd starve as a songwriter, and hoped that theater might be something he could fall back on–Menken joined the BMI Musical Theater Workshop run by Lehman Engel, a famed Broadway musical guru. "Joining the BMI workshop was like putting a huge amount of ammunition into a cannon," says Menken. "'Cause I just basically *shot* out of there . . . the combination of meeting very talented people and being forced to write up to certain standards just honed my craft."

It was through a friend in the workshop, fellow composer Maury Yeston, that he met Howard Ashman. "At that point, I was exclusively a composer/lyricist, but I decided to just write music with Howard . . . he was somebody who was very into using clearly defined musical styles as part of the message. He had musical *ideas*. And he could sing–but composing ability, no. That's the one thing he lacked, so he was stuck with having a composer in the room. I loved Howard, but I knew it was always a frustration to him–the elements he couldn't control directly, he had to at least control the *people* who controlled them directly," Menken laughs.

But Ashman's zeal didn't stifle Menken's work–rather, it left Menken in awe of what Ashman could help him accomplish. "He really responded to my talent. I began working with him, and I was flipped out by *his* talent–as a writer, lyricist, director. . . . I'd never seen anybody who could go seamlessly from book into songs the way he did. His sense of originality . . . and an incredibly strong compass artistically, was just a dream come true. I had done other shows with other people, and I had done other shows on my own . . . but it had never been an experience like working with Howard, where I just had a sense that we were going in the right direction."

As they began their collaboration, Alan Menken and Howard Ashman brought a fresh, contemporary sense of humor to their songs, along with a distinctly Broadway-flavored musical sensibility. Their partnership would bring out the best in each of them, from their first project, *God Bless You, Mr. Rosewater* (1979) on stage, to their last, *Aladdin* (1992) on screen.

Menken learned a great deal from his gifted collaborator, including the courage to make stylistic choices in his work. "*Specificity* of choice, I got from Howard. When an audience goes, 'Oh, I get it!' If you're not making a specific choice stylistically in a song . . . you're squandering an opportunity to communicate faster with an audience."

Menken acknowledges that this approach differs from some traditional theories about composing for the theater, whereby an audience gradually warms up to a musical style–"There's an entire school of musical theater which says, 'I didn't get that musical on first listening . . . on second listening, I got a lot more from it . . . but, on *third listening*, oh, I really got it now.'" For Menken and Ashman, the audience had to be moved the first time. "The way I write is, I really want a direct visceral connection as fast as possible. I learned from Howard, I learned from Lehman Engel . . . I learned from a lot of people the power of songs and what they can accomplish in a moment. And the power of the music. And I long ago lost my fear of writing in a very, very predictable style, if it's in service of a lyric that uses it in some way."

Sometimes, Menken would tell Ashman what type of music he had in mind, and Ashman would write lyrics accordingly. With this base, the real creativity would begin. "When we wrote 'Be Our Guest' [for *Beauty and the Beast*], I gave Howard a piece of music. And I said, 'You write the lyric and then, when you bring it back, I'll write the *real* music. But this is sort of a palette you can work from. A French music hall tune.' And so, he brought back this lyric:

Be our guest, be our guest
Put our service to the test
Tie your napkin 'round your neck, monsieur
And we'll provide the rest

"I tried all these different ways to set it, and, finally, [singing the main theme] *ba-da-da, ba-da-da, ba-ba-dum, ba da-ba-dop* was the way to do it. There was just no way around it. And it worked like crazy. . . . I learned that *I* may think I'm going directly at something and it's so simple and predictable that there's nothing original in it–but there are always original twists. And there's a line you walk. . . . I mean, you try to find ways to package it as

Composer Alan Menken.

originally as possible, but keep the accessibility. But then, there are the moments where you go, 'Oh, okay, I'm gonna go into uncharted territory now. Now I'm gonna do something *not* quite so accessible, but it's okay because what's led up to it has been very accessible.'"

The songs always come first for Alan Menken, and the score grows out of the songs. "Really, I started scoring to *protect* the songs," he explains. "When it came time to do *Little Mermaid*, Howard said, 'Y'know, you already do the music *into* the songs and the music *out of* the songs. . . . *You* should do the score.'" When Menken replied that he didn't know how, Ashman, who was executive producer of the film, simply replied, "Do it."

Menken admits that he was terrified. "Because I had never done it. I mean, as it was, I'm sure the fact that I won the Oscar for best score for *Little Mermaid* must make people grit their teeth. Because it was a completely primitive score . . . I was unskilled. On talent, it still worked–good melodies, good musical ideas . . . basically cluttered, and a little artless. But it had some charming things in it–the charm of somebody approaching a form for the first time, and it also had the power of these songs, and this *magic* . . . which I understood in my bones, 'cause it came *out* of my bones."

In order to help him learn the proper techniques of film scoring for *The Little Mermaid*, Menken enlisted the services of orchestrator Tom Pasatieri, a respected opera composer. He believes it was a difficult job for Pasatieri. "I think he probably saw me as somebody who was musically naïve . . . walking away with this unbelievable musical triumph on this first attempt. He did wonderful orchestration, but after that, I think it was hard for him to want to continue in that role, and I understand that." Of course, as Menken points out, he no longer needed a teacher after *The Little Mermaid*.

To illustrate how low his confidence level was initially, the composer recalls attending an early recording session to lay down a multipart cue for a scene in the film. The action began with the mermaid Ariel and her buddy Flounder poking their heads up to see a sunken ship, and ended with them escaping from a shark. As Menken listened to the first cue being played, his heart sank. "I sat there, and said, 'Oh my God, this is garbage . . . I've written utter garbage.' I heard the orchestra playing it, [but] I wasn't used to the fact that, when an orchestra first sight-reads through a piece of music, the performance isn't shaped yet."

To Menken's mounting horror, everyone there–Howard Ashman, [directors] Ron Clements and John Musker, Tom Pasatieri, and John Richards, the engineer–was huddling and whispering. All the composer could think was, "Omigod . . . they're trying to figure out how to break it to me that I'm fired." Finally, Ashman came over to him. Menken blurted out, "I know, I know, it's awful!" Ashman quietly responded, "This spot here, where Ariel looks up . . . I think you should maybe have another instrument do that, instead." Menken stared at him: "That's it?"

Even though his first score was certainly not the disaster that Alan Menken thought it was, and despite the fact that he's won many Oscars and Grammies for *The Little Mermaid* and other films, he still sounds somewhat tentative on the subject. "I still don't really know how to get out of the way as much as I should . . . because I'm very thematically driven. And I'm very into supporting the songs and the song themes, which can tug the ear and tug your attention. . . . I mean, John Williams is a fabulous film scorer. And yet, John has the other side of the coin to deal with. He often writes songs, and wants to fit the songs in . . . and sometimes it's hard for him to move into that very high profile song mode and then back into the invisible scoring mode. It's hard for *me* to combine the same two elements."

Clearly, Menken considers himself a songwriter first and foremost. "Oh, absolutely," he affirms, tossing off a few of his tune titles. "'Part of Your World,' 'Colors of the Wind,' 'Beauty and the Beast,' 'A Whole New World,' 'Under the Sea,' 'Friend Like Me,' 'Go the Distance,' 'Some Day' . . . it's *songs* that people know. When you write songs, especially for a project that's high profile, if you don't write something that either is totally infectious, totally charming, totally funny, or totally moving, you have just wasted the biggest opportunity. Because it's so possible to do that, and you should never even think of delivering a song that doesn't do one of those things."

Even so, it isn't possible to wallop a home run each and every time you come to the plate. Menken admits there have been songs that he wasn't entirely satisfied with, but they had to stay because they were integral to the story. He cites as an example his work on the score to *Hercules*, written with David Zippel. Menken had accepted the assignment knowing full well that *Hercules* was to be narrated musically by a female Greek chorus of gospel-singing black Muses, and that he was about to tread on familiar territory. "I did it to protect myself. I didn't want *someone else* doing a pastiche of *Little Shop of Horrors*, especially at Disney. And I also love working with John and Ron." Still, he didn't feel he was repeating himself, exactly. "Not musically, I wasn't," he explains. "It's gospel as opposed to R & B. But I don't feel like I was able to fully deliver–I would have loved that score to be more like *Candide*. More fun classical, almost operatic. It might not have been commercial, but then, that's not the main thrust of what we do."

Despite his occasional misgivings, Menken is generally satisfied with what he's accomplished so far. "I'm pretty happy with all the songs," he says. "I don't think there's a song in *Little Mermaid* I'm not happy with . . . 'Daughters of Triton' is a little slight, but it needs to be." The composer had initially resisted putting the Gilbert and Sullivan-esque number into the film–since it didn't match the rest of the songs stylistically–but ultimately relented because the plot called for it. "You have to just let it go and do it. And you are a slave to the story. If I disagree with something, the best way to prove it is to do what somebody asks. And either it's gonna work or not . . . there's no point in just debating with them."

Howard Ashman's companion, Bill Lauch, describes how Menken and Ashman would write together, and the give-and-take that was part of their working relationship. "Alan usually came down to Howard's place, and sat at the piano. They had a little tape recorder that they used," Lauch recalls, "and their songs were kind of banged out at the piano . . . and they'd sort of write as they go. Howard would often have a rough set of lyrics and a general notion of song structure before they started . . . and they would work on it, and mold it, and the lyrics would change and the music would change and it'd be back and forth. . . . The tapes would always end up all over the place–and that's what I would hear at the end of the day. They'd fast-forward and reverse, and get to the part they liked and say, 'What did you think of *that*?'"

That's a longhaired Alan Menken seated at the piano behind the now-deceased Howard Ashman, smiling at the camera during their early days.

As you'll find with most artists, if asked to pick out favorite songs or film scores from his own body of work, Alan Menken will first tell you he can't. Eventually, he admits that "the musical world that's created by *Little Mermaid* is the most special because it was the first," and, "in a way, I'm proudest of *Aladdin*. Because Howard died in the middle of work on it, and I had to finish the score with another collaborator. I was afraid that, after Howard died, I was going to find that what was special about me was what Howard brought to the collaboration . . . and that I would never hit those heights again."

Menken first learned of Howard Ashman's illness shortly after they won their Oscars for *The Little Mermaid*. He knew his collaborator hadn't been feeling well, but never dreamt that it was anything serious. "The night of the Oscars, we sat there with these statues in front of us, and he said, 'When I get back to New York, we need to have a talk.' 'What about?' 'Not tonight, not tonight. But I want you to know I'm really happy with what we've done.'

"So I went to his house, and he was sitting in the living room. He shut the door. And I said, 'What?' I thought he was going to say 'I need to work with other people.' He said, 'Well, you know.' 'Know what?' 'I'm sick. I'm HIV positive.' And so then, all the pieces sort of went *click, click, click, click* . . . everything added up. . . . And he said some wonderful things. He said, 'I'm so glad that you won the Oscar. I know now that you're taken care of.' It was very moving . . . it was an expression of commitment and love from someone with whom I was not able to share that. I'd always felt that I was the straight collaborator who lived in a separate world from Howard and his support group. And, especially in that time, there was almost a tribal protectiveness among his friends. . . . So it was an expression that there was a relationship here that was extremely important to both of us. And the basis of that was what we brought to the earth together."

Even with Ashman not well and getting sicker by the month, the team continued working. "The *emotion* of losing Howard found its way into *Beauty and the Beast*, more than *Aladdin*, in a way," recalls Menken. "'Cause it was really played out during *Beauty and the Beast*."

Artist Sue Nichols helped develop both films' stories and characters, and remembers the team's massive contribution as well as Ashman's deteriorating condition. "Howard and Alan were wonderful to work with, 'cause they weren't just songwriters who would write something and then tell you, 'Stick it in wherever you have a spot'. . . . They really worked with the overall story, [discerning] what part of that story would be best *as* a song, and then they'd write the song to fit the story . . . so it really was integrated perfectly," Nichols says. Although Ashman was fighting for his life, few on the crew of *Aladdin* or *Beauty and the Beast* knew the truth. "We had to go to New York to meet with Howard. It was very rare that he came out to L.A. He did, once or twice, but by *Aladdin*, he wasn't coming out at all. They kept it pretty quiet, so we didn't know why they were spending so much money to send us all over to New York. . . . We found out as we were working, through the rumor mill . . . but they didn't come out and tell us directly."

Once they finished all the songs for *Beauty and the Beast*, Menken and Ashman turned their attentions back to *Aladdin*–a project Ashman had initiated at Disney. It was he who'd first suggested turning the story of the Chinese street urchin into an animated musical feature. (No need to clean your glasses–it's true; Aladdin was the son of a poor Chinese tailor in the ancient folktale, "Aladdin; Or The Wonderful Lamp"!) In 1988, Ashman penned a forty-page treatment, envisioning the film as a thirties-style musical featuring a Cab Calloway-esque, singing, dancing Genie. Menken and Ashman had even created six new songs based on that initial draft of the story, which focused on Aladdin, his widowed mother, and his buddies Babkak, Omar, and Kassim.

When Howard Ashman passed away in 1991–not living to see *Beauty and the Beast* released six months later–he thought his work on *Aladdin* was finished. In fact, the story would undergo radical changes, requiring half the songs to be discarded. "They cut the mother, so now there had to be a new ballad. And they cut the buddies," Menken notes. "The last song Howard wrote was called 'Humiliate the Boy.' In that song, Jafar is taking everything away from Aladdin–he's taking away his clothes, his ability to do this, and do that–until Aladdin is standing there with nothing. Howard and I always used to sing our demos together . . . now, I was just singing them on my own, and he was having to watch it. The parallel was chilling, and it was painful."

Alan Menken briefly considered completing *Aladdin* as both composer and lyricist–even recording a demo for one song called "Count on Me"–but decided instead to team up with a new collaborator, Tim Rice (*Jesus Christ Superstar*, *Evita*, and, later, *The Lion King*). However, that involved considerably more than just creating new songs, as Menken explains: "It was also the challenge of taking over Howard's role–because the role that Howard assumed in his work at Disney, and everywhere, was being *the* musical theater dramatist. And I, temporarily, at least, took on the mantle of 'I'm going to be the musical theater dramatist here.' Working with Tim Rice, I want to make sure that everything Tim and I do is compatible with what Howard and I did, or would have done . . . and I had to be the one to stand up to whoever, and say, 'No, we can't cut this song and this is the reason why.' So I had to stay in the trenches, in a way that I hadn't had to prior to that."

It was a lot of extra baggage to carry, especially while trying to remain creative. "That was the period in which I was doing everything," he elaborates. "At one time, I was finishing *Beauty and the Beast*, working on *Aladdin*, doing *Newsies*, doing *Weird Romance*, doing *Lincoln*, starting work on *Pocahontas*. After Howard died, there was a period in which I was not even thinking. . . . I was just inside of the process . . . you could say, in a zone. So, I guess *Aladdin* was very much in the center of that."

Tim Rice found himself in an awkward spot, suddenly stepping into somebody else's shoes–formidable shoes, at that–to complete another man's work. "He was very sensitive about it," Menken recalls. "He's a very graceful person, and has an ease about him that's neat to be around. He was completely selfless in saying, 'You tell me what you want me to do.'" Thus, when they wrote "One Jump Ahead," they molded it in the style of Ashman and Menken's previous work.

However, Rice did find a way to instill a bit of himself into the work. In the reprise of "One Jump Ahead"–and in many of the film's other numbers–Rice's particular sense of humor really shone through. "It's very much his personality that makes those songs . . . he's got a tremendous gift," Menken remarks. Though Menken found both men brilliant, Ashman and Rice were very different in personality and temperament. "Howard was more cutting, and New York urban acerbic . . . very hip. Tim is also very hip, with more English references, to a degree–rock 'n' roll references, and cultural references. Tim was the other side of the world, in many respects. . . . It opened up a door that allowed me to move into another place emotionally."

Menken's work on *Beauty and the Beast* and *Aladdin* netted him four more Academy Awards, four Golden Globe Awards for Best Original Score and Best Song (for "Beauty and the Beast," written with Ashman, and "A Whole New World," written with Rice), and seven more Grammy Awards.

It was, literally, a whole new world for Alan Menken, once he knew he'd be able to go on without Howard Ashman. His next collaboration was with famed Broadway composer/lyricist Stephen Schwartz (*Godspell*, *Pippin, The Magic Show*), on Disney's *Pocahontas*. "No, it can't compete with the emotional back-story of what those first three had," Menken concedes. "Yet, I had always admired Stephen Schwartz. And he was a wonderful, respectful collaborator. A very demanding artist, very high standards."

The work they did together–both on *Pocahontas* and *Hunchback of Notre Dame*–was marked by a sense of mutual respect. "On those projects, I had a very strong collaborator–in certain ways, like Howard–with very strong opinions, and very strong temperament," Menken notes. "And I had to stand up and go, 'I know what I want.' I know that I'm not always as articulate as other people sometimes, and I don't have a wellspring of detailed theories . . . but I have incredible marrow, and incredible instincts. So I learned with Stephen to just bring my instincts into the room, and I found that he respected me immensely. Actually, I'm able to think on my feet, almost more like an athlete than an intellectual."

Although he's found his other projects "hard to compete with *Mermaid*, *Beauty*, and *Aladdin*," Menken describes them as incredible experiences just the same. Pausing to reflect on his success to date, he attributes it to the fact that he loves the job. "I think I'm basically *good* at doing one thing, and things related to it . . . my life consistently has been focused on composing and songwriting, and observing, and experimenting with the visceral effects on people of music and songs. It's just so much in my blood . . . and, I guess, through that, my ability to be a chameleon . . . to sort of crawl into any style and just use it. And that really came from Howard Ashman."

CHAPTER 11
NOTHING PERSONAL; IT'S JUST BUSINESS
A Peek Behind the Glamorous Façade of the Toon Trade

"WARNING: If you are of an artistic disposition and didn't know that animators do it for the money, this book may shock you!"

—Terry Gilliam, animator/director and author, *Animations of Mortality*

While animation is an art form, it's also very much a business. And, like any other business, it's filled with wild success stories and dismal failures, all whipped together with politics, contracts, strikes, negotiations, distribution, merchandising, publicity, focus groups, test screenings, elation, heartbreak, and all that jazz. That's right, baby–it's *showbiz.* Not for the fainthearted or weak-kneed.

This is the stuff they *don't* teach in school, and maybe it's just as well. The fact is, most artists and writers are lousy businessmen. We don't really want to have to worry about all that–hell, we just want to be left alone to create. That's the weird dichotomy about the *business* of entertainment: art and commerce are sort of like oil and vinegar... they don't blend naturally, but, if you shake 'em up together, you get a palatable mix. They can even help each other, which is why artists and writers and filmmakers and composers need agents and managers and lawyers and studio execs. We're really very different types of people, but working together, in harmony, we can do great things.

This chapter, one that I couldn't resist including, is a glimpse of the business of animation: how we got to where we are today, what goes on (and has been going on) behind the scenes, what some of the network and studio execs at the top are really thinking and planning, and why things sometimes go wrong . . . and occasionally right–because all that is a part of makin' toons, too.

Cartoons—The New Wave

The Toon Boom Hits TV

The animation landscape a few decades ago was generally a barren wasteland. Films were going through a major lull while TV found itself dominated by reruns of old Saturday morning shows and junky new syndicated series fueled by toy companies.

Then, slowly at first, something interesting began to happen. Animators around the world had never stopped making short, personal films, and hungry audiences–who'd been weaned on classic Warner Bros., Hanna-Barbera, and Disney as kids–began hitting the festival circuit to see them. By the early to mid-eighties, the International Tournée of Animation had grown into one of the largest, thanks to the tireless efforts of Terry Thoren, who'd decided to make toons the focus of his life. Thoren later started *Animation Magazine* and the World Animation Celebration (the industry's largest business convention), eventually becoming president/CEO of Klasky Csupo.

"It was all to promote the idea that animation was not just cartoons for kids," Thoren explains. "That was our credo. We *hounded* the studios in L.A., and the broadcasters, and everybody . . . that they need to open their eyes and see animation the way *we* see animation."

The toon scene on television changed dramatically when cable outlets like Nickelodeon and Cartoon Network were born, and with the growth of Fox, WB, and MTV as purveyors of new programming. For a long time, TV animation fell under the domain of the big three broadcast networks–ABC, CBS, and NBC–and they had their own way of doing things. That way was frustrating to many creative people in the industry.

Writer/producer Paul Dini, who'd worked on his share of network shows, came away with strong feelings about an internal approval process where content was continually watered down, mostly out of fear of ever offending anybody. At the networks, Dini says, "You've got these so-called creative executives. It's no wonder that, by the time a cartoon finally reaches the air, it looks stale and boring. . . . If anything is truly interesting or funny in it, that'll rub some creative exec the wrong way, 'cause he hasn't seen it before and simply isn't familiar with it, and he'll want it out. Y'know, they're the boss, they're in charge, they're paying the research zombies to just tell 'em whatever they want, so they're very comfortable in their own little corndog-style blanket of ignorance." Equally frustrated at the networks' constant meddling with content, producer Joe Barbera once observed, "If Charlie Chaplin, Buster Keaton, or Harold Lloyd had to work with NBC, CBS, or ABC today, they'd throw up their hands in disgust and walk away."[1]

Since cable outlets have basically cornered the marketplace on innovative toons, the networks seem unable (or unwilling) to try and compete. "For years–you could even argue that to this day–the most creative stuff is still coming out of Nickelodeon and Cartoon Network," declares Paul Germain, who co-created *Rugrats* with Arlene Klasky and Gabor Csupo. "There's this sense of . . . almost like the independent filmmaking of animation is really happening there."

"I envy TV animation today," admits Tom Sito. "They're getting away with a lot more stuff than we were able to get away with. In the eighties, on *He-Man*, we had a staff child psychologist. He had the right of veto over any script or storyboard, to make sure we weren't screwing up kids' brains. He'd put little pink memos on each script."

Sito recalls the kind of overly cautious approach he and others were forced to take back then. "He-Man would be attacked by a giant lump of broccoli or something, so he'd pull a tree out of the ground and beat him over the head with it. And we'd get a note saying He-Man cannot kill a tree. Or my favorite one: He'd pick up Beast-Man and throw him three miles–and the guy would always land in a mud puddle or a bale of hay. You couldn't do anything 'violent' in cartoons. And then ya got *The Simpsons* and *Ren & Stimpy* and *Beavis and Butt-Head* going crazy, throwing all the rules out the window and becoming monster hits! All that changed the television landscape."

The trend toward innovative, unfettered TV animation exploded at the end of the eighties. Around 1990, Vanessa Coffey went to work for Nickelodeon as vice president of animation, and began developing their first cartoon series. "This idea of doing original animated programming for Nickelodeon was an interesting business decision for them," Paul Germain observes. "For the first time, really, they were in a position where they could not only put original shows on, but they could *own* the shows. The networks at that time could not own their own shows. That was beginning to change, but it hadn't yet. Nickelodeon was a cable network–but technically, it wasn't a *network* . . . it was a really fudged distinction, yet it was legal. So there was this extra incentive for them to produce original programming."

For three weeks, Coffey took dozens and dozens of pitches. Out of that barrage of ideas, three new animated shows emerged: *Doug*, *Ren & Stimpy*, and *Rugrats*, followed eventually by *Rocko's Modern Life*. When Coffey heard a pitch that she liked, she gave a quick green light to its creator–something that's almost unheard of in this industry. "I actually liked to give 'yes' and 'no' right in the room," she says, "'cause I know if I like something or not. That's also the way Gerry Laybourne ran the company. Her theory was, 'You surround yourself with good people and you let them do their jobs.'"

Once the shows were put into development, Coffey worked very closely with the creators, helping them hone and refine their ideas. Since she couldn't do it all alone, she surrounded herself with a core group of talented producers, assistants, and development people, including Eric Coleman, Mary Harrington, and Linda Simensky. Many of them have since moved on to become major players in the animation world.

As the network grew, they decided to physically produce their own shows rather than just hire outside studios. Producer Mary Harrington made the move from New York to L.A. to set up such a facility, so that Nick could produce *Rocko's Modern Life*. "We started in January of '93, and we delivered the shows in September," she recalls. "And we were working with a creator, Joe Murray, who had never worked in television before. It was worth it, and it was a fantastic crew. We had all the usual problems–y'know, the first season of any show is difficult. You're honing the creative team . . . you hire people, but not everybody is going to work out . . . there's that whole list of problems."

The Nicktoons studio eventually expanded, moving to larger facilities in Burbank, where they're still located to this day. Among the network's many popular shows turned out there: *SpongeBob SquarePants*, *Dora the Explorer*, and *Hey Arnold*. "One of the best things about Nicktoons is bringing unique, interesting talent in," says Harrington. "Being able to give new creators a chance."

In 1992, Turner Broadcasting launched Cartoon Network, eventually luring some personnel away from rival Nickelodeon. Linda Simensky was one of them. She felt it was the right move for her, even though her new job wasn't exactly a step up so much as a step across.

"I started out as director of programming," Simensky says. "A lot of people said they thought I was stupid because I didn't get a promotion. I was changing departments, I was sort of going back to programming . . . but I think anybody that has a clue would know that if there's a company you really wanna work at, *make* a lateral move! I kept thinking that, once I got there, I could probably turn the job into whatever there was a need for."

Simensky's hunch paid off, and she quickly moved up the ladder at the new network. She and her boss Mike Lazzo displayed considerable business

The crew of Nickelodeon's first in-house cartoon production, Rocko's Modern Life. *Just behind Rocko to the left is series creator Joe Murray, in a white V-neck shirt; to Rocko's right, in glasses, is Tom Kenny, who voiced Heffer on the show and SpongeBob SquarePants a few years later; to his right sits producer Mary Harrington, wearing a vest; clutching the grass just in front of her is Carlos Alazraqui, the voice of Rocko. Note the cardboard drawing of Steve Hillenburg, absent that day, in the back, far right.*

acumen and solid taste in new programming, helping to turn Cartoon Network into a major player in just a few short years. In less than a decade, they amassed a lineup of great cartoons including, *The Powerpuff Girls*, *Dexter's Laboratory*, *Cow and Chicken*, *Courage the Cowardly Dog*, *Johnny Bravo*, *Samurai Jack*, and *Justice League*.

Simensky brought along some very definite ideas of how she feels a network should be run. For one thing, it means taking some risks. "Gerry Laybourne at Nick used to say, 'You are *expected* to make mistakes.' And I try to live by that. If you don't, you're not trying, you're not being interesting, and you're not experimenting."

Still, she explains, the network tries to pick shows that they truly feel are a good fit. "In a lot of cases, we pick up shows based on the creator's sensibility. And we try not to work with people that are really off base–one of the problems I had at Nickelodeon was we tended to work with people who were inexperienced, or their vision of the show was different from what the network wanted [as in what happened with *Ren & Stimpy*]. When you have that situation, you end up with a lot of fights."

In order to find such compatible creators, Simensky, referring to herself as a "hunter/gatherer," spends a good deal of time searching for new talent and taking a lot of pitches. And she emphasizes that the pitch should be more casual than formal. "I always try to tell people, 'Don't feel like you're pitching me. Just tell me about your idea, and we'll talk about it.' If people walk in with a fully thought-out show, it's not really fair to them," she remarks. "I mean, how were they supposed to know exactly what we're looking for? I think if they walk in willing to hear feedback–but still with a good idea and an open mind–and just wanting to have a casual discussion about their idea, y'know, not big foam-core presentation boards, but some sketches and some thoughts, you pitch your idea much more easily. I don't respond to people who are too professional and too slick. . . . No real artists act like that. Those are businesspeople–and businesspeople don't wanna make shows, they wanna make *deals*."

Furthermore, Simensky looks at development as something that continues into the first season. "Most series seem to need six episodes–or thirteen–to really find themselves," she adds. "I've never worked on a show that didn't need that. It's animation . . . there's that knowledge that a unit takes twelve to thirteen episodes to really coalesce. And we can't change that."

Simensky takes a dim view of meddlesome network execs. Her role, she says, is not to barrage the animators with creatives and consultants and nitpicky direction from upstairs. "If a project needs that much help," she conjectures, "*don't do it*–'cause clearly, there's something wrong with it."

Instead, she favors maintaining the necessary balance of keeping the show moving in the right direction *and* allowing the artists some autonomy in creating

Cartoon Network's Linda Simensky, as drawn by Paul Rudish.

the show. Of course, Simensky does give notes when it's necessary. "But if you're giving notes," she warns, "you don't give notes like 'Change *this* to *this*' because you personally think it's funny. Y'know, you're the network executive, not the show creator. They've gotta live with this; their dignity's on the line, more so than yours. Hire people that you feel you can completely trust, and then back their vision. That's your job. Your job is not to write gags for the creators. And if you think it is, then go get a job writing for that creator!"

She likens her network's relationship with its creators to that of editor and author. "Your editor wouldn't rewrite pages for you; your editor would say, 'I'm reading this, and you know what I'm getting from it? I'm getting that your guy's a mean guy. You want that?' Inevitably, the person says no. So you say, 'Well, I think you've gotta lighten it up a little bit.' Or you read something and you say, 'Y'know what? You've got twenty-two minutes here, and you've spent twenty of them setting this up, and then you rush through the ending. Don't do that. Reverse it. You should spend *two* minutes setting it up, and the next twenty doing all that funny stuff.' And the person will say, 'Oh, I didn't even realize that.'"

Similarly, Simensky tries to act as "the first audience" for the cartoon creators–an honest voice who is helping the creator shape the vision of what he or she has promised to the network. "That's what I've tried to be, and that's what my department has tried to be: an advocate for the creators to the network, and an advocate for the network to the creators. A lot of shows, during their first season, have trouble . . . they're fine-tuning. A smart creator would appreciate good notes. And our goal has always been to help them get it right, so you won't need to do it later. After that, every time you get a board that you don't have to give notes on other than *standards* notes, you can say to yourself, 'I'm a good development person. I brought in a project that doesn't need a lot of help.' It means I've brought in the right project, and that's good."

Whoops! Why Some Shows Fail

The prevailing wisdom in entertainment is that it's usually a miracle when anything gets made. For every single success story that you've read about, there are a zillion failures. Why do they fail? Sometimes, a great idea isn't executed properly. Sometimes, a show just wasn't a great idea, like *Laurel & Hardy and Bozo* (I'm not making this up), a toon series that was actually produced in 1997 but went nowhere. Other times, a show isn't given proper support by its network, and it dies without enough people ever getting to view it. I'm sure you've all fallen in love with a TV series that was well-written and absorbing, one that you looked forward to watching every week . . . only to see it cancelled after a month. But the fact that it even made it onto a screen in the first place has to be considered pretty amazing.

In the end, it's all a crapshoot. Any number of things can derail a project, and it may have nothing to do with how good or bad the show is. Networks have picked up new series and shifted their time slots so often that viewers didn't know when they were on. Other times, they'll fund a new show, have high hopes and the best of intentions . . . and then just not know what to do with it. In 1996, Gary Cooper and I were hired by producer Nina Elias Bamberger to develop a new series called *Big Bag*. Cartoon Network bought the show from Sesame Workshop and planned to air it as the cornerstone of a block of animated pre-school series.

Big Bag was conceived as a showcase for six new cartoons every week, all wrapped around an educational and entertaining story featuring live actors and Henson Muppets. It was showered with love critically, splashed on magazine covers, won a slew of awards, and only lasted two seasons. How can that happen? Because Cartoon Network discovered that preschool programming was not *their* big bag. They decided to focus on their core audience and not try to be everything to everyone. Young kids and their parents were already used to tuning in to PBS and Nick Jr. for those kinds of shows, and, mostly, didn't know our series was on. We ended up running between 5:00 A.M. and 6:00 A.M. on Sunday mornings, before the roosters were even awake. And that's how it goes sometimes: It's nobody's fault in particular; it just happens.

Then, there's a syndrome not unlike the great California Gold Rush, where everyone and their fourth cousin sees fortunes to be made, so they charge headlong into the fray. Over the last decade, there were possibly hundreds of kids' cartoon series created worldwide, marketed to TV networks and stations everywhere from Tasmania to the North Pole. Few survived.

When (against all prevailing wisdom at the time) *The Simpsons* unexpectedly turned into a smash hit for Fox, it triggered a tidal wave of attempts by producers to duplicate its success. From the early 1990s on, a horde of new prime-time toons premiered, ran for awhile, and then disappeared. You may recall some of the casualties: *Fish Police* (CBS, 1991), *Capitol Critters* (ABC, 1992), *Family Dog* (CBS, 1993), *The Brothers Grunt* (MTV, 1994), *The Critic* (ABC, 1994), *Æon Flux* (MTV,

1995), *The Head* (MTV, 1995), *Stressed Eric* (NBC, 1998), *Downtown* (MTV, 1999), *Dilbert* (UPN, 1999), *Clerks* (ABC, 2000), *God, the Devil, and Bob* (NBC, 2000), *Spy Groove* (MTV, 2000). *Sammy* (NBC, 2000), *Gary & Mike* (UPN, 2001), and *The Oblongs* (WB, 2001). Some, like *Duckman* (USA, 1994), *Bob and Margaret* (Comedy Central, 1998), *Family Guy*, *Futurama* (both Fox, 1999), and *The PJs* (premiered on Fox in 1999 before moving to WB) managed to last a few seasons before they bit the dust. All of these series varied in quality–ranging from awful to excellent–but, ultimately, couldn't lure enough viewers for execs to justify keeping them on the air. Even Cartoon Network and Nickelodeon have had their recent casualties–*Sheep in the Big City* (2000), and *Invader Zim* (2001), respectively.

"Prime-time animation is very difficult to do these days. It's always been difficult to do," said Brad Turrell, the WB's executive VP of network communications. "*The Simpsons* is an anomaly. . . . It will go down as one of the greatest shows in the history of television. Some people have it even higher than that on the list. It raises the bar to a very high level. All the shows that have followed have been judged against *The Simpsons*. I think prime-time animation is hindered because *The Simpsons* is so clever and well-defined. Nothing can quite live up to it. That's not to say that prime-time [animation] will not work."[2]

Successful series just need to be original and well written, have a good time slot, be promoted properly so audiences will watch them . . . and then get very, very lucky.

THEATRICAL TOONS

Triumph and Turmoil

"When I started in animation in the mid-seventies, there *was* no business. Everybody said, that's a dead art form," recalls Tom Sito. "Back then, if you said, 'I wanna do animation like *Bambi*, or Tex Avery, or Bob Clampett,' people thought you were crazy. They said, 'That was born of Depression-era economics, and you'll never see that kind of stuff again.' An old cartoonist actually showed me a transcript from the National Board of Advertisers in 1976 that said, 'Animation is too labor intensive, and takes too long to yield significant profit. And it's not worth the investment.' So it was a problem."

Back then, scores of newcomers were just starting out–assistants, in-betweeners, and apprentices, most in their early twenties–then, there were the animators, all seasoned veterans in their fifties and sixties. "There was nobody in the middle," Sito notes. "By the mid-1970s, the studios realized,

'Oh shit, we're mortal; we'd better start training people.' So the second generation came in, and that's when the CalArts animation department began. Punk kids like John Musker, Ron Clements, and Mike Gabriel were all getting their training."

Which goes a long way in explaining why so many first-time directors were helming animated feature films throughout the late eighties and nineties. "You have to understand, these weren't considered big-budget feature films at the time," Disney producer Don Hahn recounts. "*The Little Mermaid* hadn't come out yet. . . . Animation was our core business, yet there was nobody you could turn to who was a forty-five-year-old experienced feature director. There were none–there's a missing generation in animation."

The theatrical toon biz began to change dramatically in the late eighties and early nineties, with the enormous successes of *Who Framed Roger Rabbit*, *The Little Mermaid*, and all the subsequent Disney hits. "The funny thing is, working on the big Disney films ... from the outside, everybody goes, 'Oh yeah, Disney just cranks out one hit after another!' From the *inside*, we were sort of like a stand-up comic who wonders how long it's gonna last," Sito relates.

After the phenomenon of *Who Framed Roger Rabbit*, Sito and the others at Disney weren't so sure about *The Little Mermaid*. They'd figured the latter was a bit too old-fashioned. "So Jeffrey Katzenberg tells us, on *Little Mermaid*, 'This is gonna be the first animated film to make $100 million,'" Sito recalls. "And we were like, 'You're crazy.' The film did $88.7 million, just domestically. He was right. Even the marketing guys were astounded. Howard Green [in publicity at Buena Vista Pictures] told me that

Animation director, story artist, and former union honcho Tom Sito in his cozily cluttered home studio.

Little Mermaid merchandise was earning as much four years later as the year it came out. Ariel didn't need the movie anymore to be a real character–she was now a reality, like Bugs Bunny."

The Little Mermaid also kicked off the home video animation boom, which became an enormous source of revenue for the studios. "The video was the huge thing," director John Musker notes. "It sold millions."

But, as with their trepidation about *The Little Mermaid* as a feature film, the Disney folks weren't sure at first that a video release was prudent. "There was hesitation–there was controversy about putting *Mermaid* on video. Because they had done it with some of the older classics, but this was the first time they put a brand-new movie right onto video, and we thought that would hurt its reissue appeal," says co-director Ron Clements.

Shortly before the video was released, Musker was visiting his family in Chicago when he got a phone call from Roy Disney. As Musker recalls the conversation, Disney said, "I just wanna tell you, y'know, they twisted my arm. They were gonna release this video in the spring–and I argued against it, and they just wore me down, and I just wanted you to hear it from me that they're gonna do this." Both Clements and Musker were upset. Up to that time, Disney classics had been reissued every seven years–extending the life of the works and grossing profit after profit for posterity. Such would not be the case for *The Little Mermaid* if it were released on video, they feared.

Happily, however, Clements and Musker were mistaken. "Putting it on video just opened it up to a huger audience than had ever seen any of these things," says Clements. "It helped *Beauty and the Beast*, *Aladdin*, *Lion King*–there was a whole chain reaction," Musker adds. "So it ultimately was a good thing, but, at the time, we thought it was bad."

Disney's modern-day success hit its apex in 1994 with *The Lion King*–one of the most popular motion pictures of all time, either animated or live. By the following year, artists, directors, and animators working in the industry were starting to wonder why they weren't sharing the wealth. And then their prayers were answered: DreamWorks set up shop (green-lighting *Prince of Egypt*), and Warner Bros. Features began producing films again (*Space Jam* and *Quest for Camelot*), setting off a bidding war among the three studios for talent.

"Everybody thinks DreamWorks began the bidding wars, but actually, it was Warner Bros.," says Sito. "The average salary around that time, in 1994, was about $1,200 to $1,500 a week for an animator. Warner Bros. was the first one to offer animators $2,200 a week. And as soon as we heard that, we went, 'Ooooh!'"

Suddenly, all through the industry, salaries skyrocketed. "It became $3,500 . . . then $5,000 a week . . . there were even cleanup assistants making $3,500, and getting $80,000 signing bonuses. It was a real seller's market–you could name your price. But then, starting [in] '98, things began to go down . . . there were a lot of animation disappointments. *Emperor's New Groove* didn't do well, *Iron Giant* didn't do well for whatever reason, *Osmosis Jones* [co-directed by Sito] didn't do well, *Atlantis*, *Anastasia*, *Titan A.E.* . . . it was a mess."

To make matters worse, there were long slack periods between productions in which crews were retained but had little to do. Eventually, the accountants took notice and wondered, "Why are we keeping all these people?" And so the layoffs began.

At around the same time, CG-animated films continued to rise in popularity. Aside from the cel-animated *The Rugrats Movie* (1998) and *The Rugrats in Paris* (2000) from Klasky Csupo and Nickelodeon, and Disney's *Lilo & Stitch* (2002), the big moneymakers at the box office in recent years have all been computer generated.

Thomas Schumacher, former president of Disney Feature Animation, feels we must understand the public's natural affinity for CG toons. "Let's separate the technology from the look," he says, "and recognize what I call the 'deliciousness of dimensionality.' Walt [Disney] did it, and people fell over themselves for it. When Giotto came into the Renaissance and said, 'Look what you can do with dimensionality,' people went crazy. Dimensionality is something everyone has quested for. When you look at *Tarzan* [the 1998 Disney feature which employed a new process, dubbed 'deep canvas,' to convey a striking sense of depth], you go, 'Oh my gosh!' You can't deny it; people love dimensionality." Naturally, all this has prompted many to speculate that the end is at hand for "traditional" animation.

Not so, says Schumacher. "If you look at the sixteen movies [Disney has] in production through the TV animation group, and the seven movies in production with the feature animation group, will [they] continue with traditional? Yes," affirms Schumacher, before posing an interesting hypothetical question. "By the time [they] make the 2007 movies, might they *look* traditional but will they be made in a different technique? Will there be systems to automatically do in-betweens–is all that going to change? You know, fifty percent of the background department already paints on computer. Will [they] be using more technology, regardless?"

Of course. Without question, it will impact on the nature of the workforce. And yet, animated feature films will continue to provide jobs not only for computer programmers, but for animators, designers, painters, writers, directors, producers, composers, editors, voice artists, and all the other human talent integral to the creative process. Factor in Cartoon Network, Nickelodeon, The Disney Channel, and television's voracious appetite for programming in general, and it's clear that cartoons will be around for a long, long time.

BIBLIOGRAPHY

BOOKS

Beck, Jerry. *The Fifty Greatest Cartoons*. Atlanta: Turner Publishing Inc., 1994.

Beck, Jerry, and Will Friedwald. *Looney Tunes and Merrie Melodies: A Complete Illustrated Guide to the Warner Bros. Cartoons*. New York: Henry Holt and Company Inc., 1989.

Blanc, Mel. *That's Not All Folks!* New York: Warner Books Inc., 1988.

Brion, Patrick. *Les Dessins de Tex Avery*. Paris: Nathan Image, 1988.

Brooks, Tim, and Earle Marsh. *The Complete Directory To Prime Time Network TV Shows*. New York: Random House, 1992.

Burton, Tim. *Tim Burton's The Nightmare Before Christmas*. New York: Hyperion Press, 1993.

Cabarga, Leslie. *The Fleischer Story*. New York: DaCapo Press, 1988.

Canemaker, John. *Before the Animation Begins: The Art and Lives of Disney Inspirational Sketch Artists*. New York: Hyperion, 1996.

Cartwright, Nancy. *My Life As a 10-Year-Old Boy*. New York: Hyperion, 2000.

Culhane, John. *Disney's Aladdin: The Making of an Animated Film*. New York: Hyperion, 1992.

Dini, Paul, and Chip Kidd. *Batman: Animated*. New York: HarperCollins, 1998.

Gilliam, Terry. *Animations of Mortality*. London: Routledge Kegan & Paul, 1979.

Grossman, Gary H. *Saturday Morning TV*. New York: Dell Publishing, 1981.

Jones, Chuck. *Chuck Amuck: The Life and Times of an Animated Cartoonist*. New York: Farrar, Straus and Giroux, 1989.

Katz, Ephraim, Fred Klein, and Ronald Dean Nolen. *The Film Encyclopedia*, 3rd ed. New York: HarperCollins, 1998.

Kurtti, Jeff. *The Art of Mulan*. New York: Hyperion, 1998.

Lasseter, John, and Steve Daly. *Toy Story: The Art and Making of the Animated Film*. New York: Hyperion, 1995.

Horn, Richard. *Fifties Style: Then and Now*. New York: William Morrow & Co., 1985.

Maltin, Leonard. *Leonard Maltin's 2002 Movie and Video Guide*. New York: Penguin Putnam, Inc., 2002.

____. *Of Mice and Magic: A History of American Animated Cartoons*. New York: Penguin Books USA, 1987.

Scheuer, Steven H. *The Movie Book*. Chicago: The Ridge Press/Playboy Press, 1974.

Solomon, Charles. *The Disney That Never Was*. New York: Hyperion, 1995.

____. *Enchanted Drawings: The History of Animation*. New York: Alfred A. Knopf, Inc., 1989.

Thomas, Frank, and Ollie Johnston. *Disney Animation, The Illusion of Life*. New York: Abbeville Press, 1981.

ARTICLES

Baisley, Sarah. "South Park: Where It's Cool to Break a Rule." *Animation Magazine*, vol. 11, no. 10 (November 1997).

Culhane, John. "Katzenberg's Magic Lamp." *Animation Magazine* 6, no. 1 (fall 1992).

Daly, Steve. "Disney's Got A Brand-New Baghdad." *Entertainment Weekly* (4 December 1992).

Deneroff, Harvey. "Matt Groening's Baby Turns 10." *Animation Magazine*, vol. 14, no. 1 (January 2000).

Desowitz, Bill. "Blue Sky Comes Out of the Ice Age for Fox." *Animation Magazine*, vol. 16, no. 3 (March 2002).

"Monsters, Inc.: What's the Big Deal?" *Entertainment Weekly* Web site, *www.ew.com*, 22 October 2001.

LaRue, Bill. "Matt Groening: Loves The Toys," *SimpsonsCrazy* Web site *www.CollectingSimpsons.com*, 1998.

Levine, Bettijane. "SpongeBob Creator Feels Wrung Out." *L.A. Times*, 13 April 2002.

Mallory, Michael. "Sketches from an Old Hand: Ed Benedict." *Animation Magazine* 6, no. 1 (fall 1992)

Province, John. "Seldom RePeeted: Bill Peet, a Career Reminiscence by Disney's Master of the Story-Sketch." *Hogan's Alley* 1, no. 1 (autumn 1994).

Raiti, Gerard. "Prime time Animation Fills Growing Niche TV." *Animation World Magazine*, vol. 5, no. 8 (November 2000).

RADIO AND TELEVISION

Brodax, Al. "21st Century Radio's Beatles Yellow Submarine Special Journey." Interview by Bob Heironimus, WCBM 680 AM, Baltimore, 6 March 1994.

Noble, Maurice. "Chuck Jones: Extremes & In-betweens, A Life in Animation." Interview, *Great Performance*. Produced by Thirteen/WNET New York. Public Broadcasting System, 22 November 2000.

Silverman, David. Interview by James Young. *Talk Is Cheap*. 3RRR Radio, Melbourne, Australia, 19 August 1998.

SPECIAL PUBLICATIONS

Groening, Matt. "The Musical Prehistory of *The Simpsons*." *The Simpsons, Songs in the Key of Springfield; Original Music from the Television Series,* Rhino Entertainment Company, 1997.

Hochman, Steve. *The Music Behind the Magic*. Companion Book, Buena Vista Pictures Distribution, 1994.

Illustration Credits

Drawings on page 133, courtesy Michael Giaimo.

Drawings on pages 126 and 130, courtesy Eric Radomski.

Photo of Gary K. Wolf and Roger Rabbit on page 3 courtesy Gary K. Wolf.

Photo of David Silverman and Margot Pipkin on page 197 courtesy Margot Pipkin.

Photo of Gabor Csupo and Gyorgyi Peluce on page 34 courtesy Gyorgyi Peluce.

Photo of Paul Germain on page 36 courtesy of Paul Germain.

Photo of Ken Bruce and Tom Copolla on page 39 courtesy Ken Bruce.

Photo of Roger Allers, Jeff Albert, Lisa Keene, Brenda Chapman, Chris Sanders and George Scribner on page 108 courtesy Brenda Chapman.

Photo of The Beatles maquettes on page 140 and Mufasa sculpt on page 143 courtesy Pam and Bob Martin, and Kent Melton.

Photo of Andreas Deja on page 175 by Greg Preston.

Photo of Susan and Eric Goldberg on page 188 by Greg Preston.

Photo of Brenda Chapman, Don Hahn, and Sue Nichols on page 208 courtesy Sue Nichols.

Photo of Jay Ward, June Foray, and Bill Scott on page 217 courtesy Tiffany Ward.

Photo of Alan Menken and Howard Ashman on page 243 courtesy Bill Lauch.

Photo of Alan Menken on page 240 by Dave Cross.

Photo of Pat Carroll on page 220 courtesy Pat Carroll.

Photo of Billy West on page 224 courtesy ICM and Billy West.

Photo of John Leguizamo on page 229 courtesy IDPR and John Leguizamo.

Photo of *Rocko's Modern Life* crew on page 253 courtesy of Nickelodeon and Mary Harrington.

Caricature of Linda Simensky by Paul Rudish on page 254 courtesy Simensky.

Photo of Tom Sito on page 258 by Greg Preston.

Caricature of Allan Neuwirth on back cover by Glen Hanson.

INDEX

Note: Page numbers in *italics* refer to illustrations.

BOOKS FROM ALLWORTH PRESS

Mastering 3D Animation by Peter Ratner (paperback, includes CD-ROM. 344 pages, 8 × 9⅞, $35.00)

The Education of an Illustrator edited by Steven Heller and Marshall Arisman (paperback, 6¾ × 9⅞, 288 pages, $19.95)

Shoot Me: Independent Filmmaking from Creative Concept to Rousing Release by Roy Frumkes and Rocco Simonelli (paperback, 6 × 9, 272 pages, $19.95)

VO: Tales and Techniques of a Voice-Over Actor by Harlan Hogan (paperback, 6 × 9, 256 pages, $19.95)

Technical Film and TV for Nontechnical People by Drew Campbell (paperback, 6 × 9, 256 pages, $19.95)

Documentary Filmmakers Speak by Liz Stubbs (paperback, 6 × 9, 240 pages, $19.95)

Producing for Hollywood: A Guide for Independent Producers by Paul Mason and Don Gold (paperback, 6 × 9, 272 pages, $19.95)

Directing for Film and Television, Revised Edition by Christopher Lukas (paperback, 6 × 9, 256 pages, $19.95)

Hollywood Dealmaking: Negotiating Talent Agreements by Dina Appleton and Daniel Yankelevitz (paperback, 6 × 9, 256 pages, $19.95)

The Screenwriter's Legal Guide, second edition by Stephen F. Breimer (paperback, 6 × 9, 224 pages, $16.95)

Writing Television Comedy by Jerry Rannow (paperback, 6 × 9, 224 pages, $14.95)

Get the Picture? The Movie Lover's Guide to Watching Films by Jim Piper (paperback, 6 × 9, 240 pages, $18.95)

The Directors: Take Three by Robert J. Emery (paperback, 6 × 9, 240 pages)

The Directors: Take Four by Robert J. Emery (paperback, 6 × 9, 256 pages)

Please write to request our free catalog. To order by credit card, call 1-800-491-2808 or send a check or money order to Allworth Press, 10 East 23rd Street, Suite 510, New York, NY 10010. Include $5 for shipping and handling for the first book ordered and $1 for each additional book. Ten dollars plus $1 for each additional book if ordering from Canada. New York State residents must add sales tax.

To see our complete catalog on the World Wide Web, or to order online, you can find us at *www.allworth.com*.